The Battered Child

The Battered Child

Edited by
Ray E. Helfer and C. Henry Kempe

Second Edition

The University of Chicago Press

Chicago and London

THE UNIVERSITY OF CHICAGO PRESS

CHICAGO 60637

The University of Chicago Press, Ltd., London

© *1968, 1974 by The University of Chicago*
All rights reserved
Published 1968. Second Edition 1974
Second Impression 1975

Printed in the United States of America
LC 73–87303
ISBN: 0–226–32629–2

RAY E. HELFER is professor in the Department
of Human Development, College of Human
Medicine, at Michigan State University.

C. HENRY KEMPE is professor of pediatrics at
the University of Colorado Medical Center
and Director of the National Center for the
Prevention and Treatment of Child Abuse
and Neglect.
[1974]

We respectfully and affectionately dedicate
this volume to Anna Freud who, more than any
other single person, has for many years enlightened,
challenged, and inspired all persons, lay and professional,
who wish to understand, comfort, and protect children
through the vicissitudes and the opportunities of their
early years.

Contents

Foreword

If the merits of a book were judged purely on the basis of its subject matter, this one might remain unread. For there are few topics in modern life that are more repugnant to consider than the abuse of a child by the very persons entrusted with his care. Yet the fact is that some people of every socioeconomic, educational, religious, and geographical background in our society continue to abuse their children.

Popular awareness of the widespread nature of child abuse has increased tremendously in recent years, owing in large measure to the work of some of the contributors to this book. Now all of our fifty states have passed laws providing for mandatory reporting of suspected cases of child abuse. The Children's Bureau is proud to have had a part in stimulating this legislation.

But we are a long way from being satisfied. The need for community follow-up services is great. When a doctor reports a suspected instance of child abuse, he is simply stating the case. It is up to the individual communities to solve this problem and prevent its repetition. Children who have been abused require protection and rehabilitation, and their parents need professional guidance to help them understand, accept, and cope with their parental roles.

This book, I am sure, will be invaluable in setting forth the essential medical, social, and legal framework through which this problem must be faced.

KATHERINE B. OETTINGER
1968

Chief, Children's Bureau
Department of Health, Education, and Welfare
Washington

Preface to the Second Edition

There are fifteen women in a house of correction just outside one of our larger cities. All of them are there for the same reason: they have been convicted of crimes against children—cruelty or manslaughter. Geraldine is one of these women. Still young, she was reared in a traumatic, motherless atmosphere, ran away from home as a teen-ager, became pregnant, married an emotionally ill college graduate, and began to have more children after placing her first child up for adoption. Her second child died in its first year of life from the effects of severe physical abuse. The third was born in prison.

The "justice" achieved by the criminal court after sentencing her to from two to four years in prison is exemplified by the sentencing judge's response to a request for early parole. No one knew who killed the baby—the mother, the father, or both—but a confession had been obtained from the mother, and so she was tried and convicted; the father, remaining at home and now on welfare, cares for the prison-born child. An attempt was made to have Geraldine released so that a program of social and psychiatric treatment could be initiated. The judge, emotional and removed from the reality of the situation, chided proponents of the therapeutic program and suggested that he would approve early parole only if the mother submitted to sterilization.

Geraldine is still in prison, but in another year she will be free and reunited with her emotionally disturbed husband and her new baby, with (no doubt) more to come; the process of criminal rehabilitation has again been flaunted. And in the same institution there are fourteen other women convicted of similar offenses.

In spite of the Geraldines, there is evidence of slow but definite progress. Since *The Battered Child* was published in 1968, understanding has deepened, many more people have become involved, some courts have improved, treatment programs are being developed all over the country, and abuse and neglect are generally recognized at a much earlier point in the child's life. For example, in 1972 almost ten thousand cases of suspected abuse and neglect were reported in New York City alone (see appendix A). This fact is encouraging to many, since the feeling is that the lid is now off and solutions must and will be found.

A second book, *Helping the Battered Child and His Family* (Lippincott, 1972), has been published; the mass media have shown increasing interest and willingness to be helpful; and a few foundations have expressed interest in funding service and research projects. The biggest lack remains the apathy of federal agencies in the field of child welfare. Time is even changing this.

In the second edition of *The Battered Child,* the editors have deleted material no longer applicable, updated other contributions, and added more recent information. A chapter on the New York experience has been added. The section on the reporting laws, pathology, and X-ray has been extensively revised. Certain discussions, covered in greater detail in *Helping the Battered Child and His Family,* have been removed and duplication avoided. The classic chapters by Steele and Pollock and by Davoren, however, have been left untouched.

Adequate demographic data which provide up-to-date evidence of the true incidence of significant child abuse in the United States are not available. Comparing current reporting of child abuse under state laws, we find that many communities are running a rate of 375 reports of suspected abuse per million population per year. No one has tried to compare the reported rate of suspected child abuse to the actual incidence—only a house-to-house, block-to-block intensive study can give us this information. Even so, such a ratio would only be valid in the community studied, because the number of reports compared to the true incidence depends on many variables, including physicians' interest and education, community attitudes, receptivity of the public agencies—especially the child-protective services—and, of course, the police and the juvenile courts.

In the absence of detailed information on incidence, it is still possible to assess the experience of a large metropolitan area such as New York City. For this reason, the appendix shows the report of the Select Committee on Child Abuse authorized by the New York State Assembly. It provides information which can be used quite readily by other metropolitan areas and is a valuable contribution to the study of a difficult problem in a major center.[1]

The editors are convinced that recognition and treatment of battered children will accelerate during the seventies. The involvement and interest of both professionals and lay workers are encouraging. Geraldine, her husband, and her family see it differently, however. They will continue to withdraw, and their children will run the risk of repeated injury until many more devoted and informed individuals proliferate into every nook and cranny of our service agencies, police, hospitals, courts, schools, and, above all, our communities.

R.E.H.
C.H.K.

[1] The New York City data (see appendix C) are confusing in that the state requires the reporting of both abuse and neglect. There is no specific way of separating the N.Y.C. report into these two categories of the abnormal rearing problem. In 1972, therefore, the New York City rate for *both* entities was 1,200 per million population.

Preface to the First Edition

Tens of thousands of children were severely battered or killed in the United States in 1967. This book is written about and for these children. Who are they, where do they come from, why were they beaten, and most important—what can we do to prevent it?

Presented herein is a multidisciplinary approach to the problem. There is both agreement and controversy among the contributors, but each has one goal in mind—to provide the reader with all of the available information which can hopefully be utilized to change the fate of these children and their parents.

We would like to express our sincere appreciation to all of the contributors and their staffs for sharing with us their experiences and research in the field of child abuse. We are also greatly indebted to Miss Katherine Oettinger and Dr. Arthur Lesser and their staff at the Children's Bureau for their continued help and support. Miss Jean Rubin, a former member of the Children's Bureau, was most helpful during a critical period in our study.

Each of our patients has provided us with a unique learning experience. We would like to express our appreciation not only to these children but also to their parents, who for the most part have been cooperative and helpful in making this work possible.

R.E.H.
C.H.K.

Introduction

*Let us speak less of the duties of children and
more of their rights.*—JEAN JACQUES ROUSSEAU—1712–78

More than one hundred years after Rousseau made this observation the incident involving Mary Ellen (cited in chapter 1) occurred in New York City. In many areas of the world the rights of animals were placed before those of children.

During Rousseau's time and for hundreds of years before him, the duties of children (even the very young) were clearly placed before their rights. Children even had a duty to learn rather than a right to be educated. The Spartans (fourth century B.C.) had their whip bearer, who held a high place in their educational system, and the English school for gentlemen (seventeenth century) had its cane in the corner of each classroom. It was truly heretical for such exemplars of education as Comenius and Loyola (sixteenth century) and Locke (seventeenth century) to advocate that learning should be a pleasant experience.

During the past one hundred years the rights of children have gradually been recognized. The duties of small children, on the other hand, are less easily defined, especially when one considers the child's responsibility to his parents. Do children have the duty to satisfy the emotional needs of their parents? Many of the parents described in this book believe that they do: Jody's mother commented, "I waited so long to have my baby, and when she came, she never did anything for me."

> Jody was four years old when her parents brought her to Colorado General Hospital. She had suffered from severe child abuse all of her life and demonstrated one of the most severe cases of malnutrition that we have seen. She weighed only seventeen pounds and was covered with bruises and abrasions. Radiological studies revealed a fracture of the skull and arm and two fractures of her hands. She also presented a high intestinal obstruction due to a hematoma in the lumen of the duodenum.

xv

For years Jody's mother had expressed to her husband and other members of the family and community her concern about this child and the manner in which she was able to care for her. No one had been willing to accept his responsibility, and no help was offered the mother.

Shortly after Jody was admitted to the hospital, the mother was told that we would not recommend that she be sent home because of our concern for her welfare. Without hesitation the mother in a very relieved tone stated, "I would be more frightened than you if she were sent home."

Jody's progress in the hospital was dramatic. During the six months following discharge, she grew six inches and showed considerable developmental improvement. She has been permanently removed from her home and is now awaiting adoption.

Jody's case, as do all cases of child abuse, required the close cooperation of many disciplines. The pediatrician, psychiatrist, social worker, local child welfare worker, county district attorney, local sheriff, parents' lawyer, and nursing personnel were all intimately involved. The compilation of these monographs was stimulated by our conviction that a multidisciplinary approach is of primary importance. It is the intent of the editors to provide the many disciplines involved in helping the battered child and his parents with a frame of reference, which they may use in their approach.

It is our hope that all the Jodys everywhere will benefit from this endeavor.

R.E.H.
C.H.K.

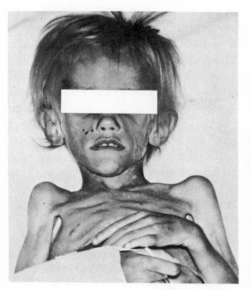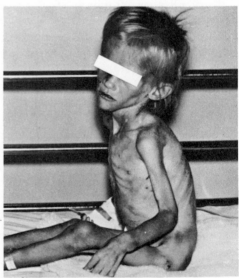

Jody upon admission to the University of Colorado Medical Center

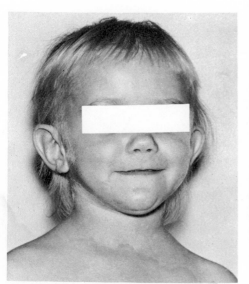

Jody five weeks after admission

PART 1

The Past

A History of Child Abuse and Infanticide

Samuel X Radbill

Graduate School of Medicine
University of Pennsylvania, Philadelphia

Maltreatment or Discipline

Maltreatment of children has been justified for many centuries by the belief that severe physical punishment was necessary either to maintain discipline, to transmit educational ideas, to please certain gods, or to expel evil spirits. Whipping children has always been the prerogative of teachers, as well as of parents. In the schools of Sumer, five thousand years ago, there was a "man in charge of the whip" to punish boys upon the slightest pretext (1, p. 11). Justification for maltreatment has also been based on religious beliefs and practices, and in ancient times boys were flogged by their parents before the altars of Diana (2, p. 195).

"Spare the rod and spoil the child" was a dictum backed by the Bible and expressed in 1633 in the *Bibliotheca Scholastica*. There was a time in most Christian countries when children were whipped on Innocents Day to make them remember the massacre of the innocents by Herod. Beatings to drive out the devil were a form of psychiatric treatment especially applicable to children, and where epilepsy was attributed to demoniacal possession, the sufferer was thrashed soundly to expel the demon. There was a sacred iron chain in India expressly for this purpose.

The ancient philosophers beat their pupils unmercifully. Parents, teachers, and ministers alike believed that the only cure for the "foolishness bound up in the heart of the child" was repression, especially by use of the rod, and the schoolmaster was

Dr. Radbill is lecturer in the history of pediatrics.
This paper was read at the Pediatric History Club, American Academy of Pediatrics, October 26, 1965.

proverbial for his severity. The ferule, a tough stalk of the giant fennel (*ferula*), was used by Roman schoolmasters as the instrument of punishment. In England and America all pictures of pedagogues showed them armed with the birch. Michael Udall, headmaster at Eton during the reign of Elizabeth I, was noted for his addiction to the use of four apple twigs; his cruelty led Roger Ascham (sixteenth century) to write *The Schoolmaster* in which he advocated love instead of fear in teaching children. John Locke, a century later, pleaded for schoolmasters to reserve the rod for moral faults only. Severe forms of punishment were used; not only were they condoned and supported by law, but they were usually considered salutary, although occasionally parents did intercede on behalf of their children (3, pp. 191–210).

Throughout history there are accounts of the customary extremes in the chastisement of children. Pepys beat his boy until he (Pepys) was out of breath; John Wesley, Frederick the Great, Lady Jane Grey, and many others in adult life complained bitterly of their treatment in childhood. It always was taken for granted that the parents and guardians of children had every right to treat their children as they saw fit. When Henry VI, who was king when still in his cradle, grew old enough to put up an argument, his tutor had to appeal to council for assistance "in chastysing of him for his defaults." Thus regular flogging produced a most unhappy person in King Henry VI, even if it did make him a scholar and a gentleman (4, p. 119). Charles I was more fortunate for he had Mungo Murray available as a whipping boy to substitute for him when punishment was indicated.

History reveals that there were influential personages other than Henry VI to speak out against the maltreatment of children. Plato in 400 B.C. advised teachers to "train children not by compulsion but as if they were playing," and Plutarch, 500 years later, decried the use of the *scutica* (a whip made of leather thongs).

The beating of very young children, for a time, raised many objections which led to some mitigation. But then as the Calvinistic views that children were imps of darkness became popular, they were again whipped. In 1570, Thomas Ingeland became incensed by this practice and wrote a protest skit which he called *A Pretie and Merie New Interlude Called the Disobedient Child*. The climax came when a boy "through many stryppes was dead and cold" (4, p. 165).

Discipline oscillated between entire abandonment of the rod and its excessive use to the point of savagery. The German-born Queen Caroline complained that the English were not well bred because they were not whipped enough when they were young. The Lady Abergane is said to have severely beaten her own child of seven in a fit of passion. When the father complained, she threw the child so violently to the ground that his skull was fractured, and he was killed (4, p. 239).

In 1646 the Massachusetts courts adopted the Mosaic law, which imposed the death penalty on unruly children; and in 1651 Connecticut followed suit; but public whipping was commonly substituted for this stringent law. However, the parents had to prove they had not provoked their children by extreme and cruel correction (5, p. 38).

Western education gradually began to yield to the demands of exemplars of modern thought, such as Erasmus, who although he brought up his own children with harsh formality, was greatly influenced by Sir Thomas More, who used peacock feathers to beat his daughters. There were others who protested vigorously against child abuse. During the reign of Henry VIII there was a group of reformers in educational methods who urged gentleness; among them was John Colet, founder of St. Paul's School in London. When Richard Mulcaster, a schoolmaster, wrote his little book on education, he was criticized by Fuller, who said "others have taught as much learning with fewer lashes" (6, p. 309). John Peter Frank, at the end of the eighteenth century, was a pioneer in the establishment of legal regulations curbing corporal punishment in the schools (7, pp. 257–68).

Pressure against child abuse was also exerted by those outside the educational system. In 1611, Roger L'Estrange published a book, *The Children's Petition*, pleading for more leniency from parents toward their children. In 1698, another book appeared in England entitled *Lex Forcia, A Sensible Address to Parliament for an Act to Remedy the Foul Abuse of Children at Schools* (8, p. 297). Over 150 years passed before public opinion was aroused in the United States. In 1861, Samuel Halliday, a reformer, reported many instances of child beating by sadistic parents in New York City (9, p. 102).

The Mutilated Child

What may be an unacceptable practice in one culture may be commonplace to another. Even though certain practices are socially acceptable, medically they often can be classified as mutilating procedures. Children have always been the victims of mutilation practices, the most common site for mutilation being the sex organs. Circumcision in one way or another is still performed even by the most highly civilized people. It is probably the oldest surgical procedure on record, having been practiced as a religious rite since the stone age. In spite of its questionable value, it is the most common operation performed today. Even though Moses was an adult when he was circumcised by his wife, the Hebrews since his time must perform the operation on the eighth day after the boy is born. In different cultures it is done at different ages, and girls are not always spared.

The eunuch played an important role in certain societies. One need only refer to the Bible and to Shakespeare to realize that castration was an acceptable procedure.

Another ancient form of mutilation was foot-binding of female children among the Chinese. This was done for cosmetic purposes and has only recently been discontinued. Various other forms of bindings to produce fashionable configurations in the arms, legs, and other parts of the body are still seen, especially in Africa.

Cranial deformation is encountered in many different parts of the world. It has been discovered in ancient skulls in the Crimea, was mentioned by Hippocrates, was common among the American Indians, and is still practiced in the Solomon Islands. The Indians favored flattened heads, while the Melanesians shaped their heads into elongated cones. Although it was lovingly done, and as a rule purely for cosmetic purposes, the Viceroy Toledo, recognizing it as a form of child abuse, in the sixteenth century forbade the practice in a series of regulations promulgated for the care and hygiene of infants in South America.

Another curious operation, practiced for generations among the Berbers of North-

ern Morocco, was uvulectomy. It is done soon after birth by the sexton of the neigh-
borhood mosque or by a barber-surgeon, not only to facilitate breast feeding and
speech, but even to insure better health throughout life.

Forms of mutilation which were clearly vicious were done by speculators who traf-
ficked in children to set them up as professional beggars. M. Annaeus Seneca, father
of the famous philosopher, at about the time of Caesar listed among the deformities
inflicted upon children to arouse pity (thereby making them good beggars)—gouged
eyes, amputated or twisted arms and legs, and broken and deformed feet.

Slavery was another of the abuses children often had to endure, or perish. In days
gone by the rights of a father included the right to sell his child into slavery. Infant
girls were sold to be raised as prostitutes, and boys were sold to toil. Children suffered
many cruel effects from the African slave trade when it flourished.

Infanticide

A child was once virtually its father's chattel. The *Patria Postestas* of the Romans
endowed the father with the privilege to sell, abandon, offer in sacrifice, devour, kill,
or otherwise dispose of his offspring. Fortunately, this right was practically never invoked. A vestige of this tradition in the United States still makes rearing children the
responsibility of parents, but now there are social and legal restrictions to safeguard
them. No parent now has the right to kill his child, and there is no distinction between
infanticide and murder. The legal limits to chastisement of children, however, are not
clearcut; such limitations have to be supplemented by public opinion.

In ancient times infancy was a dangerous time of life. The child was not considered
human until certain ceremonies were performed. The Egyptian midwife had to pray
for the soul to join the newborn infant, and the Babylonian father had to impart his
spirit into the child by blowing into its face and then giving it his name or the name
of one of his ancestors, thus bestowing upon it a soul. In this manner a child was
assured of life. The Frisian father could destroy or otherwise dispose of his infant only
before it had taken food—here, to give food was lifegiving. In Athens the amphidroma
ceremony was performed as a rule on the fifth day of life, when the new baby was
carried by its nurse around the ancestral hearth to receive consecration and a name.
If the child was not wanted, the father had to dispose of it before the amphidroma.
In general, the longer a child was permitted to live, the more the parents became
attached to him, and thus the longer he survived the greater his chances for social
recognition and parental care.

Reasons for Infanticide

Anthropologically, infanticide refers to the killing of a newborn with the consent
of parent, family, or community. Many reasons lead to this seemingly inhuman act
(10, p. 193). Population control is the motive most often assigned, especially among
peoples who do not know how to prevent conception or to produce abortion. Knowledge of contraceptive measures must perforce reduce the incidence of infanticide.
Actually, war, famine, disease, and accidents have been more effective in population
control than deliberate infanticide. The individual family size can be controlled, how-

ever, when children are abandoned, sold, or slain. In some cultures a limit of three children per family was set, and those born after the third were either killed or otherwise eliminated. In Papua and in Cochin China, where infanticide was an acceptable method of family planning, a mother was despised and likened to an animal if she had too many children.

Illegitimacy is another prime cause of infanticide (11, p. 68). Even if not willfully murdered, illegitimate babies have, in some societies, a slim chance for survival. The mortality rate during the first year of illegitimate babies' lives is frequently reported to be twice as high as their legitimate counterparts. Many illegitimate children are born prematurely, usually owing to their inadequate prenatal care. If they survive the neonatal period they are, either for reasons of shame or lack of financial support, neglected, abused, surreptitiously abandoned, left in the care of others or institutions, or killed. Economic stress was especially difficult for the mother; consequently she often selected her female infant to be killed thereby sparing her her own fate in later life. This was especially true of the American Indian squaw.

The dishonor of bearing illegitimate children often led the Arabs to kill their young girls. The Cameroons, when oppressed by their German conquerors, had a similar custom, but they were solaced by the belief that their children would return to earth when the Germans left (12, vol. 1, p. 130).

An infant often had to be sacrificed if his mother, because of illness, death, youth, debauchery, or demands made upon her by the needs of older siblings, was unable to care for him (13, p. 45) (Fig. 1). When a child was born too soon after a sibling, it might be killed because of feeding problems or because of the taboo which kept the mother away from the embraces of her husband during the lactation period. Such infants were especially in peril in a polygamous society, for the husband could find comfort from another wife too easily.

Greed for money led to infanticide. Eighty per cent of the illegitimate children put out to nurse in London during the nineteenth century died. Unscrupulous nurses collected their fees and then promptly did away with the babies. When babies were farmed out to foster care, their lot was usually an unhappy one. Although foster care is an ancient system mentioned both in the Code of Hammurabi of 600 B.C. and in the Bible (14, p. 27), neglect, ill usage, and starvation were the rule, even though the law required registration of the foster home. In spite of severe penalties, the law was widely evaded. Still, foster care may really give the baby a better chance to live than institutional care. Constant supervision in foster homes by interested, devoted people became necessary.

Other schemes that victimized infants flourished. Edwin Chadwick called attention to the insurance system, the so-called burial clubs. For an investment of about one pound sterling, from three to five pounds profit could be realized when a child was buried. Unscrupulous and greedy midwives were also a threat to the infant's life. They sometimes accepted fees to "arrange for" the death of the newborn child.

Greed for power, as when kings feared to be replaced by the new heir, could be lethal to the child. The twins Romulus and Remus were the classical examples of this motive. Although the king ordered them to be slain, they were exposed instead. Suckled by a wolf, they lived to become the symbol of Rome's infancy. When Herod

Figure 1

"Gin Lane" by William Hogarth

feared the coming of a messiah, he ordered the massacre of the innocents; and when Pharaoh feared the Jews, he likewise ordered the slaughter of innocent newborn males.

Superstition can lead to infanticide. Man fears the unusual, so that twins, monstrous births, or congenital defects frequently bode evil. When an astrologer in antiquity was consulted at the birth of a child, the poor tyke had little chance of survival if he was ill-omened. In China, India, and throughout the Orient deformed children were usually destroyed at birth; and in sixteenth-century Europe, Martin Luther ordered mentally defective children drowned because he was convinced they were instruments of the devil. Although the Thebans made infanticide and exposure of infants a capital offense, these offenses were frequent in Egypt. The Greeks, and to some extent the Romans, as well as many others, killed their weak or deformed infants in the vain hope that only the strong would survive. This belief in the survival of the fittest to strengthen the race was held by Plato, Aristotle (15, p. 347), and many others. The Roman Law of the Twelve Tables forbade rearing deformed children.

Athenian children were exposed at the Cynosarges, one of the gymnasia, and in Sparta parents were obliged to bring the newborn child to a *lesche* where a council of elders examined it. If judged weak or deformed, it was cast from Mount Taygetus into a deep canyon, called Apotheta. During the period of the Caesars, infanticide, always legal in Rome, received the approbation of philosophers like Seneca. Morals decayed, broken marriages became common, and exposure of infants frequent. Sometimes the hapless infant was simply thrown into the Cloaca Maxima where it empties into the Velabrum (16, p. 72).

Ritual sacrifice accounted for countless infant deaths. Hecate, Chthonian deity to whom sacrifices were made at the crossroads on the night of the last day of the lunar month, was called Infanticida, when she demanded children. In certain fertility rites in China, India, Mexico, Peru, and elsewhere children were cast into rivers as offerings to water gods to bring good harvests or other good fortune. In the Bible there are many allusions to ritual sacrifice which brought down the denunciation of the Lord: "Thou shalt not give any of thy seed to be consecrated to the idol, Moloch," He decreed.

Kings were deified, but when they failed in their divine duties, as shown by crop failures, blight, or public catastrophe of any kind, they might be sacrificed to appease the wrath of superior gods. Later the kings hit upon the bright idea of substitutes— and what better substitute than the most precious heir to the throne? The first-born came to be the most popular victim for human sacrifice. In time, animals as scapegoats became acceptable. When a Greek oracle demanded a girl, a goat dressed as a girl was supplied instead. The Jews developed the *Pidyon Haben* to redeem the first born with gold or silver.

Closely allied to the belief that infants could transfer fertility and growth was the belief that the blood and flesh of slain infants could confer health, vigor, and even youthfulness. Not only were infants slain for medical uses, but there are reports of feeding the flesh to mothers to produce strong offspring and to favored siblings to make them stronger and healthier. Cannibalism, mentioned in the Bible, in the Greek Cronus myth, and elsewhere, is met occasionally in the history of infanticide, but usually under extreme famine situations, rather than just for lifegiving virtues.

Superstitions also accounted for the belief that slain infants would benefit the sterile woman, cure disease, or bring good crops. To insure durability in certain ancient structures some living creature was sometimes buried under the foundations of important buildings. It is said that even as recently as the sixteenth century, children were buried alive beneath the doorsteps of public buildings in Germany (8, p. 308).

The methods used in infanticide have not changed much throughout history (17, p. 99). Blood is rarely shed. Drowning, smothering, strangulation, burial alive, incineration, and beating are still most common (18, p. 56). Ritual sacrifice, usually by fire or sword, is practically non-existent today. Wherever the use of cordials and narcotics exist, poisoning occurs. Overlaying, always a common cause of death in infants, during the nineteenth century was most frequent on Saturday nights, for obvious reasons (19, p. 85).

The Abandoned Child

Abandonment usually results in death to the infant, although this always gives the infant at least a sporting chance.

Legend and myth have dramatized abandonment of infants from the beginning of time. Many a famous character in history has glorified his humble start in life as a foundling. Moses, Romulus and Remus, Sargon I, mighty king of Agad about 2850

B.C., and even Horus, the adored infant god of the Egyptians shown nursing at the breast of Isis in innumerable statuettes, had to be exposed when born. After Horus was rescued by a poor water-carrier, Pamyles, the gay festival of the Pamylia long celebrated the incident.

In Imperial Rome at the height of its moral decadence the favorite places for exposure were at the Columna Lactaria in the produce market, where nursing mothers gathered either to hire out as wet nurses or to hire wet nurses for their own children, and in the Lake Velabrum region at the foot of the Aventine Hill where prostitutes habitually gathered. The rescued infants could be adopted, but were more often raised in slavery or used as piteous beggars after being deformed by the speculators in the baby market.

Foundlings were especially numerous in times of war or social upheaval. From the earliest days of Christianity, institutions were founded by the Church for these unbaptized waifs. These institutions received the full support of Justinian in A.D. 530. The first modern foundling hospital was established by Datheus, the archpriest of Milan, in 787 (15, p. 359). During the crusades fervent zealots left a trail of foundlings all along the course of their pilgrimages to the Holy Land. Pope Innocent III, about 1200, encouraged institutional care for these foundlings to discourage infanticide, and the Hospital of the Holy Ghost and the Order of the Holy Ghost were assiduously devoted to the welfare of foundlings. During the reign of Louis XIII, when poverty-stricken hordes inhabited Paris, the frightful number of slaughtered infants induced St. Vincent de Paul to act on behalf of foundling institutions. In Russia Catherine II, moved by the plight of abandoned children, built a foundling hospital. A basket with warm clothes was ready outside the hospital night and day to receive babies, with no questions asked. Later, the famous "tour," or turning box, was fashioned to conceal the identity of the mother and spare her from shame and harassment. The "tour" was discontinued in France during the French Revolution, but it was reinstituted and the Sisters of Charity were recalled by Napoleon to care for the foundlings because he wanted to save as many children as possible for the armies of France.

In the United States, where there were no foundling homes in the early nineteenth century, abandoned babies were taken to almshouses. Since artificial feeding was not yet possible, the demand for wet nurses in these almshouses reached critical proportions. The Bellevue Almshouse in New York City was, therefore, forced to place these infants in foster homes as soon as possible, but the neglect and abuse to which they were subjected led to frequent public anguish and outcries for reform. When the almshouse on Blackwell's Island was established, the foundlings were assigned to the care of pauper women there. Every morning a steamboat brought them to the island, and every afternoon it carried back an equal number for burial in Potter's Field. In 1869, the New York Foundling Asylum was established on Randall's Island (Fig. 2). This was evidently an improvement, because two years later John S. Parry, at a meeting of the Social Science Association convened in Philadelphia to consider the problem of infant mortality, read a paper on the necessity for a foundling hospital in Philadelphia.

During the year 1873, 1,392 foundlings were left at the asylum on Randall's Island. That same year the *Medical Register of New York* (p. 362) reported 122 infants found

Figure 2

New York Foundling Asylum, Randall's Island

dead in the streets, alleys, rivers, and elsewhere. The Howard Mission and Home for Little Wanderers attended to 1,285 destitute and neglected children; the New York Juvenile Asylum, a reformatory for vicious children, received 1,153, and the House of Refuge, 1,358 juvenile delinquents. More than thirty organizations of the city were concerned with children in need of help.

The Nursery and Children's Hospital of New York City was established in 1854 by mothers employing wet nurses for the purpose of providing care for these wet nurses' own children. The appealing incident which led to the founding of this hospital was told by Mrs. Thomas Addis Emmet. A "sick nurse" (midwife) called upon a well-known wealthy lady whom she had attended at childbirth, and while looking at the baby, was surprised to find the infant's wet nurse in tears. Inquiry revealed that the wet nurse had turned over her own infant to a foster mother. The midwife went to see this wet nurse's child and found the foster mother sick in bed in a small, dirty, basement room. The foster mother's own child was dead of smallpox, and the wretched, squalid infant of the wet nurse was under the bed in a basket of soiled clothes. To this child the Nursery and Child's Hospital owes its origin.

The early colonial apprenticeship system, under which children as young as four years of age were bound out to servitude, was responsible for many battered children. Thus, a master of Salem, Massachusetts, in 1630 was tried for murdering his apprentice. The jury acquitted him because the boy was "ill disposed," although the master's correction was thought to be unreasonable in that the autopsy disclosed a fractured skull. In Boston, on the other hand, where a master "by sundry stripes and ill usage" over a period of time killed his boy in 1643, the brutal master was said to have been executed. A postmortem examination of another child, in Plymouth in 1655, revealed such terrific battering and cruel tortures that the community was aroused and the master was brought to court (5, p. 122). When, in Maryland in 1660, an orphan boy was so ill treated that "the voice of the people crieth shame thereat," the unhappy boy, indentured at the age of nine, was set free from his master (5, p. 124). In England as early as 1687 Edward Stephens sought relief from the wrongs perpetrated against these enslaved children (20). "Pity those little creatures," Josiah Quincy wrote as early as 1801, at a time when child labor was still viewed in this country as beneficial to society as well as to the child. He found children from four to ten years old employed in cotton mills "with a dull dejection in the countenance of all of them." Not only were they physically battered, but they were battered in mind as well (5, p. 174).

Child Martyrs to Industry

Urbanization and the machine age led to other forms of child abuse and to increasing mortality. Children had always worked, but when the reign of the machine began, their work often became synonymous with slavery. They may have sometimes suffered from the ignorance or brutality of parents, but in the main, children sharing in the work of the family has always been considered a good thing. With the coming of the machine age, however, mere babies were subjected to terrible inhumanity by the factory system. When parents rebelled against these conditions and refused to send their children to work, pauper children from the workhouses, who had no parents to speak in their behalf, were put to work in the mills. Children from five years of age upward were worked sixteen hours at a time, sometimes with irons riveted around their ankles to keep them from running away. They were starved, beaten, and in many other ways maltreated. Many succumbed to occupational diseases, and some committed suicide; few survived for any length of time.

A movement for child labor reform, begun by Robert Owen and aided by Sir Robert Peel, led to the first factory act, passed by Parliament in 1802. This broke up the pauper apprentice system. Traditional rights of the parents over their children persisted, however, and thus the act did not apply to children under the supervision of their parents. Children who went into the mills with parental consent still had to work twelve hours a day and were often brutally whipped with leather thongs by tyrannical supervisors (Fig. 3). Sometimes they were dipped head first into cisterns of cold water to keep them awake. The machine became the Moloch to which the children of the eighteenth and nineteenth centuries were sacrificed (10, p. 140).

A most forlorn waif of the cities during the same period was the chimney sweep. Skinny elves with a natural proclivity for climbing were bound out to clamber up narrow flues and scrape off the soot. None of the work for children was more odious. Working night and day, their efforts usually hastened by some strong-hearted master burning straw behind them, they were subjected to all kinds of brutality. People were callous to their sufferings. When a certain woman, touched by an accident that occurred to one small sweep in her own home, befriended them as a class, her kindness was suspect. These children quickly deteriorated both mentally and physically. Not only were they subject to cancer of the scrotum, the so-called chimney sweep's cancer described by Percival Pott in 1775, but they also succumbed rapidly to the ravages of pulmonary consumption. Owing to the many serious accidents to which they were prone, the practice of sending boys up chimneys was finally abolished in England, when social reform pertaining to children was well on its way in the nineteenth century.

Figure 3

Child beating in an English woolen mill, around 1850
(Courtesy of Bettmann Archive)

The Society for the Prevention of Cruelty to Children

Even though the child stirs the most tender emotions in mankind, cruelty to children has always prevailed. Fontana (21, p. 8) reports the story of Mary Ellen, who was being maltreated by her adoptive parents. The child was being beaten regularly and was seriously malnourished. Interested church workers were unable to convince local authorities to take legal action against the parents. The right of parents to chastise their own children was still sacred, and there was no law under which any agency could interfere, to protect a child like her. The church workers were not discouraged; rather, they appealed to the Society for the Prevention of Cruelty to Animals (SPCA), which promptly took action. They were able to have Mary Ellen removed from her parents on the grounds that she was a member of the animal kingdom and that there-fore her case could be included under the laws against animal cruelty.

As a direct result of this incident the Society for the Prevention of Cruelty to Chil-dren was founded in New York City in 1871. Following the example of the New York Society, many other societies with similar objectives were formed in different parts of this country. The Philadelphia Society to Protect Children from Cruelty was founded in 1877. In Great Britain in 1899 thirty-one such societies united to form the National

Society for the Prevention of Cruelty to Children with Queen Victoria as patron, and Parliament passed an act for prevention of cruelty to children which was dubbed "The Children's Charter" (22, p. 30). In New York City, Samuel B. Halliday stirred the public consciousness with his work on behalf of destitute children (8), and in London Thomas John Barnardo, forcing upon the public conscience awareness of the existence of gangs of homeless children, succeeded in the establishment of the chain of homes and vocational schools that earned for him the title of "Father of Nobody's Children" (23).

Laws Against Child Abuse and Infanticide

The Code of Hammurabi about four thousand years ago provided that if a nurse allowed a suckling to die in her hands and substituted another, her breast should be amputated (24, p. 18). In ancient Egypt infanticide was common, but it was not legal. The Thebans made it a capital offense, and there is an Egyptian record of a child murderer who was ordered to carry the slain infant in her arms for three days and three nights. Even though the *Patria Protestas* gave a father supreme right to sell, mutilate, or even kill his offspring as far back as the reign of Numa Pompilius (about 700 B.C.), infanticide was relatively uncommon in ancient Rome. The Laws of the Twelve Tables (about 450 B.C.) modified the *Patria Protestas* so that a son could be sold only three times, and the *Lex Julia* and *Lex Papia* of Augustus Caesar in A.D. 4 checked the *Patria Potestas* and indirectly aided children; but the exposure of children, a common theme in the comedies of Plautus and of Terrence, continued unabated. Child welfare laws and agitation on behalf of children were frequent under succeeding emperors. Tiberius ordered the death penalty for Carthaginian priests who sacrificed children in the fire to Moloch, but the practice continued in secret even in the lifetime of Tertullian, over a hundred years later. The empress Faustina, during the second century, established foundations to save female infants from destruction, but apparently her efforts were ephemeral because the next century proved to be an evil one for children (24, p. 42).

The Hebrews interdicted infanticide, and so did their religious offshoots, the Christians and the Mohammedans. God frequently exhorts all of them in their holy books, the Bible and Koran, against this sin. Philo Judaeus in the first century after Christ proclaimed it a crime, and in the next century, Tertullian, one of the fathers of the Christian Church, in speaking of infanticide, said "murder is murder in any shape" and a sin against the commandment, "Thou shalt not kill." Through the influence of Christianity, edicts against infanticide and the sale of children into slavery were issued by Constantine (A.D. 315 and 321), by Valentinian, Valens, and Gratian (A.D. 374), by Valentinian II, Theodosius, and Arcadius (A.D. 391), by Honorius and Theodosius (A.D. 409), by Theodosius II (A.D. 438), and by Valentinian III (A.D. 451). Infanticide by exposure or otherwise had been established as a crime by Barnabas in the time of the apostles; in A.D. 305 a sentence of excommunication for life was decreed, but in 314 this was reduced to ten years and in 524 to seven (24, p. 55).

The Council of Nicea (A.D. 325) ordered the establishment of a *xenodochion*, a hospital for the benefit of paupers, in each Christian village. Some of these institutions became *brephotrophia*, asylums for children. The Council of Vaison (A.D. 442) provided a means for the Church to receive abandoned children and care for them. This provision was reaffirmed ten years later at Arles and again at Agde. There a marble receptacle was set up to receive the children at the church door. At the Council of Toledo (A.D. 589), clergy and civil authorities were enjoined to unite their efforts to prevent infanticide. The Council of Constantinople the year before had compared infanticide to homicide, and the Theodosian Code prescribed the death penalty for this crime. Even though capital punishment was prescribed repeatedly thereafter, it was rarely carried out. Sixtus V and Gregory XIV in the sixteenth century and Frederick the Great in the eighteenth issued stern edicts against infanticide (24, p. 57), but as long as poverty, illegitimacy, and other social problems exist such laws will always be futile.

In 1556, Henry II of France decreed death to women who concealed the birth of a child; and not long after, James I, King of England, passed a similar law, but it subsequently had to be repealed. For "dropping" (abandoning) an infant in eighteenth-century England, a woman might have been sentenced to a month at hard labor, but many women still secretly murdered unwanted babies. "There is scarce an assizes," wrote Addison in 1773, "where some unhappy wretch is not executed for the murder of a child. And how many more of these monsters of inhumanity may we suppose to be wholly undiscovered or cleared for want of legal evidence?" (25, p. 38). An act of 1803 placed women tried for the murder of bastard children under the same laws as those pertaining to murder in general and with the same penalties. In this country, too, there has never been any legal distinction between the murder of adults and the killing of a newborn infant, or an infant at any age, legitimate or otherwise. As soon as the child is born it is a citizen with full protection of the law.

Other peoples and nations also had early infanticide laws. The Roman historian, Tacitus (A.D. 55–119), noted that the Germanic tribes considered infanticide a crime, and the Germanic law codes, the Salic law, and the Hispanic laws, contained penalties for this crime. The Visigothic King, Chindaswinth, who reigned A.D. 632–49, was the first monarch to set the death penalty; penalties were also severe under Charles V, and the Austrian Penal Code prescribed life imprisonment. It should be noted, however, that everywhere the penalty meted out for killing illegitimate infants was much less severe. Under Czar Alexis in 1647 the punishment for infanticide was extremely moderate (26, p. 822).

One of the vexing forensic problems in cases of infanticide has always been how to determine that the baby was born alive before it was killed. Obviously you cannot kill a dead child. For this reason Swammerdam's discovery in 1667 that fetal lungs will float on water after respiration has taken place was one of the most important medico-legal contributions of the seventeenth century. This was first put to practical application by Johann Schreyer in the case of a fifteen-year-old peasant girl accused of infanticide in 1681; the infant's sinking lungs dramatically secured the mother's acquittal. A letter by Schoepffer in 1684, published many years later in a book on infanticide based on eighty-eight autopsies, likewise corroborated this test (27, p. 45).

During the early days of the American Republic, when the public took measures against various aspects of juvenile delinquency, abused and neglected children were gathered into the law enforcement net. In New York, in 1825, the New York Society for the Reformation of Juvenile Delinquents established a House of Refuge, Philadelphia following with a similar institution in 1828. In Boston, the civil authorities acted instead of voluntary agencies, and the City Council founded a House of Reformation 1826. These institutions were primarily for wayward children, but when the first House of Refuge was proposed in New York the memorial to the legislature advocated also that neglected and abused children be admitted. This memorial pointed out that the laws of New York did not, as in Massachusetts and some other places, authorize magistrates to use compulsory measures with parents who grossly abused their charge and yet refused to resign their children to the guardians of the poor; and so such a law was recommended for New York. In Boston the City Council ruled that among others to be committed to the House of Reformation by the courts would be children whose parents, "from drunkenness or other vices," neglected their children. While the intent here was to confine the children who by their own fault or that of their parents were a nuisance or menace to the public, the act also had the germ of the law which permitted a social agency to take custody of a battered child. When the parents demanded their children back, state courts rejected their pleas. Then in 1838 the Supreme Court of Pennsylvania ruled that under certain circumstances natural parents could be superseded by the *parens patriae*, or common guardian of the community, thus establishing another legal precedent for removing children from the danger of incompetent parents. This decision noted that the right of parental control is natural, but not an inalienable one. The courts thereafter considered the institution and organization *in loco parentis* and prevented injudicious interference from parents (5, p. 672).

After the Franco-Prussian war Theophile Roussel (1816–1903) became an outstanding protagonist of the infant-welfare movement. The "loi Roussel," of December 23, 1874, for the protection of infants sent out to nurse and his law of July 25, 1889, for the protection of abandoned or maltreated children earned for him renown as "the advocate of abandoned children" and led to a long-continued social reform movement that extended well into the twentieth century (24, p. 155). This was actually the first law protecting maltreated children, including under its protective wing the abandoned, neglected and ill-treated child, and providing for visitors to investigate cases in order to prevent maltreatment and neglect. The law was amended in 1901, 1907 and again, to meet the changing needs and attitudes in 1921. In 1935 there was a further outcry about violence and maltreatment of children, and again the government reacted by passing another law (28, p. 151). In England the Infant Life Protection Act of the latter half of the nineteenth century regulated foster homes but was ineffectual because it did not provide for regular inspection. It was not until 1908, when a particularly lurid case of infanticide by an avaricious foster mother reached the front pages, that the Infant Life Protection Act required registration and inspection of foster homes, providing for the appointment of visitors to supervise the care received by foster children.

In the United States by this time state governments were entering the field of child welfare. In 1909, the first White House Conference was convened, and the American Association for Study and Prevention of Infant Mortality was founded. With the creation of the United States Children's Bureau, the trend for federal concern began. At the White House Conference on Child Health and Protection of 1930, an American "Children's Charter" was adopted, which among many other ambitions promised every child a home with love and security, plus full time public welfare services for protection from abuse, neglect, exploitation, or moral hazard.

Soon it became evident that the cause of child abuse evolved from complex psycho-social backgrounds. Dr. Janet E. Lane-Clayton in 1920 advised health visitors to attempt "parent persuasion" in order to effect "astonishing transformation" in child abusive parents and the use of special social service agencies when drastic treatment is necessary, instead of relying on law enforcement agencies (29). Another writer, in a study of illustrative case reports largely drawn from newspaper accounts and court records, listing all the sickening stigmata of the battered child syndrome, pointed out that cruelty to children can be active where physical violence or deliberate torture are employed, or passive in the form of neglect, starvation and so on. This author analyzed the psychological aspects behind the battered child occurrences in great detail, and from a present day point of view, concluding that it is prevention, rather than cure, that is needed; and that such prevention begins at a far more fundamental level than punishment, or even treatment, of parents who have already offended (30, p. 116). It was suggested that in every case there be obligation placed upon some authority to examine the parents concerned and treat them (30, p. 131).

Medical Aspects

The physician, up to the end of the eighteenth century, as a rule knew so little about infantile pathology that when an inquest was made into the causes of death in a very young infant it was more likely a midwife or some old granny who was called upon to view the body and report the cause of death. These women treated the children in health and in sickness and were able to recognize abnormalities in children sometimes better than physicians. Yet the physicians were called upon when matters proved too difficult for these wise old women. Hippocrates discussed the childhood conditions and so did Galen. Rhazes was the first, in the tenth century, to gather the medical information about young children into a single monograph. In it he mentioned, casually, that ruptures can occur when children cry or scream a great deal, and that it may be from being struck intentionally (31, p. 376).

Injuries to children are recorded consistently throughout the medical literature. Paul Zacchius, in a medico-legal work of 1661, outlined the postmortem findings in battered persons and mentioned the daughter of Nerius in the Hippocratic writings who died nine days after she was struck by a little girl friend with the flat of the hand on the sinciput (32, p. 351). Theophilus Bonet in 1679 reported numerous autopsies on children dead from various injuries which he collected from the literature as well as from his own experience (33, p. 1595).

Postmortem findings were always of great importance in forensic medicine. Ordinarily, accidents and injuries were not the problem of medical men before the nineteenth century, being in the realm of the surgeons. There were some popular medical books written for the guidance of mothers which do mention deliberate injuries to children. There was, for example, almost always a warning about the choice of a nurse ever since Soranus warned that an ill-tempered nurse can be like a maniac and sometimes lets the child drop from her hands, or overturns it dangerously when she is unable to restrain a crying baby (34, p. 93). One grandmother strongly warned against the danger of indiscriminate blows to children, saying "nothing should induce anyone to give the slightest blow above the head or neck; what is called a box on the ear may be the occasion for incurable deafness," and asserting that blows on the head could produce water on the brain, possibly an early allusion to subdural hematoma in a pediatric text (35, p. 340).

In 1860 Ambroise Tardieu published a medico-legal study of abuse and maltreatment of children which, as Silverman points out (37) presented clearly all the features of the battered-child syndrome of Kempe. Since Tardieu did not enjoy the benefit of radiology to provide him with living anatomical information, his study relied heavily on autopsy findings. He quoted Zacchius and appended descriptions of 32 children battered to death by whipping, burning, and so forth (38, p. 361–98). The same year Athol Johnson at the Hospital for Sick Children of London called attention to the frequency of repeated fractures in children (39, p. 28). Influenced by Malgaigne, he attributed these to the rickety condition of the bones. Rickets was at that time almost universal among children, but in the cases which he described as due to successive slight accidents we can strongly suspect there were unrecognized battered children among them. He quoted Gibson of Philadelphia reporting a rickety boy with twenty-four repeated fractures, all uniting without difficulty; and mentioned a skeleton of a rachitic female in France presenting traces of 200 fractures at different periods. Yet the official London records of 1870 reveal that among 3,926 children under five years of age who died by accident or violence, 202 were listed as manslaughter, 95 neglect, 18 exposure to cold—all obviously dead of child abuse. However, the rachitic theory persisted well into the twentieth century (40, p. 612).

The "Battered Child Syndrome"

Abuse of children has excited periodic waves of sympathy, each rising to a high pitch, and then curiously subsiding until the next period of excitation. We owe the present wave of excitation to the relatively new discipline of pediatric radiology. Thomas Morgan Rotch as early as 1906 was presenting studies in infant X-rays, ten years after Roentgen's original discovery. Twenty years later Ralph Bromer was to head the nation's first X-ray department in a children's hospital. It was not until 1946 that Caffey reported his original observations regarding the common association of subdural hematoma and abnormal X-ray changes in the long bones (41). A few years later Silverman (see chapter 4) reported similar findings and clearly defined the traumatic nature of the lesions (42). In 1955, Wooley brought out the startling fact that the trauma noted on the X-rays was in many cases willfully inflicted (43). The news reached the radio, television, and press and electrified the public, as well as many social agencies.

Kempe was alarmed, in the early sixties, by the large number of children admitted to his pediatric service suffering from non-accidental injury. He contacted some eighty district attorneys in an effort to obtain a more accurate picture of the true incidence of the problem (44). In 1961, the American Academy of Pediatrics conducted a symposium on the problem of child abuse under Dr. Kempe's direction. To direct attention to the seriousness of the problem, he proposed the term "the battered child syndrome." This symposium, which attracted a large number of people, was the stimulus for the beginning of present-day interest. The Children's Bureau awarded grants for the study of child abuse, and the American Humane Society uncovered 662 cases in a single year. Every state and every social class was represented in this group. Twenty-seven per cent of these 662 cases represented fatalities; many more had permanent brain damage.

As a result of this recent surge of interest, the problems of the battered child are taking on a new phase in our history. It is one of the most serious concerns facing society. The progress made in the last decade is only a beginning of man's attempt to change the lot of these unfortunate children.

References

1. Kramer, Samuel Noah. 1956. *From the tablets of Sumer: Twenty-five firsts in man's recorded history*. Indian Hills, Colo.: Falcon's Wing.
2. Ryan, William Burke. 1862. *Infanticide: Its law, prevalence, prevention and history*. London: J. Churchill.
3. Earle, Alice Morse. 1926. *Child life in colonial days*. New York: Macmillan.
4. Godfrey, Elizabeth. 1907. *English children in olden time*. London: Methuen & Co.
5. Bremner, Robert H. 1970. *Children and youth in America*. Cambridge: Harvard University Press.
6. Still, George Frederic. 1965. *The history of paediatrics: The progress of the study of diseases of children up to the end of the XVIIIth century*. London: Dawsons of Pall Mall.
7. Aries, Philippe. 1962. *Centuries of childhood: A social history of family life*. New York: Alfred A. Knopf.
8. Dunn, Courtenay. 1920. *The natural history of the child*. New York: John Lane.
9. Halliday, Samuel B. 1861. *The little street sweeper; Or, life among the poor*. New York: Phinney, Blakeman & Mason.
10. Balestrini, Raffaello. 1888. *Aborto, Infanticidio ed Esposizione d'infante*. Torino: Bocca.
11. List, Georg Dietrich Karl. 1784. *Über Hurerei und Kindermord*. Mannheim: Tobias Loffier.
12. Briffault, Robert. 1927. *The mothers*. 3 volumes. New York: Macmillan.
13. Parsons, Elsie Clews. 1906. *The family: An ethnological and historical outline with descriptive notes*. New York: G. P. Putnam Sons.
14. Slingerland, W. H. 1919. *Child-placing in families*. New York: Russell Sage Foundation.
15. Remacle, Bernard-Benoit. 1838. *Des hospices d'enfans Trouvés en Europe, et principalement en France, depuis leur origine jusqu'à nos jours*. Paris: Treuttel et Würtz.

16. Curatulo, G. Emilio. 1902. *Kunst der Juno Lucina in Rom*. Berlin: August Hirschwald.
17. Tardieu, Ambroise. 1868. *Etude medico-legale sur l'infanticide*. Paris: J-B Bailliére et Fils.
18. Young, Leontine. 1964. *Wednesday's children: A study of child neglect and abuse*. New York: McGraw-Hill.
19. Ashby, Hugh T. 1922. *Infant mortality*. 2d ed. Cambridge: University Press.
20. Stephens, Edward. 1687. *Relief of apprentices wronged by their masters*. London.
21. Fontana, Vincent J. 1964. *The maltreated child: The maltreatment syndrome in children*. Springfield, Illinois: Charles C. Thomas.
22. Allen, Anne, and Morton, Arthur. 1961. *This is your child: The story of the National Society for the Prevention of Cruelty to Children*. London: Routledge & Kegan Paul.
23. Williams, A. E. 1966. *Barnardo of Stepney: The father of nobody's children·* London: George Allen & Unwin, Ltd.
24. Garrison, Fielding H. 1965. *Abt-Garrison History of Pediatrics*, reprinted from *Pediatrics*, Volume I. Edited by Isaac A. Abt. Philadelphia: W. B. Saunders Co.
25. Caulfield, Ernest. 1931. *The infant welfare movement in the eighteenth century*. New York: Paul B. Hoeber.
26. Gradewohl, R. B. H. 1954. *Legal medicine*. Edited by T. A. Gonzales. New York: Appleton-Century-crofts.
27. Buettner, Christoph Gottlieb. 1938 [1771]. *Kindermord*. Koenigsberg and Leipzig. Masson.
28. Bourguin, F. 1938. *La protection sociale de l'enfance en France*. Paris:
29. Lane-Clayton, Janet E. 1920. *The child welfare movement*. London.
30. Chesser, Eustace. 1952. *Cruelty to children*. New York: Philosophical Library.
31. Radbill, Samuel X. 1971. The first treatise on pediatrics. *Am. J. Diseases of Children*. vol. 122.
32. Zacchius, Paul. 1661. *Quastionem medico-legalium*. Leyden.
33. Bonet, Theophile. 1679. *Sepulchretum*. Geneva.
34. Temkin, Owsei. 1956. *Soranus' gynecology*. Baltimore: Johns Hopkins Press.
35. *Advice to young mothers on physical education of children, by a grandmother*. 1823. London.
36. Alcott, William A. 1836. *The young mother*. Boston.
37. Silverman, Frederic N. 1971. "Unrecognized trauma in infants: The battered child syndrome, and the syndrome of Ambroise Tardieu." The Riegler Lecture presented in Minneapolis, Minnesota, 21 October 1971.
38. Tardieu, Ambroise. 1860. Etude médico-légale sur les sévices et mauvais traitments exercés sur des enfants. *Annales d'hygiène publique et de médecine légale*, 2d ser., vol. 13.
39. Johnson, Athol A. W. 1860. *Lectures on the surgery of childhood*. London.
40. Barrett, Howard. 1875. *Management of infancy and childhood in health and disease*. London.
41. Caffey, J. 1946. Multiple fractures in the long bones of children suffering from

chronic subdural hematoma. *Am. J. Roentgenol. Radium Therapy, Nucl. Med.* 56 (1946): 163–73.

42. Silverman, F. N. 1953. The Roentgen manifestations of unrecognized skeletal trauma in infants. *Am. J. Roentgenol., Radium Therapy, Nucl. Med.* 69 (1953): 413–27.

43. Wooley, P. V., Jr., and Evans, W. A., Jr. 1955. Significance of skeletal lesions in infants resembling those of traumatic origin. *J. Am. Med. Assoc.* 158:539.

44. Kempe, C. Henry; Silverman, Frederic N.; Steele, Brandt F.; Droegemueller, William; and Silver, Henry K. 1962. The battered-child syndrome. *J. Am. Med. Assoc.* 181:17.

PART 2

Medical Aspects

2 | The Responsibility and Role of the Physician

Ray E. Helfer

Department of Human Development
College of Human Medicine
Michigan State University
East Lansing, Michigan 48823

The family physician or pediatrician has a clear responsibility both to the child and his family. He must see this responsibility as an involvement with the total family unit and not find himself caught up in the complex situation of alienating the parents in his attempts to help the child. He must make use of every talent, both his own and others, available to him, constantly keeping in mind his role as the *family* physician (1). This is a difficult and delicate position to be in and it is hoped that the comments herein will serve to enable the physician to feel more comfortable and to understand his role and responsibility more clearly when he finds himself involved in a case of child abuse.

Physical, nutritional, or emotional abuse is one of the most common maladies of the young child, and yet it is one which general practitioners, pediatricians, and other specialists have been unable and unwilling to diagnose. The medical profession has exhibited almost a complete lack of interest in this problem until recent years. Pediatrics, the pioneers of the preventive aspects of child care, had to turn to radiology and pathology to shed light upon the true nature of this problem (2, 3, 4). In some areas of this country and in many areas of Europe pediatrics continues to lag behind certain social and legal agencies in providing leadership, service, understanding and even research in the field of child abuse. We in pediatrics have found ourselves in the position of saying, "We must hurry and catch up, for we are their leader." It is the responsibility of the medical profession to assume the leadership in this field.

The family physician with the assistance of his psychiatric and social service colleagues must make the diagnosis, protect the child, counsel the parents, report his findings, and follow up, both medically and socially, to assure that the proper disposition has not only been made but also carried out. Many physicians are unwilling to accept this responsibility. This attitude cannot prevail much longer for the problem

25

is too immense and the responsibilities too clear to be ignored. Emotional ties with the family, lack of understanding of his legal (much less moral) obligations, denial of the facts, inability to obtain these facts, lack of experience, and "busy attitude" are only a few of the handicaps (5).

The family doctor has one of the most difficult roles to play in dealing with the abused child. His first and foremost responsibility is to the child and his family. He may have to assume several other roles including marriage counselor, medical counselor, social worker, legal consultant, reporter of the facts, testifier in court, and frequently, psychiatrist. To add to his burden, the family physician is often emotionally attached to the family and child. He may have been caring for this family for many years and would thus find it difficult to fulfill his obligations. It is of the utmost importance for the physician who finds himself emotionally involved with the family of a battered child to immediately refer the child to a physician who is not so attached, preferably one who is familiar with this type of problem. All of us who have handled battered children over the years have seen unfortunate situations where the family doctor is unable to fulfill his role and yet unwilling to ask for help.

If the family and doctor are from a small town the problems are considerably increased. The physician has not only been attached to the family for many years, but also both he and the family are frequently friends of the law enforcement and child welfare personnel, public health nurse, and local judge. This situation leads to a most inefficient and ineffectual handling of the case, and the one to suffer is usually the child. In small communities the personnel who are required to handle the case frequently have had no previous experience in cases of this type. Some states are beginning to make available consultation services for welfare agencies and law enforcement personnel in small communities. Many of these people are unwilling to ask for help and blunder their way through, only to find that their mishandling has caused antagonism, anger, and long drawn out court proceedings. Again, it is the child who suffers. When a child is returned home prematurely by a welfare worker or judge inexperienced in this field, death or severe injury may ensue.

State, municipal, and private agencies have a responsibility to the smaller communities to provide experienced consultants to assist them in the handling of these cases. The physician at the private or state medical center who has repeatedly dealt with the problem of child abuse can be most helpful to the family doctor. Every medical center should provide a readily available team of consultants, headed by a capable pediatrician, to assist the house staff, private physician, and other community personnel. This team must also assume the role of educating their colleagues as well as the members of allied fields in the community.

This education must extend to the members of the press. The news media can be most helpful to both the community and professional people working with the problem of child abuse. Sensationalism (6) may sell newspapers, but it does nothing to help the people who deal with this problem. There is nothing to be gained by this approach and a great deal to be lost. The press can be most beneficial if it is willing to assume its proper role and report to the public through feature articles on certain aspects related to the battered child syndrome. We have found that when the press cooperates in this manner the results are most helpful (7).

The Immediate Care of the Child

Once the injury has occurred the physician's first and immediate responsibility is to the child. When the parents bring their abused or neglected child to the physician, early diagnosis and treatment is essential. Treatment not only consists of medical and surgical care but also of provisions for the protection of the child. In almost every case the first step is to admit the child to the hospital (8). This is done whether or not the actual medical or surgical findings are severe enough to warrant admission. The child is both patient and victim (9). The main reason for admitting the child to the hospital other than for assessing the degree of injury is to protect him. It should be a straightforward admission for the purpose of evaluation. No accusations should be made and the experienced physician must restrain his zealous, and often accusing, house staff and ward nurses, who frequently blunder in their questioning of these parents. This does nothing but antagonize the parents and makes future communication most difficult.

The admission to the hospital provides time for more relaxed conversation with parents and permits a more thorough evaluation of the child. If the child is old enough, he frequently becomes less frightened and is willing to talk to the physician, thereby assisting him in his evaluation. It is common for parents to be willing and often relieved to admit a child to the hospital, if the case has been handled properly from the beginning and the house staff or the referring physician have not antagonized them. If the parents are kept well informed of everything that goes on and what is found they are usually willing to keep the child in the hospital until some definitive plan can be made. This point will not be difficult to understand if it is realized that the majority of parents who injure their children want help. If this help is offered without resorting to threats and accusations, the parents are usually most cooperative.

Medical Aspects

The medical and physical evaluation of the child must be handled thoroughly and expeditiously (10, 11). Emergency care is often required if the child is acutely ill. No attempt will be made to discuss in detail the frequently necessary neurological, orthopedic or neurosurgical care of these children. These aspects of acute trauma in children are well covered in the standard textbooks.

The most common urgent problem is the subdural hematoma, in which case the physician should very early in the period of the child's care request the consultation of a neurosurgeon. Early handling of the subdural hematoma improves the prognosis (12, 13). The neurosurgeon not only can give surgical assistance but also can provide expert opinion if the case comes to court. It is not uncommon to see documented subdural hematomas in the absence of demonstrable fractures of the skull or evidence of external trauma. The most common omission in the evaluation of these children is serial head measurements. This may be the only change noted during the early stages of this problem.

The child who has been severely beaten may present with a very acute problem related to the gastrointestinal tract such as an acute obstruction owing to a hematoma in the intestinal wall (14), a perforation of the intestine resulting in peritonitis or abscess formation, or lacerations of other abdominal organs (15). These are, of course, acute surgical emergencies and should be handled accordingly (16). Many children who have been battered require immediate orthopedic consultation (17) which will improve the long-term prognosis in cases of both complete fracture as well as severe epiphyseal or metaphyseal damage owing to recurrent trauma. Traumatic eye injuries may also occur, requiring emergency care by an ophthalmologist (18).

At the risk of arousing the anger of some of my surgical colleagues, I feel that the non-surgical aspects of the case, such as parental counseling, communications with community agencies, and medical care of the child should be handled by the family physician or pediatrician and not by the surgical consultant. The battered child syndrome is a pediatric problem and should be handled by the pediatrician with the assistance of his surgical colleagues as consultants.

Every child who has had a serious unexplained injury should have X rays of the long bones, ribs, and skull. This is the physician's most important diagnostic tool and should be utilized in all situations involving possible child abuse. If the child is seen soon after the initial trauma the evidence of the trauma may be missed on the X rays. If suspicions are high, repeat X rays of the long bones in a two- or three-week period should be performed to completely rule out trauma to this area. There are a few entities that must be considered in the differential diagnosis, most of which can be ruled out by an adequate history and physical examination. Both of these points are very adequately covered in chapter 4. A radiologist who is aware of the problems of child abuse will not only be helpful in making the diagnosis but will also be most useful in the area of case finding. It is not unusual for a good radiologist when viewing routine X rays to point out suspicious areas and request additional films to confirm these suspicions.

A consultation with the hematologist is most desirable in all instances of severe bruising. In our experience it is most unusual to see bleeding tendencies in children who are battered, although a frequent explanation on the part of the parents is that "my child bruises easily." It is important, both for medical and legal reasons, to rule out the fact that the child in question does not have a bleeding disorder. Our Pediatric Hematology Section sees all of the battered children with severe bruises who are admitted to our hospital and performs a coagulation survey. It is their feeling that to rule out all known coagulation defects no less than six tests must be performed. Unless each of these is completed, the physician is deceiving himself by depending upon the results of any one of them. These are as follows: platelet count, bleeding time, prothrombin time, thrombin time, partial thromboplastin time, and tourniquet test. None of these are beyond the routine capacity of the laboratory and can be easily performed.

When a coagulation defect is found, it presents difficulties in diagnosis because of the possibility that this defect might have been responsible for the multiple ecchymoses. We have seen only one child who has had an abnormality in any one of these studies. She was a five-year-old child who was reported to have fallen down the cellar stairs. She was covered with ecchymotic areas, some older than others. X rays were negative. She had pneumonia, possible sepsis, and pancytopenia. Her platelet count was less than 50,000/mm^3, which rose when the infection responded to treatment. The nutritional status, neighbor's reports, and severe ecchymoses gave every indication that the child had been severely abused, but no court action was taken and the child was sent home. Her infant brother appeared one year later at another hospital suffering from a subdural hematoma.

Cases in which children are beaten and ecchymoses are the only physical findings usually are difficult to handle. It is important, therefore, for the physician to consider the use of photography. Colored slides are most helpful in documenting findings to various law enforcement agencies and courts, as well as assisting in teaching house staff and medical students. Colored pictures may not be admissible as evidence in some courts, thereby necessitating the obtaining of black-and-white photographs as well. Surprisingly, we have not found it difficult to obtain parental permission if the case has been handled properly. In difficult situations court permission can usually be obtained within a short period of time.

When the medical and surgical evaluation has been completed the physician is confronted with the difficult task of gathering all the data together and making a definitive diagnosis. He should constantly be aware of *discrepancies* between the degree of trauma and the history given to explain these injuries. In many cases the diagnosis is easy. The X-ray determinations are clear cut and the physical findings reveal, without question, that the child has been severely injured. It is the indefinite case such as an isolated subdural hematoma without a history of trauma, fracture, or bruising that poses a difficult problem. What recommendations should be made to the parents or community agencies? The physician is fully aware that the subdural hematoma by and large cannot be explained on any basis other than trauma (meningitis usually not entering the picture) and yet the parents are unable or unwilling to give him the necessary history. Children with extensive ecchymoses and no other physical findings also present a difficult diagnostic problem. Every physician who has had any experience with these children has experienced the most unfortunate circumstance of having a child return home only to come back to the hospital or another hospital much more severely injured or even dead. And yet, we must not falsely accuse parents of injuring children (19, 20, 21). The problem of the difficult case will be discussed in more detail, hopefully providing the physician with suggestions as to how situations of this type might be handled. There is no easy solution.

The Physician's Responsibility to the Parents

Once the child has been admitted to the hospital and his medical evaluation is under way the physician must turn his attention to the parents. It is here that experience becomes essential. This should not be the responsibility of an inexperienced house officer. A technique can be developed (it must be individualized in each situation) which enables the physician to handle this most difficult aspect of the problem reasonably well. Three points seem to be most important: first, the physician must make every effort not to render judgment or become angry; second, he must realize the parents usually want help; and third, he must always keep the parents completely informed about what is going on.

It is most difficult for any individual dealing with parents who abuse children not to demonstrate some form of hostility and anger. The importance of controlling one's emotions in this situation becomes readily apparent after a case has been mishandled by an over-zealous, emotional interviewer, be he physician, medical student, police officer, or social worker. If he is able to sit down with the parents and talk with them about the problem and the child, without demonstrating any hostility, the interview will go well and the cooperation of the parents will soon become a reality. At times, in cases of severely injured children, it is best to wait several hours before talking at length with the parents about the problem. Parents are less worried and anxious, the physician is less angered, and the problem can be approached more rationally. In practically every instance where communications break down, the case has been mishandled at the outset by a physician, student, social worker, or the police.

I introduce myself as a staff pediatrician who is interested in talking with parents whose children have been injured. I usually begin the interview with them by asking the parents how they are doing, or by indicating that I realize this has been a tough few days for them. Only after dealing with their concerns and questions do I move into a discussion about the child and his injuries. I talk with both parents individually and together while the child is in the hospital. The interview may not be completed for several days, lasting for a few minutes each day, improving rapport as well as adding new knowledge with each session.

In regard to the second point, dealing with the parents' desire for help, it must be admitted that there are times when they do not demonstrate this desire too clearly. If the physician is convinced, however, that this fact is true, the parent will eventually demonstrate in some manner his or her rather desperate longing for some form of assistance. One mother's response to my statement that I would be afraid to have her four-year-old child return home said, "You wouldn't be nearly as frightened as I would." On the other hand another mother replied, "You can go straight to hell." She finally indicated her tremendous relief when she learned the child had been placed in a foster home as a result of a court order. The rewards of working with parents who beat their children are not readily seen, and all too frequently, it may take years of follow-through of a given case before the physician is convinced that he took the right approach—and sometimes, he never is.

I have found it most helpful to be extremely honest and frank with the parents of these children. Throughout the whole interview emphasis must be toward helping the parents and the child. In the past they have rarely had anyone interested enough in them to offer assistance. If this atmosphere persists throughout the many interviews that are necessary then the antagonism, anger, and threatening aspects of the situation are diminished.

After I have explained in some detail the findings of the medical and surgical evaluation, I then outline the results of the laboratory tests, including the X rays. I tell them exactly the number of fractures that are present and interpret for them their significance. The parents seem willing to discuss in more detail some of the other aspects of the case once they realize you have honestly given them the complete medical report on a day-to-day basis. The medical findings are, if you will, a tool that, if used properly, will open the door for further discussion. Constant care must be taken not to place so much emphasis on the child that the parent is neglected or threatened.

The question arises, should the social worker assume many of these responsibilities rather than the physician (22)? It is possible that some of this work can be done very adequately by a well trained social worker (23). I personally would rather have the experienced social worker assist in the support and therapy of the parents rather than the fact finding and investigative aspects of the case (see chapter 8). It is the physician who must explain the findings to the parents, make the written report to the law enforcement agency, and testify in court. If he has not been a part in all of the foregoing discussions with the parents, then rapport breaks down and parents are difficult to work with. I do not feel that the medical report required by law should be sent by a social worker. Physicians are much too anxious to pass their responsibility on to the social worker, and the social worker is much too willing to accept it.

After the parents are convinced that the physician is truly interested in them and their problem and has been honest with them in reporting all findings to date, it is then necessary for the physician to explain that he, as a practicing doctor in the state must by law make a report. It is at this point that many physicians find their relationship with parents strained. On one hand he has explained to them all the findings of the child's evaluations and that he is most interested in helping them, and on the other hand he then must tell them that he must make a report to a state agency. Some parents are at this point convinced that the doctor, whom they had trusted, has betrayed them. The most effective way of handling this situation is to be straightforward and frank with the parents.

I usually explain that I am in a difficult position. I tell them that I have spent these last few days or hours talking with them about their problem and that I am interested in helping them. However, because of my legal obligations that I have as a practicing physician in this state, I must send a report to a state agency on every child that I see who has been injured by other than accidental means. If the case has been handled correctly, most parents at this point will respond by saying that they knew this report had to be made. Once this hurdle has been achieved then the physician should go one step further. It is his responsibility to explain to the parents what this report actually means, to whom it will be sent, what it will say, and what will be the probable response of the recipient. If the physician does not do this, then all the work to gain rapport with the family may be lost by a single, misguided, unanticipated visit by a police officer or welfare worker. It is possible for an experienced social worker to carry out this role of explaining to the family what will happen after the report is sent to the proper agency. I have found that unless the social worker is very familiar with this problem as well as with the proceedings of the police, welfare agencies, and the court, she will not be able to function effectively in this capacity.

The parents should be told that a number of possible actions may be taken once the report has been received. Occasionally, nothing is done. Certain agencies need a great deal of prodding to take an active role in the evaluation and disposition of a case. On the other hand, if an overzealous police department receives the report, they may rush to the home and demand to know why they beat their kids. Occasionally, an uninformed district attorney may pursue a given case on criminal grounds because he thinks he can "win." By "winning," he means obtaining a conviction and putting a parent in jail.

Fortunately these methods of handling this type of case are becoming less and less frequent. Welfare agencies are beginning to hire more trained personnel and many large police departments have assigned juvenile division personnel to the child welfare departments, which enables the investigations to be handled intelligently and with understanding. In this situation communications with the medical personnel is optimum. The point made regarding the inexperienced house officers' ability to handle these cases also holds true for the inexperienced welfare worker or police officer. They should not be involved without very capable supervision.

While I am discussing the possible outcome of the report with the family, I talk with them about the goals of each person involved with the case. I try to emphasize that all of our goals are the same, namely, to help the parents and do what is best for the child. The parents usually respond favorably to this approach.

If the case appears to be one that will be going to court, I strongly recommend to the parents that they seek legal counsel. I have seen very unfortunate situations in court in which the parents have not been represented by counsel, usually because they cannot afford it. At the same time I try to emphasize that they should make it very clear to their lawyer what they want and what he should be working toward. Many defense lawyers, as do some district attorneys, have the attitude they can "win" the case. In the defense lawyer's eyes this means having the child returned to the home of his clients. I frankly tell the parents that they have to give very serious thought to this fact and decide whether this is winning as far as the child is concerned. Many parents are willing to give this very point considerable thought; in fact, many are happy the point has arisen.

It is at this point that I attempt to reemphasize my interest in helping them as parents of this child. I try to find out whether or not they feel it would be helpful to talk in depth with someone about the problems they are having with this child. I ask them if they feel that psychiatric counseling would be helpful and if they would be willing to see a psychiatrist if I were to arrange it. With very few exceptions they are most anxious and willing to seek psychiatric help. It is common for one parent to be less willing than the other but yet willing to "go along with the idea." Once they have agreed to this no time should be lost in arranging the necessary consultation.

Finally, if the case does come to court and the physician is required, which he should be, to go to court and present his findings, it is most rewarding and beneficial to sit down with the parents prior to the court appearance and explain to them in detail what will happen in court. They should be told exactly what he will say in his testimony. Usually if the parents have been told the truth up to this point there is nothing new that the physician must tell them. He merely needs to reemphasize these points. With this approach they are much less frightened about going into court and the therapeutic role of the doctor can still be maintained, even though he is ordered to present the facts in the courtroom. It should be reemphasized that the physician's main goal is to help the child and his parents. Even though the parents are not in complete agreement with the doctor, his opinion and reasons for this opinion should be clearly explained to them.

A Physician's Legal Obligation

Doctors are often very negligent when it comes to fulfilling their legal obligations in regard to the battered child. For a number of reasons there is a great reluctance on the part of physicians to involve themselves in legal matters. They have many excuses which to them are quite reasonable and justified. The physician must realize, however, that when it comes to child abuse he does have a responsibility, both moral and legal, to the child as well as to the parent. If he does not accept this responsibility, 25 to 30 per cent of the time the child will be permanently injured or killed within the next several months. It is discouraging to recount the number of cases that have been seen by a private physician who was unwilling to accept his responsibility and admit to himself that the child had been maltreated. I have seen private physicians elated over a bleeding time that was one minute longer than normal, which to them explained the child's extensive bruises. One physician told the parents of a severely injured child that he would not report the case if they agreed to go to a psychiatrist.

All 50 states require physicians who see children injured by unexplained means to make a report to a given agency. The agency to which the physician must make the report is variable (see chapter 10). This report usually consists of a phone call at the time of admission, followed by a letter to the referring agency. I do not feel that the report should be made until the parents have been told of the necessity of making the report. It is much easier for parents to understand and accept the need for reporting if this has been explained to them prior to the report. When this is not done unfortunate situations may develop, which are impossible to rectify. In most states the physician is protected from suits of libel as a result of this report. This is relieving to the physician's mind and is an important part of any law requiring reporting of unexplained injuries to children.

Theoretically, the physician is relieved of any necessity of investigation or making charges in a given case (9). It is very apparent, however, that the physician's report is heavily relied on by the agency receiving the report. Unless he is willing to state that the child is severely injured and should not be discharged from the hospital to the home and is willing to support this in court, the welfare or law enforcement agency is usually unable to pursue the case with any degree of authority. The doctor must take a firm stand. The letter below exemplifies the type of report that should be sent to the proper agency by the physician. It places the final responsibility for disposition on them, but states clearly where he stands.

> Dear Sheriff:
> In compliance with the Colorado State Legislation regarding injury to children other than by accidental means, I am sending the following information on DB. This girl is 4 years old and was seen in our emergency room on August 30 having been brought here by her parents. The chief complaint was that she would not eat and was vomiting for 2 or 3 days. The child was admitted directly to the hospital.

I talked with both parents personally and they stated that she had been doing reasonably well until a few days prior to admission. The only history of trauma was a fall from a fence a few days prior to admission. They stated that she had always been a poor eater, but the parents did not feel this had been any worse until the vomiting began.

On physical examination the child was extremely emaciated and malnourished. The photographs enclosed will serve to better exemplify this point. Even though the child was 4 years of age she weighed only 17 pounds. She had multiple bruises over her entire body, as well as many scratches, abrasions, and sores. When the child was asked how she was injured, she replied, "My mommy did it."

Laboratory studies included a hematologic survey, which indicated the child does not have any bleeding tendency or easy bruisibility. X rays of the child's bones revealed a large skull fracture, a healing fracture of the left forearm, and a small fracture of both little fingers. There is no X-ray evidence of any disease that would cause this child to fracture easily. We have as yet found no evidence of organic disease which would explain this degree of malnutrition, bruises, or fractures. We also have X-ray evidence of a high intestinal obstruction, which is probably due to a hematoma (blood clot) in the wall of the intestine. This has resolved and the vomiting has ceased.

This child represents one of the most severe cases of malnutrition that has been seen in this hospital in recent years. We have colored slides which delineate the findings which could be seen on admission. It can be stated without hesitation that there is no known medical explanation for such severe malnutrition, fractures, and bruises other than severe neglect, abuse, and physical trauma.

From the above information, I trust it is apparent that I am unwilling to discharge this child back into the home of her parents. I will await your disposition before making any arrangements for discharge.

Very sincerely, ...

When the doctor finds a given agency uncooperative, he is placed in a very difficult position. He may feel that the child is at great risk if discharged to the parents and yet he may be unable to convince a specific law enforcement or child welfare agency to bring dependency proceedings to the court. When this situation develops, the physician has a number of alternatives. He occasionally can convince the parents that it is best for all concerned for the child to go into a foster home for a temporary period of time. At this point, I should state that uncontested voluntary removal of children from the home becomes very difficult unless the welfare agency is supported by a court order. Too many parents, after they voluntarily give the child to the welfare agency, rescind this relinquishment and ask for the child back. Unless the court has given the order to have the child placed in a foster home it becomes almost impossible to work with the parents for any length of time. In voluntary placements parents may constantly pester the welfare worker. She finally weakens and returns the child, often with disastrous results.

In addition to working with the parents in these difficult situations in which no action is taken, the physician may go either to the district attorney or directly to the juvenile court judge to ask for assistance. One of our children was still at home after his eleventh fracture because the child welfare agency was unwilling to file a dependency petition. He was not removed from the home until the judge upon our request forced the agency to file on the child's behalf.

Even though the following point is discussed very adequately elsewhere (chapter 10), it should be reemphasized at this time. The physician must understand the difference between criminal proceedings and dependency proceedings. It is our contention that with very few exceptions cases involving abused children should go into court under dependency proceedings. This usually requires the child welfare agency to file a petition in court on behalf of the child. They ask the court to make them responsible for the child on a permanent or a temporary basis. In this situation the case is usually heard in juvenile court, and the doctor is asked to testify. In dependency proceedings it is not necessary for anyone to prove that the child was beaten by a given individual but only to prove that in light of the medical and social findings the given child has not been properly cared for. In this situation the physician is in a good position to present his findings. The child can be removed from the home, and the parents are then free to take care of their other children as well as receive counseling and psychiatric help.

If criminal proceedings are brought by the district attorney's office, the prosecuting attorney must prove that a given parent or person beat this child. This may be most difficult. Even if the case is "won," the parents usually receive probation or a short jail sentence. In this situation the parents are usually antagonistic and unwilling to receive psychiatric care. In most situations there is nothing to be gained by criminal proceedings and a great deal to be lost. (For an opposite point of view see chapter 8.)

If the doctor who is confronted with the problem of an abused child is unwilling to accept his legal responsibility, then he should refer the child to another physician who has previously handled cases of this type. The physician who is to be condemned is the one who is not only unwilling to accept his responsibility but also unwilling to refer the case.

To avoid serious problems in court the physician must remember to keep accurate records while the child is being treated. If a member of the house staff has taken the initial history and performed the physical examination, the physician must repeat this and countersign the resident's note. This becomes important in certain courts, especially where there are no juvenile court regulations, because anything that is recorded in the chart other than by the doctor giving the testimony may be considered hearsay evidence and may not be admissible. To avoid this problem, the physician should countersign or write all important notes. Fortunately, juvenile court regulations in many areas do allow the physician to give information from the chart that is not countersigned or actually recorded by the testifying physician.

It is important that the physician request an interview with the attorney representing the department of child welfare prior to his court appearance. It is at times surprising how poorly certain welfare department attorneys understand these cases and how little effort is made in preparing their presentation. The doctor must state clearly his findings and his opinion that these findings are due to unexplained but definite trauma. If he hedges, the child may be returned to the home prematurely. Defense attorneys constantly propose hypothetical situations and ask the doctor to state whether the child could have been injured in this manner. The doctor must continue to remind the court that the situation proposed by the defense attorney did not happen according to the available history.

As indicated, I have found it very helpful to work closely with the parents prior to the court appearance. They should be told what the doctor will say and hopefully they can then discuss their feelings with their attorney. I have on occasion been able to discuss the case with their attorney. In some situations we have all (parents, attorneys, and child welfare agency) been in agreement prior to the court hearing. Parents without the benefit of counsel may never be convinced that their rights were fully protected, and in some cases they are not.

When dependency proceedings are filed, I am happy to see judges who are willing to hold hearings in their chambers rather than in the courtroom. It is much more relaxed, and the ability to work with the parents is greatly increased. The formality of the court may still be maintained, and the result is usually more beneficial to all concerned. When hearings are held in the courtroom, the atmosphere is frequently not conducive to a good disposition of the case.

It is not difficult for any physician to understand the position the judge is in as he makes final disposition in cases of child abuse. A good judge is forever haunted by the realization that the child he sent back to the parents may be killed at any time. It is the physician's responsibility to the judge to be as precise as possible about his findings and to state clearly his opinions about disposition. We cannot expect the judge to take all of the responsibility, even though the responsibility of final disposition rests with him.

The Difficult Case

The most difficult situation in which the physician can find himself is the one in which the abused child is sent home prematurely. This disposition can result from court action, or more commonly, the child is sent home from the hospital without the court becoming involved. In this latter situation the child has usually suffered mild or moderate injury, which is not of sufficient magnitude to convince the doctor or any state agency that a dependency petition should be filed.

Commonly this difficult case is a child with repeated unexplained bruises without an adequate history to explain the bruises. The subdural hematoma can prove to be most difficult in making proper disposition if there is no evidence of fracture or additional trauma. The physician should not hesitate to call the local welfare agency or judge to request assistance in the proper handling of such a case.

It is in these cases that excellent rapport with parents is mandatory if the child is to be followed and protected. When the child is at home, therapy becomes essential (see chapter 6). It is in this situation that the psychiatrist, social worker, and public health nurse are most helpful. Someone must set up a positive relationship with the parents. The battering parent must feel comfortable with this individual and be able to contact her at any time. An experienced social worker or public health nurse can be life saving during these critical times.

If the child has been placed under the temporary care of a child welfare agency by the courts, the case is not over. Welfare agencies rarely request opinions of the referring physician when the case returns to court for a rehearing. Children whom the physician thinks are safe in a foster home occasionally reappear in the emergency room severely injured or dead, the case having been reheard by the judge and the patient returned home without the knowledge of the physician. It is our policy to follow up each case of temporary dependency with a letter to the welfare agency and court stating that this child should not be returned to the home under any circumstances unless the referring physician is consulted and his testimony heard at the rehearing. Unless this is done, it is surprising how often children are returned home without the knowledge of the doctor, hospital social worker, or psychiatrist who initially referred the case.

Responsibility of the University Medical Center

The responsibility of the physicians associated with university medical centers is threefold—research, teaching, and service. The future and challenge of research in this field is just being realized. Many unanswered questions remain, as the reader of this book clearly understands. The very significant problem of on-going follow-up of these children and their extremely mobile parents provides a significant obstacle as the physician attempts to make accurate observations and recordings. Predictive studies (i.e., the determination of high risk parents) look promising. This approach, if successful, should enable physicians and social agencies to determine which families must receive the most attention to assure the safety of the child or children in question. Adoption agencies could use this information in their evaluation of prospective parents.

The utilization of trained public health nurses and social workers in ongoing treatment situations warrants serious evaluation. It is to be hoped that these professionals can take on patient loads under the supervision of psychiatrists and pediatricians, thereby increasing the number of patients under treatment. Day-care centers for battered children and their parents are also being evaluated. Juvenile court judges are beginning to enter the research field, exploring various means of handling this problem.

In addition to this research responsibility the personnel at the university medical center must assume the role of teaching, not only house staff, medical students, and area physicians the proper team approach to the problems of the abused child, but also of carrying this message to community agencies (such as child welfare or local police), to elected officials (such as judges and district attorney), and to school personnel. Without this teaching effort and improvement of communications between these community agencies and the medical center abused children will continue to be neglected by the misguided efforts of the inexperienced.

Finally the medical center is obliged to provide a service to patients as well as a consultation service to area physicians. The problems involving neglected and/or battered children can best be handled by a group of hospital personnel usually consisting of a social worker, pediatrician, and psychiatrist. Additional disciplines may be most helpful and should include a public health nurse, statistical consultant, and psychologist. With each case entering the accident room the team should be called in for consultation. The pediatrician should evaluate the case, talk with the parents, and work with the house staff. The social worker can enter the picture after the immediate medical evaluation has begun and assist with the communication with necessary agencies. The pediatrician on the team should be responsible for the necessary reports. Care must be taken not to eliminate the house staff from the care of the child. Court testimony should be given by the staff physician, not the resident, since experience in this area is essential. The other members of the team will come into the picture as the case progresses and therapy for the parents becomes a reality.

There is probably no aspect of child care that can yield more rewarding results than the proper understanding and approach to care of the abused and neglected child and his parents.

References

1. Woolley, Paul V., Jr. 1963. The pediatrician and the young child subjected to repeated physical abuse. *J. Pediat.* 62:628–30.
2. Caffey, John. 1946. Multiple fractures in the long bones of infants suffering from chronic subdural hematoma. *Am. J. Roentgenol. Radium Therapy Nucl. Med.* 56:163–73.
3. Silverman, F. N. 1953. The Roentgen manifestations of unrecognized skeletal trauma in infants. *Am. J. Roentgenol. Radium Therapy Nucl. Med.* 69:413–27.
4. Adelson, Lester. 1961. Slaughter of the innocents: A study of 46 homicides in which the victims were children. *New Engl. J. Med.* 264:1345–49.
5. Bain, Katherine. 1963. The physically abused child. *Pediatrics* 31:895–97.
6. Earl, Howard Y. 1965. 10,000 children battered and starved, hundreds die. *Today's Health* 43 (September): 24–31.
7. Feature article. *The Denver Post*, January 16, 1966.
8. Committee on Accidents in Childhood. The battered baby. 1966. *Brit. Med. J.* 1:601–3.
9. Harper, Fowler V. 1963. The physician, the battered child and the law. *Pediatrics* 31:899–902.
10. Barta, Rudolph A., and Smith, Nathan J. 1963. Willful trauma to young children: A challenge to the physician. *Clin. Pediatrics* 2:545–54.
11. Connell, John R. 1963. The devil's battered children. *J. Kansas Med. Soc.* 64:385–91.
12. Greenyard, Joseph. 1964. The battered child syndrome. *Med. Sci.* 15:82–91.
13. Russell, Patricia A. 1965. Subdural hematomas in infancy. *Brit. Med. J.* 2:446–48.
14. Eisenstein, E. M., Delta, B. G., and Clifford, J. H. 1965. Jejunal hematoma: An unusual manifestation of the battered child syndrome. *Clin. Pediatrics* 4:436–40.
15. Kennedy, R. N. 1960. *Nonpenetrating injuries of the abdomen.* Springfield, Ill.: Charles C. Thomas.
16. Shaw, Anthony. 1964. The surgeon and the battered child. *Surg. Gynecol. Obstet.* 119:355.
17. Godfrey, Joseph D. 1964. Trauma in children. *J. Bone Joint Surg.* 46:422–47.
18. Kiffney, G. T., Jr. 1964. The eye and the "battered child." *Arch. Ophthal.* 72:231–33.
19. Milowe, Irvin D., and Lourie, Reginald S. 1964. The child's role in the battered child syndrome. *J. Pediatrics* 65:1078–81.
20. Caffey, John. 1965. Significance of the history in the diagnosis of traumatic injury to children. *J. Pediatrics* 67:1008–14.

21. Berant, M., and Jacobs, J. 1966. Scurvy and the battered child. *Clin. Pediatrics* 5:230.
22. Braun, Ida G., Braun, Edgar J., and Simonds, Charlotte. 1963. The mistreated child. *Calif. Med.* 99:98–103.
23. Boardman, Helen E. 1962. A project to rescue children from inflicted injuries. *Social Work* 7:43–51.

3 | Radiologic Aspects of the Battered Child Syndrome

Frederic N. Silverman

Departments of Pediatrics and Radiology
University of Cincinnati College of Medicine
Cincinnati, Ohio

The concept of "the battered child" and the recent developments in the elucidation of the condition are intimately related to the field of diagnostic radiology. Although the syndrome was recognized in practically all its manifestations and implications by Tardieu (1) in 1860, it was not until Caffey's radiologic observations 86 years later (2) that any significant impact upon medical, social, and legal activities was generated. Caffey's observations subsequently were confirmed and their significance supported by papers published primarily in radiologic journals and particularly by pediatric radiologists. The evidence of the radiologic signs of bone injury and repair provided the solid medical basis on which was built the social, legal, and psychopathologic aspects of the problem. The recent recognition of extraskeletal radiologic features has further emphasized the role of diagnostic radiology.

The patients described by West (3) in 1888 have been considered to represent some of the early instances of the battered child syndrome, but, because his report antedated the discovery of the X ray in 1895, the diagnosis cannot be substantiated. Although great advances were made in most areas of X-ray diagnosis immediately following the introduction of X rays, the radiographic features of injuries to bones of infants and their repair were not described in any detail until almost forty years later. At that time the bizarre radiographic manifestations of recovery from epiphyseal separation during breech extraction were reported by Snedecor and his associates (4). About the same time articles on unusual periosteal reactions in children which were primarily to be differentiated from those of congenital syphilis began to make their

Dr. Silverman is director of the division of roentgenology, The Children's Hospital, and professor of pediatrics and radiology.

appearance (5, 6, 7). Caffey (2), in 1946, was the first to call attention to multiple fractures of the long bones of unknown origin, which accompanied a significant number of cases of subdural hematoma. Accepting the view of Ingraham (8) that the subdural hematomas were traumatic, Caffey suggested a traumatic origin for these injuries also.

Ample support for Caffey's observations on bone lesions with subdural hematomas followed quickly (9–14). Bakwin (15, 16) reported several cases of unusual traumatic reactions in bones, among which was at least one battered child. In 1953, Silverman (17), following Caffey's lead, insisted on a traumatic basis for injuries of the type now known to occur in the battered child in a presentation of three cases of the condition without subdural hematomas. Astley (18) believed that there was a primary metaphyseal fragility of bone in affected children, but this concept was discarded by Woolley and Evans in 1955 (19). These authors reviewed material seen over an eight-year period with radiographic findings suggesting injury, with or without a history of trauma. They concluded that the radiographic manifestations of injury and its repair were identical whether a history of injury was or was not obtained and that the skeletal lesions "having the appearance of fracture—regardless of history for injury or the presence or absence of intracranial bleeding—are due to undesirable vectors of force." They also emphasized that the environmental factors surrounding the infants with the radiographic changes frequently included grossly undesirable and hazardous circumstances. Numerous subsequent reports have reinforced Woolley's and Evans' conclusions which have now become generally accepted (20–30). The radiologic aspects were dealt with in detail by Caffey in 1957 (31) and by Silverman in 1972 (47). A comprehensive report has been published in French by Rabouille (32).

Radiologic Manifestations

Radiologic examination has two main functions in relation to the battered child. It serves as a case-finding tool, and subsequently it can be used as a guide to the management of known cases.

In many instances the diagnostic bone lesions are noted incidental to examination for conditions other than known injury; more frequently, the examination is undertaken because of a history of injury, and then lesions are found which are much more extensive than would have been anticipated from the history or which demonstrate some of the features indicating that the present episode was only one of several. In instances in which the battered child syndrome is suspected, the presence of radiographic changes in the skeleton can support the diagnosis; the absence of radiologic changes does not necessarily exclude it. In well established cases of the battered child, follow-up examinations to evaluate the nature and extent of healing are helpful just as they are in the follow-up examinations of any other type of fracture.

The radiologic signs of skeletal injury and response to it are similar whether there is a history of injury or not. Gross fractures are obvious, and their characteristics are available in standard radiologic and orthopedic texts. The outstanding features of skeletal injuries in the battered child syndrome are predilection for the metaphyses, exaggerated periosteal reaction, multiplicity of lesions, and differing stages of healing and repair of the multiple lesions.

Lesions of the metaphyses are a common observation and the most typical. Their frequency is probably related to the fact that most of the injuries are incurred not so much by direct blows as by vigorous handling, as in shaking the child. The extremities are the "handles" for the mishandling. The rigidity of bone and the elasticity of ligamentous connections apparently can withstand the twisting-pulling forces of a heavy adult hand on a young extremity. In the infant under one year of age, who is the most frequent recipient of this type of maltreatment, epiphyseal separation takes place at the weak cartilage-shaft junction. This may be a gross displacement, easy to recognize, a minor irregularity in the line of radiolucent cartilage between epiphyseal ossification center and shaft with slight widening (Fig. 1) or may be so slight as to be radiologically invisible. In areas where epiphyseal ossification centers are not present for their displacement to be noted, the features are initially more difficult to recognize (Fig. 2). In any event, the healing process of the epiphyseal separation involves a

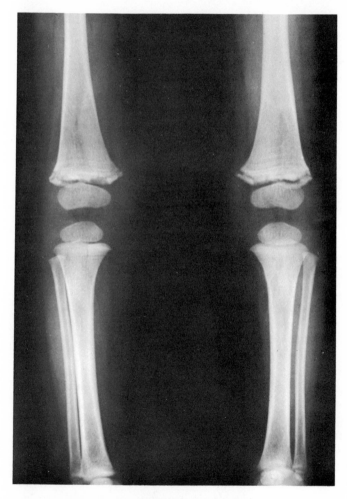

Metaphyseal fragmentation without epiphyseal displacement

Figure 1

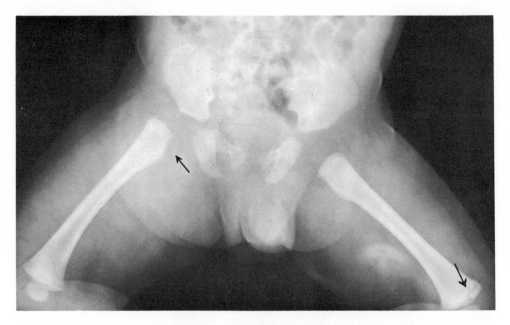

Figure 2

Traumatic epiphyseal separation of the right femoral head one week after vigorous pull on child's legs. Note soft tissue swelling of right thigh owing to hemorrhage. Displacement would be more obvious if ossification center for femoral head were present. Note also metaphyseal fracture at distal end of left femur.

revascularization which is reflected by subepiphyseal (metaphyseal) demineralization and which can be detected radiologically approximately two weeks after an injury. If there has been no immobilization, and further injury has occurred from ordinary activity, let alone further maltreatment, the destructive features are exaggerated. Rarely, epiphyseal injury is of a degree which leads to deformity and shortening.

The periosteum of young infants is relatively loosely attached to the bone in comparison with that of adults and is easily separated from it by direct physical force or by subperiosteal hemorrhage consequent to injury. In its new position, the periosteum produces new bone so that a calcified envelope (involucrum) surrounds the denuded portion of the bone (Fig. 3). The periosteum has its strongest attachment to the epiphyseal line; as a result, most of the periosteum tends to remain attached to it even in gross epiphyseal separations. It is this feature in children which permits the newly formed bone to align itself with the displaced epiphysis, and the end result of production of new bone and resorption of old bone generally is complete reconstitution. In the interval the abundant subperiosteal new bone formation may develop an appearance suggestive of osteogenic malignancy (33). Subperiosteal ossification may be delayed if there is associated infection.

The initially elevated periosteum and its underlying blood is radiolucent. Within two to three weeks following the injury, calcium is deposited on its undersurface,

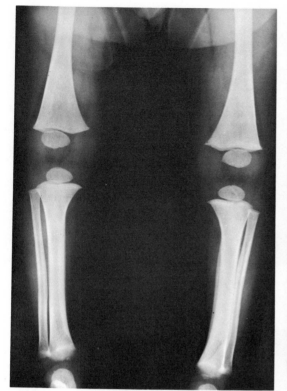

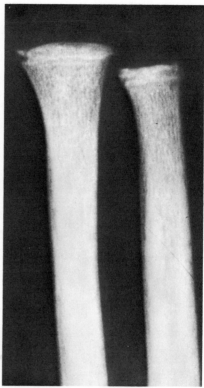

Figure 3a

Figure 3b

Lesions of different characters and ages attest to the repetition of injury. *a:* The spiral fracture in the left tibia is partially obscured by the well-organized reparative subperiosteal bone production. There is a suggestion of a recent metaphyseal fracture in the medial aspect of the distal metaphysis of the left femur. *b:* Same child, same day: recent metaphyseal injury in radius at wrist; possible remote cortical thickening along shaft of ulna. *c:* Same child, same day: recent metaphyseal injury of radius at other wrist, and remote fracture of distal humerus with exaggerated subperiosteal new bone formation. Note density of all bones.

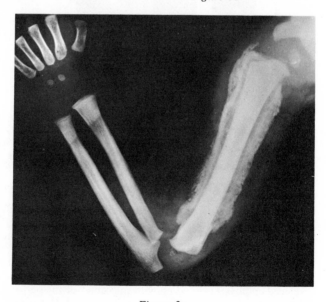

Figure 3c

46   *Silverman*

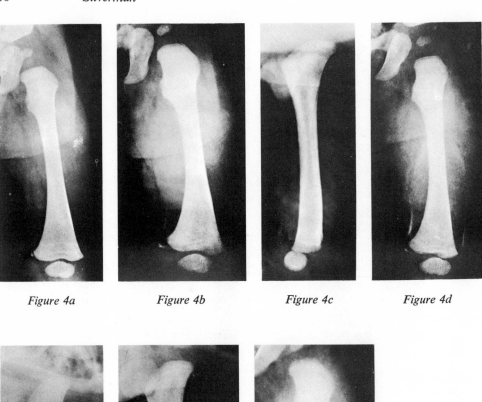

Figure 4a   Figure 4b   Figure 4c   Figure 4d

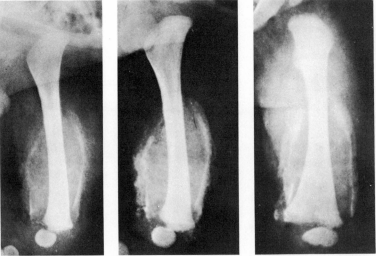

Figure 4e   Figure 4f   Figure 4g

Sequence of calcification of elevated periosteum. *a:* 4 days after unexplained swelling of knee: small chip fracture, medial end of femur at knee. *b:* 9 days after onset, chip fracture separated from bone by subperiosteal hemorrhage. *c:* Epiphyseal separation clearly shown by posterior displacement in lateral projection. *d:* 14 days after onset: the elevated periosteum is producing new bone, and the extent of the subperiosteal hematoma becomes visible. *e:* lateral projection, corresponding to *d*. *f:* 16 days after onset: subperiosteal ossification has increased. *g:* the displaced epiphysis is lined up with the center of the periosteum (involucrum) rather than the shaft from which is was separated (sequestrum). (Courtesy of *J. Am. Med. Assoc.*)

which becomes radiologically visible (Fig. 4). If additional injury has taken place or if the initial injury was sufficient to tear the periosteum, calcifying callus may extend beyond the confines of the periosteum and develop gross irregular margins (Fig. 5). Once the union of the fractured components of the bone has been accomplished, whether by fibrous or bony union, the periosteum responds to the usual stresses and strains, and the bone is remodelled to its original form; late residuals may merely present unusually thick cortices. Careful inspection of the tubular bones of children with the battered child syndrome frequently demonstrates periosteal elevations of varying degrees in different bones (see Fig. 3). This variation is testimony to the repetitive nature of the injuries to which the child's skeleton has been subjected. An injury of considerable age may be indicated by a relatively thick, dense cortex; a slightly younger injury may have obvious subperiosteal new bone formation. More recent injuries may demonstrate massive calcium production with gross irregularities, and the most recent injury may show only soft tissue swelling without any bone production whatsoever.

The possibility of subdural hematoma must always be entertained when skeletal lesions are observed and supportive evidence for subdural hematoma may be provided by the demonstration of separated cranial bones and widened sutures, other signs of

Extensive subperiosteal and metaphyseal lesions. The irregularity of the periosteal envelope suggests tears in this structure. (Courtesy of *Am. J. Roentgenol.*)

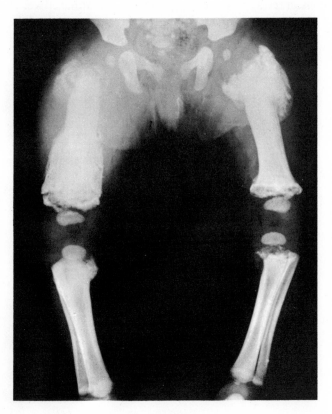

Figure 5

increased intracranial pressure, or obvious fractures of the cranial bones themselves (Fig. 6). Not infrequently, the cranial fractures are not simple linear fractures but are comminuted and resemble the multiple irregular fractures of an eggshell.

It is important to emphasize that it is the healing phase of the fractures which is generally recognized radiographically. Therefore, an injury that is too recent to demonstrate reparative change (less than two weeks old) may be missed entirely. Radiographic evidence of soft tissue edema, of obliteration of deep and even superficial intermuscular fat septa, may provide a clue that the area in question should be re-examined after an appropriate interval.

Although skeletal lesions predominate in the extremities, almost any bone can be affected. Rib fractures, recent or healing (Fig. 7), are comparable to those seen after vigorous resuscitation activities. However, in combination with a more typical metaphyseal and/or periosteal lesion elsewhere, they strengthen the case for a diagnosis of battering. Small tubular bones of the hands and feet may demonstrate reactions to repetitive beatings. Compression fractures of the vertebral bodies (Fig. 8) or fractures of spinous processes may occur following forced flexion or extension injuries (34).

Injuries to tissues other than bones are occasionally recognized radiographically. McCort and Vaudagna (35) reported the findings of infants with initially unexplained visceral trauma presenting as acute abdominal crises. The most common visceral injury was rupture of the small bowel, but lacerations of the liver and a perforation of the stomach were also noted. Laceration of the lung and subpleural hemorrhage were

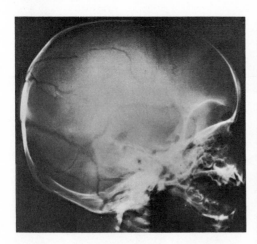

Figure 6a

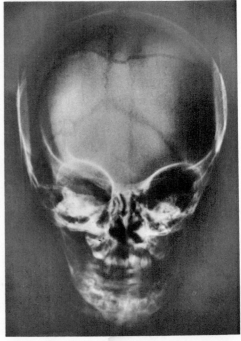

Extensive diastatic fractures of skull in child with typical extremity lesions. Subdural hematomas were present bilaterally.

Figure 6b

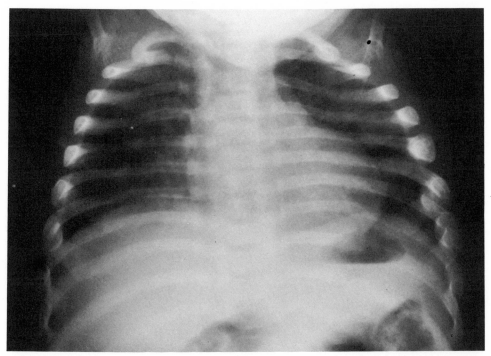

Figure 7

Rib fractures in a healing stage may present as local thickenings. This child had metaphyseal fractures in long bones, skull fracture, and a subdural hematoma.

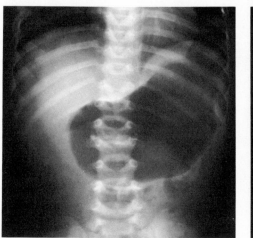 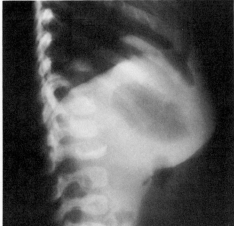

Figure 8a   *Figure 8b*

Compression fracture of vertebral body in 17-month boy with skull fracture, intramural hematoma of the duodenum, and multiple cutaneous bruises. Mother admitted punching baby in stomach.

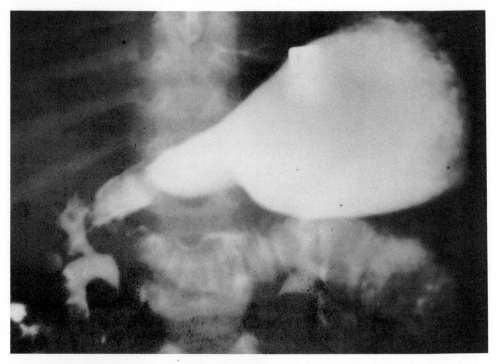

Figure 9a

Intramural hematoma of duodenum demonstrated by barium meal in same patient as in Figure 8. Intravenous pyelogram had been done just before the barium examination because of microscopic hematuria. Hematoma surgically evacuated because of progressive obstruction.

Figure 9b

thoracic findings. Both multiple visceral and skeletal lesions were found. The radiographic features were pneumoperitoneum, hemoperitoneum, and/or ileus. In one patient with a perforated duodenum there was considerable delay in seeking medical care and multiple peritoneal abscesses were found. Intramural hematoma of the duodenum (36, 37), well defined radiologically, occurs characteristically as a consequence of direct blows to the abdomen (Fig. 9). Pancreatic pseudocysts also occur and can be diagnosed radiographically (38, 39). Caffey (48) emphasizes the mental retardation sequels which he attributes to whiplash—shaking injuries to the brain and its vessels.

Radiographic signs of retarded development and of malnutrition are commonly present in battered children, but they have no special diagnostic significance.

Differential Diagnosis

In general it can be said that the skeletal manifestations of the battered child syndrome are so characteristic as scarcely to be confused with anything else. Nevertheless, from time to time there is reluctance to accept the specificity of these lesions. It is felt that these manifestations of fracture are very uncommon in relation to the number of cases of fracture which are seen by radiologists in the course of their daily work. However, the circumstances of radiographic examination in instances where there is known injury and those in which there is no history of injury are quite different. Given a known epiphyseal separation, the child is treated by mechanical reduction of the deformity and immobilization, usually in plaster. Films are taken initially after reduction has been accomplished and usually at a follow-up examination about six weeks after the injury, when healing is apt to be relatively complete. If, in the intervening time, another film is taken for any reason whatsoever and subperiosteal new bone formation or metaphyseal fragmentation is noted, it occasions no concern because it is known that an injury has taken place and these are obviously the signs of repair. Such is the situation which obtains in the newborn infant (4, 40) who has been delivered by breech extraction, has an epiphyseal separation at the knee or hip, and two-and-one-half to three weeks later shows a large calcifying hematoma (Fig. 10). The knowledge that breech extraction is an adequate explanation for skeletal trauma is generally sufficient to allay any apprehension concerning the radiographic findings. If observed incidental to examination under any other circumstances, the same findings might be alarming.

To test this interpretation, we reviewed the films of children who had had epiphyseal separations with known cause. Among the group there were several who had films obtained more than two and less than six weeks after the injury. Almost all of them demonstrated metaphyseal irregularities and subperiosteal new bone formation which was radiologically indistinguishable from that seen in the battered child (Fig. 11). In addition, children with acute epiphyseal separations were brought back for reexamination between two and three weeks after the known injury. Metaphyseal rarefaction and subperiosteal new bone formation of the same nature were observed regularly (Fig. 12), although none were so severe as occur in the battered child who does not have the benefit of immediate and usually effective immobilization.

There are several conditions which occasionally are confused with the battered child syndrome:

Scurvy

Naturally, scurvy is one of the first to come to mind, particularly with older physicians who were familiar with the massive subperiosteal hematomas of healing scurvy in days gone by. None of the children with the battered child syndrome who have been studied thus far have had scurvy, although it is quite possible for the condition to develop in the environment in which some of these children grow up. If present, scurvy would be expected to exaggerate the radiographic findings. Scurvy is a generalized disease, and although local exaggerations owing to trauma do occur, all of the bones show generalized osteoporosis. The cortices are thin, the trabecular architecture is ill-defined, and the bones have a "ground glass" appearance. The epiphyseal ossification centers are sharply demarcated by the zones of provisional calcification to produce the so-called Wimberger's ring. At the ends of the shafts of *all* the long bones, and most prominent at the areas where growth is most rapid, there are comparable dense lines in the provisional zones of calcification. The calcification of cartilage proceeds normally; the transformation to bone (ossification) is inhibited as the osteoblasts require adequate amounts of vitamin C for their function. The decreased osteoblastic activity is reflected by a low level of alkaline phosphatase in the blood. Rarefaction of bone

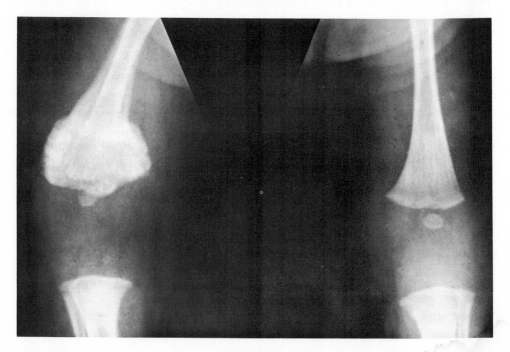

Figure 10

Exuberant calcified callus formation in sixteen-day-old infant who had unrecognized epiphyseal separation at knee as complication of breech extraction.

underneath calcified cartilaginous plates and minute incomplete fractures produce the characteristic "corner sign" of active scurvy. With subperiosteal hematomas owing to scurvy, other manifestations of the disease, such as capillary fragility and hematuria, might also be present. It is noteworthy that ecchymoses and hematuria may also occur as the result of soft tissue injuries in the battered child. It is pertinent also, that scurvy is extremely rare before the age of six months, whereas many of the infants in the battered child syndrome appear with well developed bone lesions prior to this age. In contradistinction to scurvy, exaggerated changes may be present at one end of the

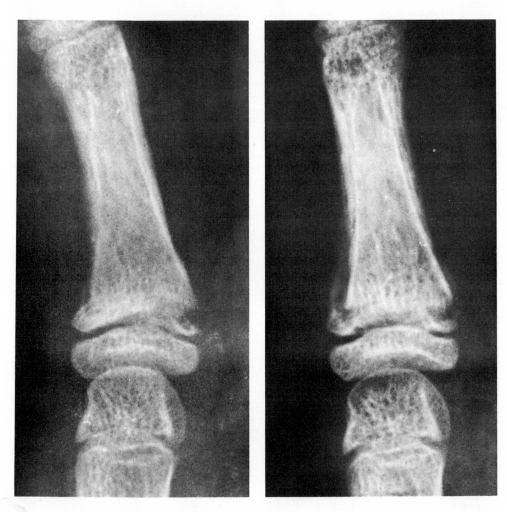

Figure 11a   Figure 11b

Epiphyseal separation in finger. *a:* On day of injury. *b:* 19 days later. In spite of known injury and attempt at immobilization, metaphyseal and subperiosteal reactions are present and are identical to those with unknown injury.

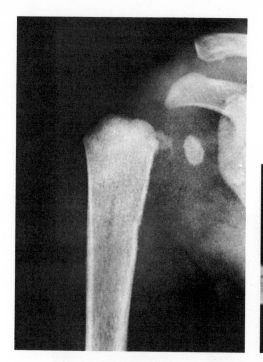

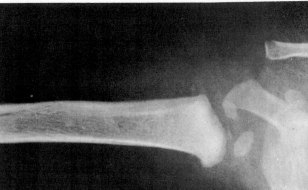

Figure 12a

Figure 12b

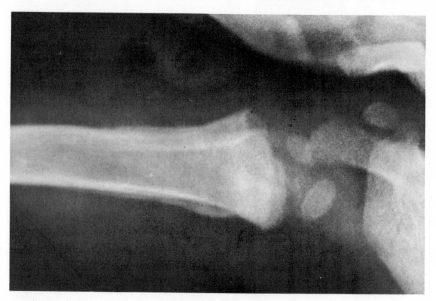

Figure 12c

Serial films in known epiphyseal displacement. *a:* At time of admission after motor car accident. *b:* 24 hours later; reduction is complete in abduction. *c:* 3 weeks after reduction, before application of new cast. The metaphysis, previously uninjured, now shows irregularity of mineralization, and a subperiosteal envelope of new bone cloaks the proximal end of the shaft. Had there been no immobilization, these reactions would have been more extensive.

bone while the opposite end or the corresponding area of the uninjured bone of the opposite extremity shows no signs whatsoever of disease.

Syphilis

Syphilis in the congenital form can result in metaphyseal and periosteal lesions resembling those under discussion, especially during the first months of life. Although there is probably a traumatic factor in the distribution of the lesions of congenital syphilis, they do tend to be symmetrical, whereas those of the battered child are generally asymmetrical; and when osseous lesions as marked as those found in the battered child are produced by syphilis, other stigmata of the disease are usually present. In any questionable case serological tests for the disease are available.

Osteogenesis Imperfecta

Osteogenesis imperfecta is also a generalized disease, and signs of the disorder should be present in bones which are not involved in the immediate productive-destructive process. In the cranium the characteristic mosaic rarefaction (multiple sutural bones) is present in the early years of life, and in children of an age to be considered as possible battered children, the fracture-like appearance of the calvarium, much more extensive than the eggshell fractures of the battered child, should be of considerable assistance in diagnosis. In osteogenesis imperfecta the fractures are more commonly of the shafts of the bones than of the metaphyses and epiphyses. Other signs of osteogenesis imperfecta are usually present in the form of blue sclerae and obvious skeletal deformities; usually, a family history of the condition can be elicited.

Infantile Cortical Hyperostosis

Infantile cortical hyperostosis is characterized by subperiosteal new bone formation, but there are no metaphyseal irregularities or defects. A healed lesion of the battered child might simulate a healing lesion of infantile cortical hyperostosis, but the clinical course can be helpful in differentiation. Involvement of the mandible occurs in approximately 95 per cent of the children with this condition but has been lacking thus far in the battered child in the absence of obvious mandibular fracture.

Osteoid Osteoma

Osteoid osteoma may produce swelling, pain, and periosteal reaction in a child. Metaphyseal lesions do not occur and the characteristic history of pain—worse at night, relieved by aspirin—is helpful if present. Osteoid osteoma is not a common disease in this age group. The presence of a sclerotic nidus in the center of the lesion is diagnostic.

Self-Sustained Injury

Fatigue fractures probably represent a variant of the battered child syndrome in which the child himself is responsible for the battering. More common in the metatarsal bones of adults, as in "march fractures," they do occur in the fibulas of children where they are present with pain and localized periosteal reaction (41). The remainder of the bones are normally mineralized, and there are no metaphyseal lesions.

The so-called "little league elbow" (42) is another manifestation of repetitive injury where the vigorous mechanical activity of throwing a ball causes incomplete avulsions (epiphyseal separations) around the region of the elbow. The productive changes may simulate those of the battered child. The age of the patient is appreciably older than that of most battered children, the remainder of the bones is in excellent condition, and a history of trauma adequate to explain the reaction is usually elicited.

Others

Multiple fractures of bones are seen in severe rickets, hypophosphatasia, leukemia, metastatic neuroblastoma, and as sequels to osteomyelitis and septic arthritis. In general additional signs of the primary disease and a history of prior disease adequate to explain the lesions can be elicited.

The one condition which imitates exactly the radiographic findings of the battered child is one which supports the hypothesis of a traumatic basis for the lesions—that is,

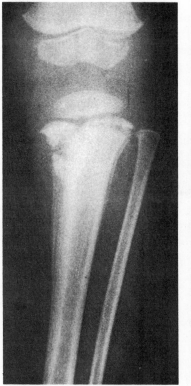 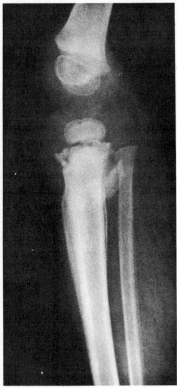

| Figure 13a | Figure 13b |

Metaphyseal fragmentation and subperiosteal new bone formation in paraplegic child with sensory defect (meningomyelocele). Swelling noted after vigorous physiotherapy in attempt to correct contractures. *a:* AP projection. *b:* Lateral projection.

neurogenic sensory deficit in relation to injury (43, 44). As has been mentioned previously, the attachment of the epiphysis to the shaft of the bone is one of the weak areas in the growing bones of the young child. If the young child also has a neurogenic sensory deficit such as that associated with paraplegia following spine injury or with meningomyelocele, separations of epiphyses in the lower extremities as a consequence of physiotherapy, or other injury whose severity is not appreciated, can give rise to radiographic findings indistinguishable from those of the battered child (Fig. 13).

Individuals afflicted with the so-called congenital indifference to pain (45) also fail to react normally to skeletal injuries, and metaphyseal rarefaction, excessive callus formation, and bone sclerosis develop as a consequence just as in children with unrecognized trauma (Fig. 14). The features of metaphyseal and physeal injuries in children with spina bifida and meningomyelocele are discussed in detail by Gyepes, Newburn, and Neuhauser (46).

Some children who have the radiographic manifestations of the battered child and whose clinical history supports this diagnosis, have certain features in their skeletal X rays which have led competent radiologists to ask whether there is not some underlying systemic disorder. All of the features of metaphyseal fractures, subperiosteal new bone formation, healing fractures in different stages of repair, and so on can be found

Metaphyseal irregularity, old cortical thickening and growth disturbance in child with congenital indifference to pain. (Courtesy of *Radiology*)

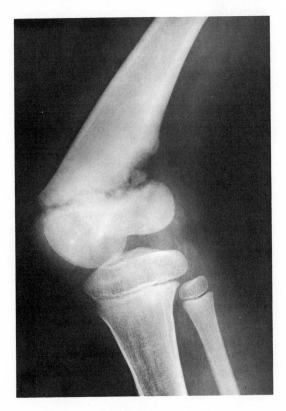

Figure 14

in these children, but they also demonstrate a "chalkiness" (see Fig. 3) in the skeleton, which calls to mind the fragility of bones of children with osteopetrosis (Albers-Schönberg disease). These children do not demonstrate any of the hematologic disorders of osteopetrosis and usually lose the sclerosis of bone as they become older. None have been shown to have hypercalcemia, but this aspect has not been studied adequately. The sclerotic changes may merely reflect productive changes in bones owing to multiple repetitive trauma insufficient to cause obvious fractures or the usual reparative changes which are diagnostic of the battered child. This group will merit further study, but it is almost certain that, regardless of any contributing factors, they will have in common with all the other children an episode, or repetitive episodes, of physical abuse.

Conclusion

The radiographic signs of the battered child are surprisingly specific. They speak for the child who is unable or unwilling to speak for himself and serve to alert the physician to a hazard of considerable magnitude which threatens the life and limb as well as the emotional and intellectual potentialities of the child. Although they may reflect the time of the injury with considerable accuracy and permit extremely accurate deductions concerning the nature of the forces producing the injury, they provide no information whatsoever concerning the circumstances surrounding the injury or the motivation of the individuals responsible. The epiphyseal separation which results from grabbing the child by a limb to prevent a serious fall is indistinguishable from the epiphyseal separation incurred while the infant is being vigorously shaken or otherwise abused by an irate, distraught adult custodian. The recognition of the radiographic changes, however, does constitute a distinct indication to investigate the circumstances surrounding the injury.

References

1. Tardieu, A. 1860. Etude médico-légale sur les sévices et mauvais traitments exercés sur des enfants. *Ann. d. Hyg. Publ. et Méd. Lég.* 13:361–98.
2. Caffey, J. 1946. Multiple fractures in the long bones of infants suffering from chronic subdural hematoma. *Am. J, Roentgenol.* 56(2):163–73.
3. West, S. 1888. Acute periosteal swellings in several young infants of the same family, probably rickety in nature. *Brit. Med. J.* 1:856–57.
4. Snedecor, S. T., Knapp, R. E., and Wilson, H. B. 1935. Traumatic ossifying periostitis of the newborn. *Surg. Gynecol. Obstet.* 61:385–87.
5. Rose, C. B. 1936. Unusual periostitis in children. *Radiology* 27:131–37.
6. Caffey, J. 1939. Syphilis of the skeleton in early infancy: The nonspecificity of many of the roentgenographic changes. *Am. J. Roentgenol.* 42:637–55.
7. Epstein, B., and Klein, M. 1936. Luesähnliche Röntgenbefunde bei un spezifischen Skeletterkrankungen im Säuglingsalter. *Wien. Med. Wschr.* 86:750–53.
8. Ingraham, F. D. and Heyl, H. L. 1939. Subdural hematoma in infancy and childhood, *J. Am. Med. Assoc.* 112:198–204.
9. Lis, E. F., and Frauenberger, G. S. 1950. Multiple fractures associated with sub-dural hematoma in infancy. *Pediatrics* 6:890–92.

10. Smith, M. J. 1950. Subdural hematoma with multiple fractures. *Am. J. Roentgenol.* 63:342–44.
11. Meneghello, J., and Hasbun, J. 1951. Hematoma subdural y fractura de los huesos largos. *Rev. Chilena Pediat.* 22:80–83.
12. Marquezy, R-A., Bach, Ch., and Blondeau, M. 1952. Hématome sous-dural et fractures multiples des os longs chez un nourrisson de 9 mois. *Arch. Franç. Pédiat.* 9:526–31.
13. Kugelmann, J. 1952. Uber symmetrische Spontanfrakturen unbekannter Genese beim Säugling. *Ann. Paediat. (Basel)* 178:177–81.
14. Marie, J., Apostolides, P., Salet, J., Eliachar, E., and Lyon, G. 1954. Hématome sous-dural du nourrisson associé a des fractures des membres. *Ann. Pédiat. (Paris)* 30:1757–63.
15. Bakwin, H. 1952. Roentgenologic changes in the bones following trauma in infants. *J. Newark Beth Israel Hosp.* 3(1):17.
16. Bakwin, H. 1956. Multiple skeletal lesions in young children due to trauma. *J. Pédiat.* 49:7–15.
17. Silverman, F. N. 1953. The roentgen manifestations of unrecognized skeletal trauma in infants. *Am. J. Roentgenol.* 69(3):413–26.
18. Astley, Roy. 1953. Multiple metaphyseal fractures in small children. *Brit. J. Radiol.* 26(311):577–83.
19. Woolley, P. V., Jr., and Evans, W. A., Jr. 1955. Significance of skeletal lesions in infants resembling those of traumatic origin. *J. Am. Med. Assoc.* 158:539–43.
20. Jones, H. H., and Davis, J. H. 1957. Multiple traumatic lesions of the infant skeleton. *Stanford Med. Bull.* 15:259–73.
21. Weston, W. J. 1957. Metaphyseal fractures in infancy. *J. Bone Joint Surg.* 39(B):694–700.
22. Fisher, S. H. 1958. Skeletal manifestations of parent-induced trauma in infants and children. *Southern Med. J.* 51:956–60.
23. Friedman, M. S. 1958. Traumatic periostitis in infants and children. *J. Am. Med. Assoc.* 166:1840–45.
24. Marti, J., and Kaufmann, H. J. 1959. Multiple traumatische Knochenläsionen beim Säugling. *Deut. Med. Wochschr.* 84:984–88, 991, 992.
25. Miller, D. S. 1959. Fractures among children. I. Parental assault as causative agent. *Minn. Med.* 42:1209–13.
26. Altman, D. H., and Smith, R. L. 1960. Unrecognized trauma in infants and children. *J. Bone Joint Surg.* 42(A):407–13.
27. Gwinn, J. L., Lewin, K. W., and Peterson, H. G., Jr. 1961. Roentgenographic manifestations of unsuspected trauma in infancy. *J. Am. Med. Assoc.* 176:926–29.
28. Kempe, C. H.; Silverman, F. N.; Steele, B. F.; Droegemueller, W.; and Silver, H. K. 1962. The battered-child syndrome. *J. Am. Med. Assoc.* 181:17–24.
29. McHenry, T., Girdany, B. R., and Elmer, Elizabeth. 1963. Unsuspected trauma with multiple skeletal injuries during infancy and childhood. *Pediatrics* 31:903–8.
30. Teng, C. T., Singleton, E. B., and Daeschner, C. W., Jr. 1964. Inflicted skeletal injuries in young children. *Pediatrics Digest* (Sept.):53–66.
31. Caffey, J. 1957. Some traumatic lesions in growing bones other than fractures and dislocations: Clinical and radiological features. *Brit. J. Radiol.* 30:225–38.

32. Rabouille, D. 1967. Les jeunes enfants victimes de sévices corporels. *These. Med.* (Nancy).

33. Brailsford, J. F. 1948. Ossifying hematoma and other simple lesions mistaken for sarcomata. *Brit. J. Radiol.* 21:157–70.

34. Swischuk, L. E. 1969. Spine and spinal cord trauma in the battered child syndrome, *Radiology* 92:733–38.

35. McCort, J., and Vaudagna, J. 1964. Visceral injuries in battered children. *Radiology* 82(3):424–28.

36. Bratu, M.; Dower, J. C.; Siegel, B.; and Hozney, S. H. 1970. Jejunal hematoma, child abuse and Felson's sign. *Conn. Med.* 34:261–64.

37. Eisenstein, E. M., Delta, B. G. and Clifford, J. H. 1965. Jejunal hematoma: an unusual manifestation of the battered child syndrome. *Clin. Pediat.* 4:436–40.

38. Bongiovi, J. J. and Logosso, R. D. 1969. Pancreatic pseudocyst occurring in the battered child syndrome. *J. Ped. Surg.* 4:220–26.

39. Kim, T. and Jenkins, M. E. 1967. Pseudocyst of the pancreas as a manifestation of the battered-child syndrome. *Med. Ann. D. C.* 36:664–66.

40. Snedecor, S. T., and Wilson, H. B. 1949. Some obstetrical injuries to the long bones. *J. Bone Joint Surg.* 31(A):378–84.

41. Griffiths, A. L. 1952. Fatigue fracture of the fibula in childhood. *Arch. Disease Childhood* 27:552–57.

42. Brogdon, B. G., and Crow, N. E. 1960. Little leaguer's elbow. *Am. J. Roentgenol.* 83:671–75.

43. Gillies, C. L., and Hartung, W. 1938. Fracture of the tibia in spina bifida vera. Report of two cases. *Radiology* 31:621–23.

44. Oehme, J. 1961. Periostale Reaktionen bei Myelomeningozele. *Fortschr. Gebiete Roentgenstrahlen Nuklearmed.* 94:82–85.

45. Gilden, J., and Silverman, F. N. 1959. Congenital insensitivity to pain: A neurologic syndrome with bizarre skeletal lesions. *Radiology* 72:176–89.

46. Gyepes, M. T., Newburn, D. H., and Neuhauser, E. B. D. 1965. Metaphyseal and physeal injuries in children with spina bifida and meningomyeloceles. *Am. J. Roentgenol.* 95:168–77.

47. Silverman, F. N. 1972. Unrecognized trauma in infants, the battered child syndrome, and the syndrome of Amboise Tardieu. Rigler Lecture. *Radiology* 104:337–53.

48. Caffey, J. 1972. On the theory and practice of shaking infants. Its potential residual effects of permanent brain damage and mental retardation. *Am. J. Dis. Child.* 124:161–69.

4 | The Pathology of Child Abuse

James Tuthill Weston

Department of Pathology
School of Medicine
University of New Mexico
Albuquerque, New Mexico

Editor's Note

A book concerning the battered child would be incomplete without including the experiences of a forensic pathologist such as Dr. Weston. This material is presented for the specific purpose of assisting other pathologists and medical examiners in the recognition and handling of child abuse. We felt it important to include data dealing with neglect as well as abuse, since they are frequently interrelated.

We would advocate a consultation with a forensic pathologist in all cases of child abuse which present external lesions due to traumatic injury. His experience may prove efficacious in substantiating the extent of injury, possible etiology, and probable time at which these injuries were sustained.

* * *

Introduction

A discussion of the pathology of child abuse cannot limit itself to descriptions of the pathological findings in children who have been subjected to abuse at the hands of their parents or siblings but must be a consideration of the entire clinical pathological syndrome, including the fruits of preliminary investigation, medical examinations, and follow-up studies. It is appropriate to consider a contemporary period of a forensic

Dr. Weston was forensic pathologist with the Department of Public Health and was also visiting lecturer in legal medicine at Jefferson Medical College, Philadelphia. He served as Chief Medical examiner, State of Utah, and Associate Professor of Pathology at the College of Medicine, University of Utah. Presently he is Chief Medical Investigator, State of New Mexico, and Professor of Pathology, School of Medicine, University of New Mexico.

pathologist's experience within several metropolitan areas such as Philadelphia and Salt Lake City and to consider in some detail all of the infant and childhood deaths which may have been the result of another person's conduct. Unfortunately, we do not have the information necessary to interpolate mortality studies of this type into morbidity statistics which accurately reflect the extent of the problem.

Procedure

Preliminary Investigation

The background of the individual conducting the preliminary investigations will vary considerably from one jurisdiction to the other. In most metropolitan areas it is the responsibility of detectives attached to the urban police force, frequently augmented by a social case worker who may have had previous contact with the family or who is regularly assigned to work with the agency responsible for the welfare of children. The pathologist himself may, on occasion, find it desirable to make an inspection of the premises and conduct much of the investigation through his own contacts. Irrespective of the background, training, and education of the individual concerned in this phase of the study, however, it is imperative that he have a thorough insight into the entire problem of childhood maltreatment. In many metropolitan areas this is accomplished by including formal presentation of the subject within the curriculum of the police academy and by annual lectures to social workers and nurses allied with any of the law enforcement agencies or health department. In addition to acquainting these persons with the ramifications of child abuse in general, any presentation should strongly emphasize the anticipated disparity between the presenting story of the parents and the circumstances as found on investigation and should endeavor to inculcate into the agency concerned a sense of responsibility for the welfare of the siblings, even in cases where only a suspicion of child maltreatment is present. This indoctrination should include specifically pointing out the social agency responsible for the welfare of the children and, specifically, how contact may be established.

If the death is reported while the body is still at the scene of demise, it is incumbent upon the investigator to immediately conduct a thorough inspection of the premises with the body in its terminal position. This examination should include a careful and objective notation of the appearance of the home, including its state of repair or disrepair, and its degree of cleanliness. This should reflect the apparent state of economic stability within the family and record the nature and quality of the furnishings, clothing, appliances, and food. Sanitary conditions should be carefully observed and similarly objectively reported. It is not sufficient in such an inspection to record a general statement such as, "The home is filthy." The report should reflect the presence or absence of trash on the floor, the state of operation of the toilet, drains, illumination, heating appliances, and the accessibility to lavatory facilities. A general description of the home should include its geographical location within the community and a general observation of the state of repair of adjoining residences, making comparison with the one in question. Evidence of insect or rodent infestation should be observed. If the home is not satisfactory for human habitation, the appropriate social agency should be notified immediately.

Careful observation of the deceased on the premises should note its location, apparent state of cleanliness, the apparent interval between death and the time originally observed by the investigator, including observation of temperature, rigor and livor mortis, and other postmortem changes. During this initial visit to the premises, the investigator should also take careful note of the condition of other siblings within the home, including their state of nutrition and general well-being. The report should reflect the apparent state of happiness of the children and the presence or absence of any indication of physical abuse. Although the initial visit is usually not the appropriate time to determine the nature of the family structure and its means of support, follow-up visits should attempt to learn the amount of support gained from public and private institutions and the manner in which these funds are expended. Investigation into the family structure should evaluate the amount of time spent in the home by members of the family, both immediate and remote. Objective evaluation of the intelligence and sincerity of the parents is also possible at the time of the initial investigation. When it seems necessary, other agencies should be involved immediately to provide for the safety and welfare of the siblings and, if necessary, the education and rehabilitation of the parents.

This initial examination of the home is much more valuable than one conducted either by surprise or appointment at a later date, since it provides an unrehearsed and unprepared representation of the home environment. It also allows the investigator and ultimately the pathologist to have first-hand acquaintance with the parents, guardians, and siblings of the deceased—all of which is sometimes of paramount importance in evaluating the pathological findings.

When the child dies after medical treatment, this inspection of the home scene should be conducted in a similar manner as soon as the appropriate authorities have been notified. Appropriate photographic documentation of all the details of the report, including the position of the body and the condition of the siblings, is desirable.

External Medical Examination

The postmortem examination should be conducted by a competent forensic pathologist who is aware of all of the implications of child abuse. The first stage of this examination should be a thorough inspection of the external appearance of the body, noting the clothing, its degree of cleanliness, and its state of repair. The description of the body of the deceased should include careful notation of all of the general external characteristics, including weight, height, the state of nutrition, and the approximate interval between death and time of examination. Special attention should be paid to the degree of preservation of the body, the degree of nutrition as reflected by the subcutaneous fatty depots, the degree of diaper rash, including the observation of secondary infection, scarring, or hypopigmentation.

This inspection should note the state of cleanliness of the body, with special attention to any obvious discrepancy between one facet of the infant's care and another—for example, severe diaper rash in conjunction with an extremely well scrubbed, clean skin and new diaper and clean dress. Special note should be made of any evidence of insect infestation. This may consist of fresh bites or evidence of old bites with extensive scarring. External evidence of specific chronic conditions which might have precipitated the state of marasmus should be diligently searched for together with indications of specific avitaminoses or congenital malformations.

In children subjected to physical abuse, the external examination should carefully record every instance of injury, paying special attention to its size, shape, location, pattern, color, and degree of healing. Special note should be made of the more obscure portions of the body which are sometimes subjected to physical trauma with the intention of obscuring this from the other parent, physicians, or social workers. One such popular location is the soles of the feet. Incision through these areas into the underlying tissue will frequently reveal the presence of resorbing subcutaneous hemorrhage not obvious externally.

After inspection of the body as it was received, description, and appropriate photography—both before and after disrobing—the external surface should be thoroughly cleansed to allow further detailed examination in which subtle trauma may be ruled out. Such examination should note carefully any asymmetry of the head, trunk, or extremities. Following this, prior to commencement of the autopsy, roentgenographic examination of the entire skeleton should be conducted. If, on such examination, subtle changes are noted, re-X-raying following evisceration should be conducted and is often more revealing. When multiple fractures, not only of the long bones of the extremities but also of the skull and ribs, are evident, a roentgenologist may be of great assistance to the forensic pathologist in establishing the fact that there were temporally two or more distinct episodes of injury to the bony structure. An essential part of his practice is devoted to evaluation of bony repair following injury. This roentgenographic scan should not be limited to those children who expire from obvious external trauma, irrespective of the alleged cause, but should routinely be conducted on children who expire possibly as the result of neglect, with or without its obvious external manifestations. The roentgenologist's evaluation of the skeletal survey should include not only appraisal of the obvious healing of recent fractures but should be of sufficient quality to evaluate the possibility of remote fractures wherein the healing is complete. Both the anatomic and the forensic pathologist often gain experience in evaluating their skill at aging wounds if these wounds, including the subcutaneous tissue as appropriate, are routinely biopsied, appropriately labeled, and subsequently examined microscopically to differentiate the interval between injury and death and determine whether or not there were two or more distinct episodes of trauma.

Following the initial documentation by photography of the child as it was received, with the clothing and all external injuries and matter intact, a careful search should be conducted on the exterior of the body for any type of trace evidence that may afford a clue to the actual assailant or the nature of the weapon utilized by the assailant. Such evidence should be carefully preserved, sealed, and submitted for appropriate laboratory examination in accordance with the well-established patterns for handling such trace evidence, maintaining the integrity of its detailed records of the chain of possession for its handling.

Internal Medical Examination

Internal examination, as in any competent medicolegal examination, should include detailed objective observation and description of all of the injuries, paying special attention to subtle color changes and other evidences of healing which make possible the dating of traumatic lesions. This examination should also include a detailed observation, inspection, and description of all of the organ systems in the body. Competent medical photography should document all of the pathologic processes with accurate color representation without artifacts.

Detailed complete microscopic examination should be conducted. In the neglected infants this serves to rule out underlying obscure chronic debilitating disease, which might lead to marasmus, and in the infants and children expiring as a result of injury, assists in evaluating the importance of any natural disease process. Microscopic examination of the injuries should be conducted to determine the degree of healing and to substantiate the repetitious nature of the injuries. To determine who is responsible for the injury when a child has been moved from one residence to another, the estimate of time of injury is also extremely important. Careful inspection of all of the contents of the gastrointestinal tract, with photographic documentation, is desirable.

In an effort to rule out exogenous poison as a contributing factor to the death of these children, appropriate qualitative and quantitative toxicological examinations should be conducted. A number of recent contributions to the literature point out the importance of this general toxicological examination in ruling out the introduction of exogenous poisons or overdoses of therapeutic agents as contributing factors to the death of these children. No contemporary discussion of child abuse could be considered complete without appraisal of the impact of the drug culture and illicit drug traffic upon the next group of teenagers. Children born out of legal wedlock in a transient commune type of domestic situation, common among the "flower children" of the drug culture, are not only much more prone to suffer from any one of the patterns of childhood maltreatment described below but are often victims of habitual addiction or sustained overdoses of depressant drugs administered to keep the child docile and tranquilized. Several references within the literature clinically document the presence of permanent brain damage, probably as the result of transient hypoxia in the course of such administration (7). During the postmortem examination, the pathologist should carefully search for the subtle, nonspecific microscopic alterations within the central nervous system which may be the only clue to substantiate such previous injury. While these examinations are usually negative, reasonable doubt is rarely ruled out in a criminal court in large metropolitan areas without this positive documentation by the toxicologist. When infectious disease is suspected, postmortem bacteriology is equally desirable in establishing the etiologic agent causing or contributing to the death.

Follow-Up

When the pathologist completes his preliminary investigation and examination, he should acquaint the investigating officer or social workers with all of the alternatives of his observations and institute a prompt and thorough follow-up investigation. This should include detailed interrogation into all of the circumstances leading up to and including the terminal episode, and medical background such as the circumstances of the infant's birth, state of its maturity, the length of postpartum hospitalization, the degree of medical attendance sought, and the agencies at which this attendance was given. This should also include the nature of the family relationship, the degree of harmony within the family, and the nature of the interrelationships between the parents and other siblings.

Questioning should not be limited to the parents but should include private conferences with siblings capable of offering vocal testimony, with the understanding that, should the siblings present testimony which might be injurious to their general welfare if returned to the hands of the parents, they would be offered permanent shelter from this type of revenge. Thorough search of all social welfare agency records should be conducted to determine if there has been previous contact with the family. The neighbors should be interrogated with considered evaluation of their statements and the motives for their testimony. When the child is born out of wedlock, careful note should be made of the mother's behavior patterns, the source of the income for the child's care, and the degree of responsibility of the father in providing for this care. Special attention should be paid to the temporal relationships in the physically injured children, with careful documentation of each interval of the child's terminal period of life, including detailed interrogation of the persons, including baby sitters and siblings who have been left in attendance with the children. Skilled interrogators working with law enforcement and social agencies should be employed whenever possible to gather this type of background information. Confrontation of the parents by the usual obvious disparity between the initial presenting story and the evidence as gathered by the medical investigator usually results in a slowly unfolding admission of misconduct. Newer refinements in investigative techniques, such as the polygraph, may be used to promptly rule out the person or persons who might be implicated in a temporal relationship. These individuals, not being responsible for the injuries, are usually willing to submit to this type of examination or to interrogation readily. Repetitive interrogation of both parents may produce admissions which provoke hostility between themselves and prompt admission of further implication. Distant relatives, grandparents, and others not in the immediate family, who live within the home or are frequent visitors, may often volunteer information which will be invaluable in interrogation of the suspected assailant or assailants. An investigator thoroughly familiar with the usual reasons offered for mistreatment or abuse by the parents is in a much better position to conduct satisfactory interrogations. Any interrogation conducted by any investigator related to a law enforcement agency should be conducted after thoroughly acquainting his suspect with his legal rights and privileges in accordance with recent court decisions.

The Pathologist in Court

The pathologist, upon reaching an opinion concerning the cause and manner of death—the principal purpose for conducting exhaustive investigation and postmortem examination in harmony with the law enforcement agency—should be able to present his findings in court in such a conclusive manner as to prove his point beyond a reasonable doubt. Nonetheless, it should be remembered that these observations are merely opinions on the part of an expert witness and he should have at his disposal all of the detailed records of observations and supporting examinations which were utilized in order to arrive at such an opinion. The rules of evidence preclude the pathologist's presenting any information except that which he derived by his own personal observations; hence, if he personally did not investigate the scene of the death, such evidence must be introduced by the investigator primarily responsible for such investigation and the gathering of this portion of the evidence.

The skilled forensic pathologist is usually the senior member of the team conducting the investigation, and, as such, he should see that all of the evidence gathered is well documented, appropriately identified, carefully kept in custody, and prepared not only for suitable presentation in court but possible examination by a designated expert for the defendant. The hospital pathologist often serves only as an adjunct to the investigating agency and, therefore, is frequently responsible only for the evidence derived from examination of the body. In either instance, however, it should be pointed out in pretrial conference and, if necessary, in the course of courtroom testimony, that neither individual, except on unusual occasions, is capable of arriving at a definitive conclusion concerning cause and manner or mode of death except by evaluation of the circumstances surrounding the death of the child in conjunction with the laboratory and pathologic findings.

When, in the course of the trial procedure, there is a determination to sequester the witnesses or restrict them from the courtroom when other witnesses are testifying, the prosecutor should take this into consideration and insure that his medical expert has all of the firsthand evidence which has been previously introduced in the course of the trial, to serve as an adjunct to his pathologic findings in establishing the mechanism of injury.

A pretrial conference sufficiently in advance of the trial should have gathered together all members of the team who have assisted in the investigation. The prosecuting attorney should thoroughly review all of his evidence at this time. When experts such as a neuropathologist or radiologist assist the forensic pathologist, their findings should be recorded independently within the body of medical evidence and these individuals should be called upon to review these findings with the prosecutor and subsequently present their testimony, if necessary. The medical expert should assist the prosecutor not only by enumerating the positive findings but by evaluating the degree of certainty of these opinions and indicating the controversial and salient negative findings from which argument in the courtroom may ensue. This type of testimony is especially important in childhood neglect cases wherein pre-existing constitutional disease must be ruled out. The medical expert for the prosecution should anticipate that counsel for the defense may well request independent evaluation of all of his evidence, including photographic documentation of the external examination, radiographic examination, microscopic preparations, and other laboratory examinations to assist him in his evaluation of the opinions concluded by the state's medical expert.

It is also well for the physician to bear in mind that no matter how emotionally involved he may have been initially or during the course of his investigation, while in court it is wise not to play the role of an advocate but that of an amicus curiae.

It may be necessary to introduce photographic documentation in court to assist the physician in illustrating injuries or the general condition of the child to the jury. On occasion, such documentation may be ruled inflammatory or to be excluded from the eyes of the jury. However, increasingly, it has been the practice of the courts to allow introduction of such evidence when it is determined that word description, no matter how detailed, does not satisfactorily portray the condition of a child. All such photographs should be completely devoid of any artifact and should illustrate only those external findings present on the body prior to autopsy. When it is necessary to illustrate internal pathologic findings, this should be done with discretion and, again, without artifactual alterations produced by the pathologist. If it becomes necessary to illustrate more subtle changes such as histologic observations, these should be accompanied by appropriate illustrations of comparatively normal tissue or when dating injuries, by comparison with injuries of known duration. Numerous authoritative references are available (1).

Patterns of Maltreatment

Although the medical literature contains numerous references to patterns of child abuse written by clinicians, social workers, psychiatrists, and others in related fields,

TABLE 1

DEATHS FROM NEGLECT AND ABUSE FOR A
FIVE-YEAR PERIOD IN PHILADELPHIA

YEAR	NEGLECT DEATHS		ABUSE DEATHS		TOTALS
	White	Non-White	White	Non-White	
1961	1	4	1	6	12
1962	1	5	0	6	12
1963	1	4	2	2	9
1964	2	5	4	8	19
1965	1	0	1	6	8
TOTALS	6	18	8	28	60

the references in the field of pathology are sparse. In classic presentations by Adelson (3, 4), the two characteristic patterns of childhood maltreatment—namely, neglect and abuse by physical injury—are well documented in a small group. In an attempt to derive reasonably accurate statistics delineating the incidence of death from parental neglect and abuse in a large metropolitan area, the author, while associated with the Office of the Medical Examiner in the City of Philadelphia, had opportunity to review the mortality of all children under 16 years of age. During the time of that period of study from 1961 to 1965, Philadelphia was not a homogeneous population but rather consisted of a central section of the community which lived virtually in ghetto-like surroundings while isolated demographic groups including Germans, Italians, and those of Jewish extraction, occupied similarly well delineated segments of the more densely populated sections of the City. Within the City boundaries, a few miles from this dense center of population, were large areas of typical suburban type developments consisting of single family, middle-class dwellings, while an even smaller segment of the community consisted of sprawling mansions, sparsely distributed over estates consisting of several acres of wooded land. Within this heterogeneous population, there was an opportunity to study not only the patterns of child abuse but the sociologic and demographic conditions of these patterns in a much more satisfactory manner than had thus far been accomplished by review of compulsory reporting after appropriate legislation had been enacted or by review of incidents reported within the public media. Table 1 reflects the incidence, age, and racial distribution of these basic maltreatment patterns over a five-year period. It may be presumed that the forensic pathologists responsible for conducting the examinations and supervising the investigations were fully alerted to the ramifications of these problems. There is no significant variation in the incidence from year to year, nor in the racial distribution: During the last five years of the author's experience within the populous Wasatch Front area of Utah, constituting a population of approximately 800,000, the Office of the Medical Examiner has positively identified 11 instances of child abuse resulting in death. In keeping with the race-population distribution within this section of the country, every instance of identified fatal child abuse within this group has been in the white population. The technique for investigation of each of the entities was similar and basically followed the outline presented.

Childhood Neglect

Twenty-four infants, varying in age from one to thirteen months at the time of their deaths, died as a result of negligence on the part of the parent or parents responsible for providing adequate nutritional and environmental needs to the child during its helpless early months. Victims of this type of abuse represent an act of omission on the part of the parent, in contrast with those suffering as the result of physical abuse or trauma. All but 1 of the infants were born with medical attendance; 16 were born at term gestation and 8 prematurely. These premature infants were retained within the hospital for intervals of two to seven weeks to establish maturity acceptable for home care. All but 3 of the infants were dead when first seen by physicians, and with few exceptions, all presented variations of essentially the same picture.

External Examination

The appearance was one associated with gross dereliction of all of the amenities of food, clothing, and sanitation, which the helpless infant is unable to provide. Extremely soiled clothing, frequently caked or matted with vermin and feces, often had to be soaked from about the genitalia and lower extremities to avoid denudation of the skin during undressing. In two instances the clothing had obviously been changed during a period immediately prior to death or postmortem, with the underlying skin obviously having been extensively scrubbed. One of these was presented postmortem in its christening gown, beneath which the new undershirt still retained the price tag (Fig. 1). Infrequent changing of diapers and bedding was reflected by severe diaper rash frequently associated with complete denudation of the skin of the genitalia and perineum. In several cases this was of sufficiently long duration to result in loss of pigmentation in negroid infants (Fig. 2). In the more advanced cases this process extended from the axilla to the soles of the feet and was associated with secondary infection and sepsis (Fig. 3). A tightly tied ligature around the penis, to prevent urination, resulted in early gangrene in one child.

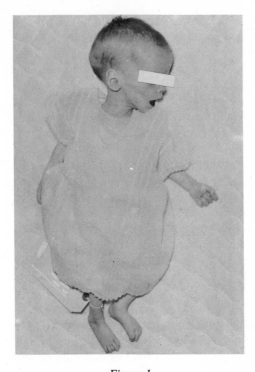

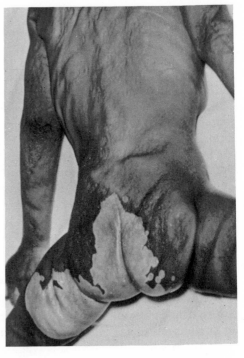

Figure 1

Starved infant, age five months, scrubbed and redressed in christening gown after death.

Figure 2

Neglected infant, age eleven months, with hypopigmentation of perineum associated with longstanding diaper rash.

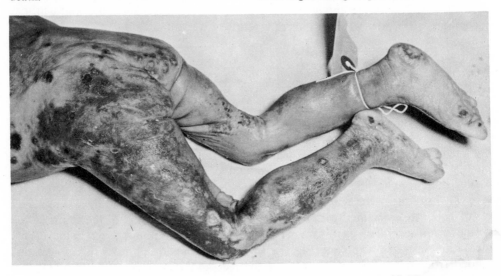

Figure 3

Weeping, secondarily infected diaper rash in neglected infant, age nine months.

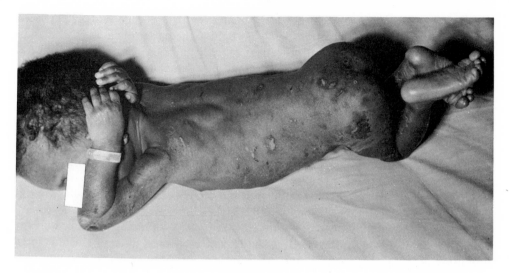

Figure 4

Scars resulting from infected insect bites on posterior trunk. Patient hospitalized at age eight and one-half months for marasmus and discharged after weight gain with feeding.

The caked, encrusted dirt was removed only with considerable effort from the infants to reveal skin with virtually no turgor or palpable subcutaneous fat, hanging loosely over the bones of the face and extremities, while the abdomen was usually retracted and the ribs on the thorax unusually prominent. Absence of intraorbital fat resulted in marked depression of the eyes, which was associated with marked concavity of the cheeks. Infestation by insects, including ants, bees, and roaches, frequently resulted in extensive bites on the skin, many of which were secondarily infected. Many of these resulted in permanent scarring (Fig. 4).

The infants seen during the terminal period of their lives in each instance reflected an extremely low state of metabolism, marked diminution in respiratory rate and volume, hypothermia, and vascular collapse which persisted until death in spite of the administration of parenteral fluids, oxygen and steroids. The clinical impression in each was that of extreme malnutrition and dehydration resulting from neglect. Often this was more repugnant to the attending physician than the trauma identified in the physically battered children.

Internal Examination

Complete autopsy was conducted on all of the infants. Absence of fatty depots within the interior of the bodies was associated with the loss of subcutaneous tissue. The gastrointestinal tract in most of these infants indicated little or no evidence of food ingestion immediately prior to death. Although terminal complications were present in several of the group, examination revealed no congenital or acquired constitutional disease of sufficient severity and duration to account for the marasmus.

Bronchopneumonia was present in 3 of the infants; sepsis complicated the celluliti, associated with the diaper rash in 3 additional infants. One child had an advanced otitis media and one an acute necrotizing laryngitis. Chemical examination of each in this series revealed no indication of lead or other exogenous element. In the several infants whose weight at death approached that anticipated in an infant of their ages other obvious external manifestations of parental neglect, such as maggot infestation, prompted including them within the group. In one infant, constant sucking of the index finger in the terminal period resulted in maceration, with the skin and nail readily slipping from the underlying tissue.

Alleged and Confessed Method of Injury

Upon initial questioning, the parents repeated a monotonously uniform story of the child being in reasonably good health until one or two days before death, when it "would not take its feeding," "had a mild diarrhea," or "had a cold" as did several siblings within the family. Repeated interrogation might elaborate the story that the youngster "never did well after birth" or had always "failed to thrive." The attempted postmortem cleaning of the children and redressing reflected sufficient parental concern at the outward appearance of their offspring to warrant correction before presentation to a physician or hospital.

TABLE 2

AGE, RACE, AND SEX OF TWENTY-FOUR VICTIMS OF PARENTAL NEGLECT

AGE (months)	WHITE		NON-WHITE		TOTALS
	Male	Female	Male	Female	
0–3	1	0	5	1	7
3–6	3	2	2	1	8
6–12	1	1	5	1	8
13	0	0	1	0	1
TOTALS	5	3	13	3	24

Table 2 shows the distribution of age, sex, and race of this group. Eighteen of the infants were male and 6 female; 16 were non-white and 8 white, during a period in which the ratio of non-white to white births was 16 to 25. The weights at death varied from 35 to 88 per cent of the expected weight, averaging 65 per cent. These were all below the third percentile, except the cases where neglect resulting in death was in an area other than food deprivation, such as complications resulting from failure to change diapers. Emphasis should again be placed upon the disparity between the presenting story of the parents and the obvious physical condition of the infants at the time examination was conducted. The degree of cachexia, dehydration, and malnutrition apparent in these youngsters was inconsistent with a history of one or two days of diarrhea, upper respiratory infection, or vomiting.

Family Background and Conditions

These children represented in each instance the last born offspring of families averaging 7 children, varying from 2 to 12 in number. Thirteen were born out of wedlock, while 9 were offspring of legitimate families. The average infant within this group was five months of age at the time of his death. The parents in most cases were described uniformly by police officers, social workers, or representatives of court as being of low intellect. Slightly more than fifty per cent of the group received all of their financial support from public assistance, while more than eighty per cent received some public support.

An attempt was made, as by Adelson (3), to contrast the appearance of the siblings and the homes of children born legitimately with those born out of wedlock. To some degree there was a comparable parallel within this group. In general, the mother caring for families of 5 to 12 who was unable to provide proper nutrition for an offspring who died was also incapable of providing an accepted state of cleanliness or repair within her home. Exceptions within this series were limited to married couples who were usually described as considerably substandard in their intellect, whose homes were in a state of extreme uncleanliness, and whose siblings were generally described as completely unkempt. Mothers of these children more often than not had offspring by more than one father and frequently housed the offspring of as many as three and four paramours, the whereabouts of whom was unknown. They were usually between eighteen and thirty years of age and were invariably held accountable for the condition of the deceased baby. They rarely lived in a residence more than six months and often shared one with another equally large family.

The most commonly encountered descriptive word characterizing the homes of these infants was "filthy," with numerous references to an odor of urine and feces permeating the residence and numerous descriptions of bedding, clothing, and floor soiled by wet and dry excreta. In more than eighty per cent the description included reference to extensive infestation by roaches. In most of the homes, all of which were examined in the course of the investigation, careful description of the food supplies revealed only sparse quantities in refrigerators and kitchens. In three homes, with siblings numbering from 3 to 8, in which the infants were found dead, there was no provision for central heat, and in one home human excreta from 17 occupants representing two families was deposited daily by the children from a bucket into the rear yard. Invariably the descriptions included references to piles of debris and trash, not only in the yard of the residence but within the house itself. Interviews of the neighbors frequently provided evidence of disinterest of the parent for the offspring. In the group it was not unusual to have the oldest, a nine-year-old youngster, providing the complete daily and nocturnal needs of his younger siblings, ranging in age from three months on up. No provision was made for clothing the preschool children in 2 of the families.

Examination of the medical history of the children revealed that the parents had sought medical attendance in only two instances after the initial postnatal immunization. For both of these children hospitalization was considered necessary. Extensive clinical and laboratory examinations failed to reveal any condition to explain the cachexia present on admission, while striking response to feeding with resulting weight gain prompted their return to the parents in a relatively short time, only to have them expire with outright starvation several months later (Fig. 5, see also Fig. 4).

No discussion of child neglect would be complete without alluding to those condi-

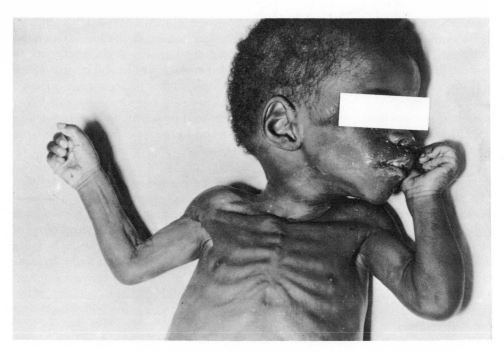

Figure 5

Infant in Figure 4 upon his death by starvation at age thirteen months.

tions in which death or disease may arise out of dereliction of parental responsibility in protection and supervision of their offspring. Such deaths frequently occur upon leaving the children unattended for long periods. Acute dehydration or heat exhaustion during the summer months may contribute to the number of sudden unexplained infant deaths. Similarly, no large urban area passes through a winter without seeing at least one, and usually several, large families wiped out by fire when left unattended by competent adult supervision. This is frequently the result of mischief by one of the younger children and is often a repetitive act occurring after several admonitions by the parents on previous occasions. Death caused by a natural disease amenable to therapy requiring constant surveillance (e.g., epilepsy or diabetes mellitus) is considered by some to be due to parental neglect when it can be shown that the parents have been properly advised, provided with the medication, and have no religious objection to its use. For a complete summary of this group of neglected infants see Table 1, Appendix B.

Children with No Previous Injury

During this same period of study, 36 infants and children succumbed as a result of proven physical injury inflicted by a member of their family, paramour, or baby sitter. In 13 of these infants (group 1) there was no indication of previous injury of a magnitude such as to leave scarring or other physical defects; while in 23 (group 2) physical

TABLE 3

AGE, RACE, AND SEX OF THIRTY-SIX VICTIMS OF PHYSICAL ABUSE

AGE	WHITE		NON-WHITE		TOTALS
	Male	Female	Male	Female	
Months					
0–3	2	0	3	1	6
3–6	1	1	1	1	4
6–12	0	0	2	3	5
Years					
1–2	2	0	2	3	7
2–3	1	0	1	4	6
3–4	1	0	2	3	6
4–5	0	0	0	0	0
>5	0	0	1	1	2
TOTALS	7	1	12	16	36

examination, internal examination, roentgenographic examination, or investigation with confession elaborated history of previous trauma.

The children in this group 1, of whom 2 were white and 11 non-white, ranged in age from one month to six years, with an average age of nine months (if the single six-year-old is excluded from the group). Seven of the children were male and 6 female. These youngsters in each instance were taken to a physician's office or a hospital either in a terminal or postmortem state.

The alleged method of injury to the child is shown in Table 4. Six of the group were described as having fallen downstairs or from a crib or lap, and in 4 of the group no injury whatsoever was acknowledged by the parents. These infants and children came from homes which were considerably better, socioeconomically, than those of the neglected infants or the majority of the repetitively injured children. In more than half, representing the middle class, the homes could be described as clean and well maintained. The parents expressed considerably more concern for the welfare of their offspring during the terminal and postmortem period than did either those of the neglected children or those of the repetitively injured children. The general appearance and nutritional status was considerably above that of the other two groups.

TABLE 4

CONTRAST BETWEEN THE ALLEGED AND CONFESSED METHODS OF INJURY—
GROUP 1

Alleged Method of Injury (number)	Confessed Method of Injury (number)
Fell from crib, lap, or down stairs 9	Struck with hand 10
Found dead in crib 6	Struck with object (plastic toy, vacuum cleaner, hairbrush) 4
I hit baby 2	Threw or pushed 2
Beat up by brother 1	Threw object at baby (plastic milk bottle) . . . 1
Overturned hot water 1	Immersed in hot water 1
Baby disappeared 1	Unknown 1
	Elbowed by baby sitters watching TV 1

External Examination

In most of this series (9 cases), there was obvious recent external injury to the body. In the children that were shown to have been struck by hands and fists, this was reflected by numerous poorly outlined red-blue bruises associated with swelling and predominantly distributed over the face, lateral aspect of the head, neck, and trunk. When the soft tissues were in apposition to underlying bony structures or teeth, there was frequently denudation of the skin with abrasion or, in the more severe cases, lacerations. These were often present in the inner aspect of markedly swollen, contused lips. When a weapon, either held in the hand or thrown as a missile, was employed, a pattern injury frequently reflected its shape; for example, a linear bruise and denudation resulted from a blow by a vacuum cleaner pipe or a hairbrush (Fig. 6). In the one baby struck in the upper abdomen by a partially filled plastic milk bottle hurled across the room, there was only a small, semicircular, sharply outlined bruise externally, lying

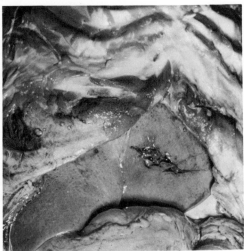

Figure 7

Laceration of liver produced by half-filled plastic milk bottle hurled across room.

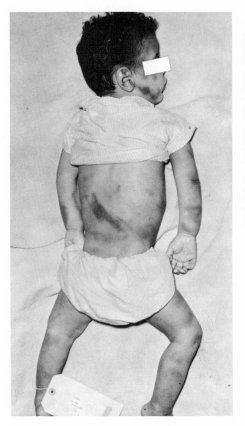

Figure 6

Posterior view of infant beaten in one violent episode without evidence of pre-existing scars.

in apposition to a similarly sharply circumscribed, slightly semicircular laceration of the underlying liver capsule (Fig. 7). This infant, observed in the hospital for three-and-one-half hours, expired as a result of intra-abdominal hemorrhage, the history of trauma having been elicited only after the postmortem examination. In 3 infants in the group there was only minimal external evidence of trauma reflected by sharply outlined, superficial red-blue bruises. In 1 of the group there was no external indication of trauma, either healing or recent.

Obvious extensive second- and third-degree burns (resulting from heat) scattered over the lower trunk and extremities resulted in irreversible shock and death in the absence of other significant findings in 1 of the group. These occurred when an older sibling, pursuing his brother to punish him by partial immersion in a pan of hot water, overturned the container and spilled the water into which the deceased slipped and fell. The brother himself was a victim of repetitive abuse, with numerous old scars, and considered the punishment to be within the scope of that expected of him as a baby sitter.

Internal Examination

The internal examination of children in group 1 reflected, in most cases, the magnitude of the external trauma as well as its location. There was no indication of any old fractures within the extremities, skull, or trunk. Recent fractures were present in the skull in 2 of the children, and within the ribs in 3. The most commonly encountered pathologic finding was that of subdural hemorrhage. This was acute with no indication of any organization and in most instances was associated with a localized area of recent subarachnoid hemorrhage and underlying contusion of the cerebral cortex identified by a light pin-purple discoloration, slight softening, and sharply outlined dark red-purple petechial hemorrhages. In the children thrown or hurled against the wall or to the floor, there was evidence, not only of a primary contusion adjacent to the scalp lesions but also of a contrecoup injury, reflected by contralateral subarachnoid hemorrhage and cerebral contusions. Examination of the galea frequently revealed numerous sharply outlined hemorrhages, which often reflected the outline of the weapon employed, even in the absence of conspicuous external bruising, abrasion, or laceration (Fig. 8). To the pathologist this multiplicity of galeal hemorrhages frequently is the only clue of discrepancy between a presenting story and the actual method of injury.

While the external examination of the anterior aspect of the thorax and abdomen may reveal only minimal, poorly outlined bruises, which may be seen only by sectioning through the abdominal wall, the underlying viscera and fractures of the ribs may reflect the impact of the trauma much more accurately. Within the thorax there may be extensive hemorrhage into the thymus and anterior mediastinum, while in the lungs and epicardium are relatively small anterior hemorrhages. In one of the series with severe anterior contusions of the lungs, involving approximately one-third of the anterior pleural surface, there was a linear vertical laceration of the anterior wall of the right ventricle of the heart. Extensive hemorrhage into the abdominal wall in scattered areas was encountered in several cases, again indicating a multiplicity of blows. In the freely movable loops of bowel, subperitoneal hemorrhages were small and widely

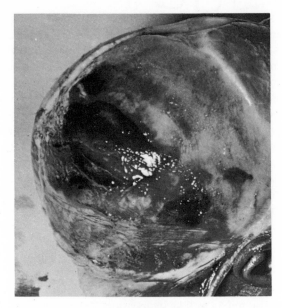

Figure 8

Scalp reflected to reveal multiple galeal hemorrhages not visualized externally.

scattered, although within the more firmly attached root of the mesentery, hemorrhage
was much more widespread. Laceration of the splenic capsule, associated with extensive retroperitoneal and intramesenteric hemorrhage, was seen in one case.

Alleged and Confessed Method of Injury

Follow-up investigation conducted upon completion of the medical examination
elaborated a story considerably different from that alleged at the hospital. Table 4
contrasts the presenting and finally confessed methods of injury. In 8 of the group an
admission of striking the child was elicited. In 5 of these no weapon was employed
except the bare hand or fist. In 3, a readily-at-hand weapon was used, including plastic
toys, a vacuum cleaner pipe, and a hairbrush. Exasperation resulting in throwing or
pushing the infant accounted for injuries in 2 additional cases. Although the internal
trauma was inconsistent with an accidental death in 1, no admission of injury was
acknowledged and consequently the mechanism was unknown.

The assailants in most of these cases were the natural parents, the father being responsible for the trauma in 5 cases, the mother in 3, a stepfather in 1, and siblings
ranging in age from fourteen to seventeen who were charged with caring for the other
children in the home being responsible for an additional 3. In each instance the story
elicited was quite similar, namely that of extreme exasperation at a time of parental
fatigue. The exasperation was most commonly provoked by what was considered excessive crying at a time inconvenient to the parent. Soiling of pants, bed, or floor by
urine and feces provoked the terminal episode in 3 additional cases. One baby, in

whom the mother attempted to force mastication by placing food in its mouth and mechanically manipulating its jaws, who still would not swallow its food, provoked exasperation to the point of physical fisticuffs on its face. The episode of injury, whether it be to the head or trunk, in most of the cases was similar and described as an episode of violent outrage arising from exasperation resulting in pummeling of the most readily available part of the baby with open hands and fists. If the baby was sitting up in a highchair or carriage, the head was most frequently injured, while if the baby was in a supine position, the injury was most frequently inflicted to the anterior trunk and abdomen, although it was not necessarily limited to this portion of the body.

Although the injuries resulting in death in some of these children may have resulted from the first episode of beating in an otherwise typical battered child situation, the advanced age of some within the group, the general state of well-being of them and of their home, and the complete absence of any preexisting trauma, suggest that this group represents a clinical-pathologic entity altogether different from the typically battered children with repetitive trauma. The complete summary of these cases is presented in Table 2, Appendix B.

Children with Repetitive Injury

Among the 23 children who expired as a result of injuries superimposed on previous injury, 6 were white and 17 non-white. The age ranged from two months to five years, with an average of twenty-four months. Thirteen of these children were male and 10 female. All of the group were presented to the hospital or attending physician in a terminal or postmortem condition, with allegations of injury acknowledged in all but 4 who were allegedly found dead in their cribs without an intervening episode of trauma. Again, the most common explanation offered was that of a fall down the stairs or from the bed or crib. In 2 instances, beating the child was acknowledged by the parents, and for one additional baby, acknowledgment was obtained that he had banged his head while attempting to withdraw from a beating.

External Examination

The external examination offered a complete range of extremes of injuries. In 4 cases there were only small, sharply circumscribed bruises associated with partially encrusted denudations, completely consistent with injury inflicted by a fall. In 19 of the group, repetitive, extensive, obvious external injury of short duration was present.

If no weapon was employed except the fist and hand, the injuries were usually limited to poorly outlined, irregular bruises similar to those noted in group 1, accompanied by lacerations when in apposition to the teeth or skull, and by moderate to marked degrees of subcutaneous swelling (Fig. 9). Weapons which leave a characteristic pattern were frequently encountered, the most common of which was a coiled lamp cord or rope, characteristically leaving a loop welt, simulating the arrangement of the cord (Fig. 10), with dark red-purple discolorations and often denudation of the skin. Older healed similar welts with varying degrees of scarring, hypopigmentation, and hyperpigmentation were frequently seen, accompanied by fresh identical patterns in which there was recent hemorrhage and superficial contusion. If a stick was employed,

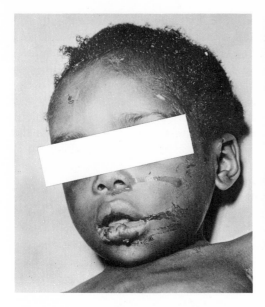

Figure 9

Face in typical repetitively beaten child marked by scars, abrasions, contusions, and lacerations of lip in various stages of healing.

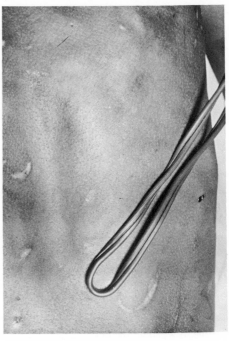

Figure 10

Commonly encountered lamp-cord whip with its characteristic loop pattern welt.

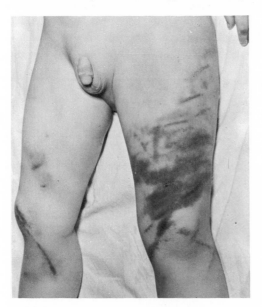

Figure 11

Numerous superimposed bruises of thighs resulting from repetitive blows by stick.

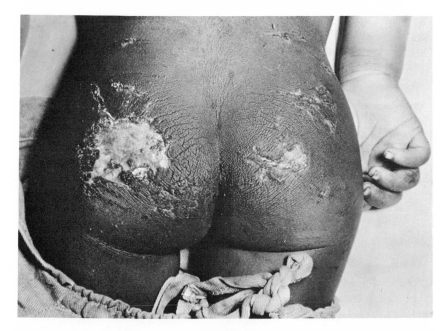

Figure 12a

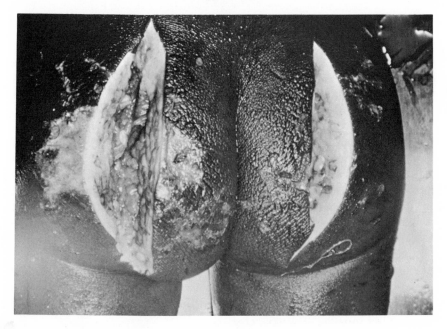

Figure 12b

Healing abrasions and contusions of buttocks with scarring resulting from repetitive beating. *b:* Incision into buttocks frequently allows visualization of old hemorrhage and scarring resulting from previous trauma.

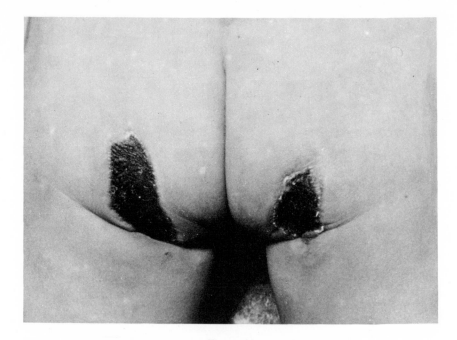

Figure 13

Healing burns on buttocks suffered when forced to sit on steam radiator to dry diapers.

frequently one or both of the sharp outlines representing the borders of the weapon were present on the bruise (Fig. 11), often accompanied by denudation and abrasion of the skin. Bruises and abrasions resulting from weapons in these infants were not confined to the face, neck, and trunk but were also distributed over the head, genitalia, and extremities. In several within the group an unusual and characteristic pattern of abrasion or contusion remained, providing a ready means of identifying the weapon used as a file or belt buckle.

Fourteen of this series showed obvious prolonged repetitive trauma, manifested by healed scars and welts in addition to recent abrasions, contusions, and lacerations superimposed on the older injuries. The number of individual scars and marks on the children numbered from 18 to 347 with the anterior and lateral aspects of the thighs and buttocks reflecting as many as 30 individual superimposed recent linear bruises inflicted by a ruler or stick, in addition to as many as 50 healed linear welts reflected by hypopigmented and hyperpigmented scars within which there often was a slight tendency to keloid formation (Fig. 12*a*). Sectioning into the buttocks and soles of the feet in several of the children revealed subcutaneous hemorrhage associated with trauma which was not obvious externally (Fig. 12*b*).

Bony prominences frequently were the site of accumulations of subcutaneous fibrous connective tissue, presenting on the head as pseudohyperostotic frontal bossing, obviously originating from old trauma manifested by extensive scarring of the overlying skin.

In 5 children within this series, there was only minimal external healing trauma, similar in nature to that noted in the more severe cases but of lesser magnitude. In 2 of the children, although there was no external indication of any healing or healed preexisting trauma, confession elicited a story of repetitive beating, and in 1, roentgenographic examination revealed a healing fracture. In 4 of the group roentgenographic examination revealed healing fractures, including those of the skull, humerus, femur, and ulna. Fractures with no evidence of healing were demonstrated in the skull in 5 cases, ribs in 3, and humerus in 2. In the one child alleged to have had a pint bottle of boiling water overturned upon him, there were second- and third-degree thermal burns extending from a sharply outlined transverse upper border on the posterior thorax over the entire buttocks, thighs, lower legs, and feet, including the soles. This infant was later proven to have been immersed in hot tap water and had a healed skull fracture from a previous punishment. On 1 child numerous healing and healed abrasions and contusions were superimposed on a symmetrical pattern-burn scar on the buttocks, resulting from forcing the child to sit on a hot gas plate in his basement when he soiled his diapers at an earlier age. Burns were also present on the buttocks of one child (Fig. 13) who was forced to sit on a hot steam radiator to dry his wet diapers.

Internal Examination

Internal examination revealed injuries essentially the same as those noted within the earlier series but of considerably greater magnitude. Subdural hemorrhage without skull fracture, associated in some instances with severe contusions of the cortex and overlying subarachnoid hemorrhage, were present in 8. Frequently this hemorrhage was revealed to be in several stages, with fresh, bright red blood bordering old, resorbed, partially organized hematomata. In 5 of the group, severe skull fractures were associated with contusions of the brain and hemorrhage in all membrane layers. Detailed neuropathologic examination of the brain may reveal tears in the white matter of the cerebral cortex which the neuropathologist by histologic examination may also be able to document as two separate episodes of trauma (11). Frequently, the multiplicity of the galeal hemorrhages, together with the indication of resorption and breakdown of blood pigment, reflected by the reddish-brown discoloration present in bruises elsewhere on the body as well, served to delineate grossly the time intervals between the various episodes of trauma. In 3 of the children, severe contusion of the brain was unaccompanied by any fracture or subdural hemorrhage. Violent trauma to the trunk and abdomen in the form of pummeling by fists was indicated in 6 of the children in whom there frequently was only minimal evidence of external trauma of the skin surface, although extensive lacerations of the liver were present in 3, in the mesentery in 2, and in the spleen in 1—all associated with extensive hemorrhage into the abdominal cavity and wall.

Alleged and Confessed Method of Injury

This group, in general, reflected the most violent treatment of any within the series. Table 5 reflects the same contrast between alleged and confessed method of injury seen in group 1. With few exceptions, most of these children came from homes of extremely low socioeconomic level, wherein the family was loosely knit, with the elder sibling serving the parental role often for several days or weeks at a time. This was reflected by the general unkempt appearance of the children. None of the families within this subgroup was in a socioeconomic group consistent with upper middle class or upper class.

The reason for abuse offered by one mother in this group was constant teasing of the parents by the child. The mother interpreted this as a desire for attention by her child, who purportedly achieved satisfaction by the parental beating which ultimately resulted in death.

Parental physical abuse and burns are responsible for all of the deaths within this series. However, more unusual methods of punishment have occasionally resulted in unexpected death. Adelson (4) has reported one death following aspiration of pepper, the ingestion of which was inflicted by the parents as punishment. Death has also

TABLE 5

CONTRAST BETWEEN THE ALLEGED AND CONFESSED METHODS OF INJURY—
GROUP 2

Alleged Method of Injury (number)	Confessed Method of Injury (number)
Fell from furniture 10	Struck with fists 15
Fell downstairs 7	Struck with hands 12
Found dead 4	Struck with weapon (belt, cord, switch, ruler,
Beat child 4	wire coat hanger, strap) 10
Banged head in attempted withdrawal 2	Banged head in attempted withdrawal 1
Fell down 1	Burned on gas burner 1
Overturned bottle of hot water on baby 1	Burned on radiator 1
Car bed collapsed on baby 1	Burned by immersion in hot water 1
Drowned in bathtub 1	Unknown 1
	Struck with hands and neglected 1

followed aspiration of vomitus following the ingestion of red-pepper sauce in one child and following aspiration of a soap solution used to wash out the mouth of one additional child.

The significance of trauma in the background of the parents is reflected by the fact that, in this group of 9 mothers serving as the assailants, several admitted that they had been beaten, not only during childhood but in the weeks and months immediately prior to the death of their offspring. The most violent beating within the group was that given by a twenty-four-year-old mother repetitively beaten by her husband who ultimately abandoned his home, leaving her with the resented child. The mother admitted to ritualistic orgies wherein she repetitively beat the child to a point of semi-consciousness on three occasions prior to the terminal flogging which resulted in death. The complete summary of these cases is presented in Table 3, Appendix A.

Repetitive torture (e.g., by cigarette burns) often reported by clinicians, was not proven in any of these cases nor was there any indication on the extremities of individuals in this group that they had been confined to their bed or room by restraints sufficiently tight to produce abrasion and scarring. Four of these children had been cared for by physicians and local hospitals in the year before their demises, with roentgenographic demonstration of fractures in 2, explained by family and physicians as being incident to a fall from a crib. One of these infants still had a cast on its femur upon its terminal admission to the hospital. In none of the children examined was there any indication of organic brain damage antedating the terminal episode.

Included in this group is 1 child who expired as a result of rupture of the mesentery and retroperitoneal hemorrhage, although the parents never acknowledged a beating of this magnitude. Herein lies one of the greatest problems to the forensic pathologist in arriving at a definitive conclusion concerning a manner of death. For if one is to say that every subdural hematoma, even every skull fracture, in a child who has evidence of welts and scars incident to beating on his trunk and extremities is a result of child abuse, an injustice may well be done since this type of punishment is observed clinically much more frequently than seen at postmortem, and it is impossible to preclude accidental injury superimposed on this type of abuse. In 2 infants studied in this same period, accurate, careful follow-up investigation was able to produce reliable witnesses capable of documenting accidental traumatic episodes consistent with the terminal injuries. This was superimposed on evidence of repetitive beating similar to that noted in the other children.

During this same period of study, an additional 10 children, ranging in age from one to thirty-six months, of whom 8 were non-white and 2 white, were examined and investigated. Externally on these infants, trauma was indicated to varying degrees from small, linear welts to massive single contusions of the scalp with underlying fracture of the calvarium. In 4, the explanation of a fall from the crib was offered, 2 were alleged to have been dropped inadvertently by the mother on the stairs, while 2 were alleged to have fallen down the stairs. The mechanism of injury was unknown or unexplained by the parents in 2 additional cases. Repetitive interrogation and extensive investigation failed to establish sufficient disparity between the alleged injury and pathological finding to establish proof of physical abuse. Within this group, fractures of the skull were present in 3, with subdural hematoma in 6, fractures of the humerus in 1 (resulting in fat and bone marrow emboli to the lungs), and bronchopneumonia was the terminal episode in 1. Although there was no evidence of preexisting bone disease within the skeletons of any of the infants examined within this group, several clinical observers have pointed out the importance of ruling out preexisting bone disease as a contributing factor to the fractures present. Detailed postmortem examination must rule out not only such bone disease, but other conditions such as diseases prompting hemorrhagic diasthesis which may tend to aggravate or exaggerate the magnitude of injury responsible for the terminal pathologic findings.

Conclusion

This study, as do others on this and related problems in forensic medicine, demonstrates the importance of teamwork between the investigating agencies and the forensic pathologist in proving the cause and manner of death. The clinician who maintains the same degree of suspicion and objectivity while caring for the injured child and who solicits the services of highly qualified law enforcement investigators and social service workers can contribute significantly to decreasing the mortality and morbidity rates of these unfortunate children.

Acknowledgment

The author is indebted to the members of the staff of the Office of the Medical Examiner in the City of Philadelphia and in the State of Utah who assisted in conducting many of the necessary investigations and examinations from which this information has been gathered.

References

1. Curran, W. J. 1965. *Tracy's "the doctor as a witness."* Philadelphia: W. B. Saunders.
2. Adelsen, L. 1964. Homicide by pepper. *J. Forensic Sci.* 9:391–95.
3. _____. 1964. Homicide by starvation. *JAMA* 186:458–60.
4. _____. 1961. Slaughter of the innocents. *NEJM* 264:1345–49.
5. Bowen, D. A. 1966. The role of radiology and the identification of foreign bodies at postmortem examination. *J. Forensic Sci. Soc.* 6:28–32.
6. Curphey, T. J.; Kade, H.; Noguchi, T. T.; and Moore, S. M. 1965. The battered child syndrome: Responsibilities of the pathologist. *Calif. Med.* 102:102–4.
7. Dine, M. S. 1965. Tranquilizer poisoning: An example of child abuse. *Ped.* 36:782–85.
8. Griffiths, D. L., and Moynihan, F. J. 1963. Multiple epiphysial injuries in babies (battered baby syndrome). *Brit. Med. J.* 5372 1558–61.
9. Hamlin, H. Subgaleal hematoma caused by hair pulling. JAMA 204:339.
10. Koel, B. S. 1969. Failure to thrive and fatal injury as a continuum. *Am J. Dis. Child.* 118:565–67.
11. Lindenberg, R., and Freytag, E. 1969. Morphology of brain lesions from blunt trauma in early infancy. *Arch. Path.* 87:298–305.
12. McCort, J., et al. 1964. Visceral injuries in battered children. *Radiology* 82:424–28.
13. Parker, G. E. 1965. The battered child syndrome (The problem in the United States). *Med. Sci. Law* 5:160–63.
14. Palomegne, F. E., and Hairston, M. A. 1964. "Battered child" syndrome: Unusual dermatological manifestation. *Arch. Derm.* 90:326–27.
15. Swischuk, L. E. 1969. Spine and spinal cord trauma in the battered child syndrome. *Radiology* 92:733–38.
16. Woolley, P. V., and Evans, W. A. 1955. Significance of skeletal lesions in infants resembling those of traumatic origin. *JAMA* 158:534–43.

PART 3

Psychiatric and
Social Aspects

A Psychiatric Study of Parents Who Abuse Infants and Small Children

Brandt F. Steele and Carl B. Pollock

Department of Psychiatry
University of Colorado School of Medicine, Denver

The Project and the Sample Studied

Our study of parental attack on infants began inadvertently several years ago when C. Henry Kempe asked one of us to see the parents of a battered baby on the pediatric ward, hoping we could find out the why and wherefore of this distressing type of behavior. We had refused previous requests because consultations on the pediatric service were not in our domain, but this time out of curiosity we acquiesced and unwittingly were launched on a long-term investigation. This first patient, an effusive, hysterical woman with a vivid, dramatic history and way of life, turned out to be a challenging "gold mine" of psychopathology. Our feelings alternated between horror and disbelief that she had actually fractured the femur and skull of her three-month-old daughter, but these feelings were soon lost and replaced by a wish to know her, to understand her behavior as fully as possible, and to find out if treatment could help. Before long, other attacking parents were seen, and it became apparent that one psychiatrist alone could not possibly handle all the available cases as a part-time "hobby." Hence, a second psychiatrist and a psychiatric social worker were enlisted to work part time on what had come to be a fascinating problem.

During a period of five and one-half years, we studied intensively 60 families in which significant abuse of infants or small children had occurred. In many cases we began our acquaintance with parents referred by the pediatric service while the attacked child was in the hospital. Other contacts were established with parents who had not injured their children seriously enough to require hospitalization, some of

Dr. Steele is professor of psychiatry and chief, psychiatric liaison division at the University of Colorado School of Medicine, and Dr. Pollock is assistant professor of psychiatry at that institution.

them referred by other physicians, social agencies, or legal authorities, and some of them coming voluntarily to seek help. Other cases were picked up when the problem of child abuse was discovered during treatment in the psychiatric hospital or outpatient clinic. One couple was first seen in jail after we read newspaper reports of their arrest for child beating.

Our study group of parents is not to be thought of as useful for statistical proof of any concepts. It was not picked by a valid sampling technique nor is it a "total population." It is representative only of a group of parents who had attacked children and who came by rather "accidental" means under our care because we were interested in the problem. We believe, however, that our data have particular significance because our haphazardly selected group provides a spectrum of child abusing behavior which negates in many respects stereotypes of the "child beater" popularly held in the past.

We began by seeing parents of severely injured children, work which was publicized under the title of "The Battered Child Syndrome" (1). The injuries included serious fractures of the skull and long bones and subdural hematomas, other less serious fractures, lacerations, multiple bruises, and burns. Soon we became aware that we were dealing only with the extreme of a much more widespread phenomenon and began including cases in which the infant was moderately bruised by severe hitting, shaking, yanking, choking, or being thrown about. It is difficult, as all those familiar with the problem can testify, to draw a line separating "real abuse" from the "accidental" signs of appropriate, albeit severe, disciplinary punishment. We feel we have been conservative in our classification of injuries as abuse.

There seems to be an unbroken spectrum of parental action toward children ranging from the breaking of bones and fracturing of skulls through severe bruising to severe spanking and on to mild "reminder pats" on the bottom. To be aware of this, one has only to look at the families of one's friends and neighbors, to look and listen to the parent-child interactions at the playground and the supermarket, or even to recall how one raised one's own children or how one was raised oneself. The amount of yelling, scolding, slapping, punching, hitting, and yanking acted out by parents on very small children is almost shocking. Hence, we have felt that in dealing with the abused child we are not observing an isolated, unique phenomenon, but only the extreme form of what we would call a pattern or style of child rearing quite prevalent in our culture.

The present report includes only cases of infants and young children predominantly under the age of three who have been significantly abused by their parents or other caretakers. Cases of direct murder of children are not included. It is our belief that direct murder of children is an entirely different phenomenon and is instigated during a single, impulsive act by people who are clearly psychotic (2). To be sure, a significant number of battered children eventually die because of repeated injuries; yet this is still considered to be quite different from death due to a single, direct attack. Physical attack of the child in an effort to make it behave is not the same as attack with intent to kill. Nor have we included cases in which abuse begins when the children are older. It is our opinion that when abuse begins on children aged four, five, or older, it is a different form of behavior and the attack by the parent is instigated by a different type of psychopathology. Attack on such older children is much more involved with matters of sexuality than is the attack on small infants.

Methods of Study

Our method of study was clinical, patterned basically after the usual methods of psychiatric diagnosis and therapeutic interviews with an attempt to reach as deeply as possible into the patient's personality. In addition to the directly psychiatric procedure, great use was made of interviews and home visits by our social worker, whereby information could be obtained about general modes of living and of actual day-by-day interactions between parents and between parents and child. Contacts were made not only with the attacking parent but also with the spouse. This was often inevitable, as it was not always possible at first to know who had attacked the child. Later such contacts were maintained or instituted because the uncovering of problems in the marriage made it obvious that treatment of both partners was highly desirable. Interviews, usually rather informal, were held whenever possible with the attacker's parents and other relatives, and occasionally we had the chance to see an abusing mother with her own mother in a joint interview and to observe their interaction. From such sources we obtained information which corroborated, corrected, or elaborated the memories which the attacker had of his own childhood and upbringing. A battery of psychological tests was done on most of our attacking parents, and in some instances, on the non-attacking spouse as well.

The duration of our contacts varied. A few parents were seen for only brief exploratory, diagnostic interviews. Most parents were seen over a period of many months, several for as long as three to five years. Reasons for not maintaining adequate contact included moving away due to job changes, divorce, living at an impracticably great distance, and going to a penal institution. Rarely, a patient was lost because we had no way of holding onto anyone who was extremely recalcitrant or uncooperative. By and large, the involvement of our study parents was quite voluntary on their part, even though on first referral they were "told" to see us. In a few instances, maintenance of contact with us depended upon the admonition from a judge that the parents' probation or the return of their child to them was contingent upon seeing us and a report from us.

Our procedure in developing a relationship with attacking parents was far from constant or rigidly designed. From the very beginning we were aware that our patients were notably difficult people to deal with. All of them, even those who came voluntarily asking for help, were quite reluctant and evasive, and contact had to be contrived by whatever possible means on an ad hoc basis. Often we had to pursue them, either figuratively by phone calls and unusual favors as to hours of appointment, or literally, as they rapidly walked away from us down the halls of the hospital ward where their child was a patient. Several attacking parents were hospitalized in our psychiatric unit—some because of mildly psychotic behavior, others for a lesser but significant emotional disturbance. Hospitalization was determined as much by a desire to have the opportunity for close observation as by medical necessity. Those patients in the psychiatric unit and those visiting their injured child in hospital were seen several times a week, daily if possible. Parents seen as outpatients had office interviews on a regular basis, one to three times a week. After a variable initial period, most patients were maintained on a schedule of a weekly office appointment with a psychiatrist and a home visit by the social worker every week or two. Later, visits were spread farther apart and eventually placed on a demand basis with contact resumed or increased at the patient's request in case of crisis or trouble. Telephone calls were a significant part of our relationships. We let patients know they could call us at any time for anything, and many of them made frequent use of this privilege. Typically, each child-attacking parent was seen by one of the psychiatrists and the social worker, usually at different times but occasionally in joint interviews. The spouse of the attacker was followed less intensively and frequently by either one of the psychiatrists or by the social worker. A few times, interviews were held jointly by both social worker and psychiatrist with both spouses. Although each parent in this study was a patient of one of the psychiatrists, all parents were at least minimally known to the other psychiatrist. Hence, all patients felt free to call other team members in case of need if their own particular therapist was unavailable.

It is obvious that in our work we were much more elastic in our treatment arrangement with patients and much more giving and available to them than is usually the case in either psychiatric practice or social work. This was done consciously and purposefully for three reasons: First, we were dealing with a group of people who required a lot of concrete evidence of interest from the environment before they believed in it at all. Second, we felt we could not accomplish our research goal of understanding child attack without developing such an involved relationship. And third, we had to be intensively and meaningfully involved in these parents' lives if we were to accomplish our goal of either keeping the attacked child in the home or returning it at the earliest possible time.

Obviously, judged by the usual standards of psychotherapy, we were working in a highly "contaminated" relationship with greatly enhanced dependencies and transference reactions, especially in the beginning. Nevertheless, in many of our patients we were able to develop and maintain a surprisingly high degree of approximation to a dynamic, psychoanalytically oriented therapy with rewarding results. Particularly in those patients with longer contacts, we encouraged free association and made use of dream material. Development of a full transference neurosis was not encouraged, but interpretation of transference reactions was used extensively.

In the following sections we present the information collected from people we got to know quite well in many hundreds of psychiatric interviews and from hundreds of home visits.

General Characteristics of the Parents in the Study Group

If all the people we studied were gathered together, they would not seem much different than a group picked by stopping the first several dozen people one would meet on a downtown street. They were not a homogenous group, but rather a random cross-section sample of the general population. They were from all socioeconomic strata— laborers, farmers, blue-collar workers, white-collar workers, and top professional people. Some were in poverty, some were relatively wealthy, but most were in-between. They lived in large metropolitan areas, small towns, and in rural communities. Housing varied from sub-standard hovels to high-class suburban homes. At both extremes they could be either well-kept or messy.

Educational achievement ranged from partial grade school up to advanced post-graduate degrees. In like fashion, determination of intellectual ability ranged from low borderline figures of I.Q.'s in the 70's to superior ratings of 130. The employment record of those with scanty education was characterized by many job changes and periods of unemployment. Those with higher I.Q.'s and advanced education were steadily employed in their professional roles or in the industrial, business, or financial fields. Several with adequate intelligence and education had poor job histories related to neurotic conflicts and difficult personality traits.

Our study parents ranged from eighteen to forty years of age, the great majority being in the twenties. One exception is an eleven year old girl who attacked two children with whom she was baby sitting. The marital situations of our group seemed not significantly different from that of others in their socioeconomic groups in the general population. A few cases were involved in separations or having only a temporary liaison. A few had been divorced and were in a second marriage. A few were in recurrent marital conflict. The great majority, however, were in a relatively stable marriage. The stability of the marriage was not always based on firm grounds of real love and a happy, cooperative relationship. Rather, it was often a desperate, dependent clinging together out of a fear of loneliness and losing everything, which held the partners together despite incompatibilities and friction. This will be discussed more fully later.

Religious affiliations included Catholic, Jewish, and Protestant. Among the latter were Episcopal, Methodist, Presbyterian, Lutheran, Mormon, Mennonite, Baptist, and Christian. Several families had no religious affiliation or only a nominal one without participation. A few were definitely antichurch. It was our impression that among those who were actively involved in their religion, there was a greater than average adherence to a strong, rigid, authoritative "fundamentalist" type of belief.

The ethnic background of most of our families was Anglo-Saxon American. There were also a few whose backgrounds were Scandinavian, Irish, German, Eastern European, and Spanish-American. We saw only one Negro family very briefly, but we draw from a population which is less than 10 per cent Negro. There were children of immigrants but no immigrants. True alcoholism was not a problem except in one family, and many were total abstainers. Among those who did use alcohol, drinking was occasionally a source of marital conflict but bore no significant, direct relationship to episodes of child beating.

The actual attack on the infant is usually made by one parent. In our series, the mother was the attacker in 50 instances and the father in 7 instances. We were unable to be sure which parent was involved in two families, and in one family both parents attacked.

These general characteristics of the parents in this study, as described above, are significantly different from those reported by Elmer[1] and others (3, 4). The incidence of poverty, alcoholism, broken marriages, and prominence of certain racial groups is not significant in our series. We do not believe our data are any more accurate than

[1] Elmer, Elizabeth, 1964, 1965, "The Fifty Families Study." Unpublished mimeographed reports from The Children's Hospital of Pittsburgh.

those of other reporters, but that different reports reflect the inevitable result of using skewed samples. Social agencies, welfare organizations, and municipal hospitals will inevitably draw most of their child beaters from lower socioeconomic strata. Our institution serves a wide range of socioeconomic groups and is closely associated with physicians in private medical practice. Obviously, our sample will be skewed in a quite different way. Our data show a great majority of women as child beaters. Other reports show a roughly fifty-fifty distribution between male and female, and some a significant predominance of men. We suspect that our low incidence of male attackers is related in part to a low incidence of unemployment among the males in the group. There were less hours of contact between males and infants than between females and infants—therefore, less exposure time for attack to occur by males. In samples in which women are working out of the home and unemployed men spend more time with the infant, the male attack rate would doubtless increase. While the factors of employment and unemployment have some contributing effect on the presence or absence of child attack, they are certainly not crucial. In our small series both employed and unemployed men have attacked their children.

Similar comments may be made concerning the other social, economic, and demographic factors mentioned above. Basically they are somewhat irrelevant to the actual act of child beating. Unquestionably, social and economic difficulties and disasters put added stress in people's lives and contribute to behavior which might otherwise remain dormant. But such factors must be considered as incidental enhancers rather than necessary and sufficient causes. Not all parents who are unemployed and in financial straits, poor housing, shattered marriages, and alcoholic difficulties abuse their children; nor does being an abstaining, devout Christian with a high I.Q., stable marriage, fine home, and plenty of money prevent attack on infants. These facts are well recognized by most of those who work in the area of child abuse. We have stressed them, however, because large segments of our culture, including many in the medical profession, are still prone to believe that child abuse occurs only among "bad people" of low socioeconomic status. This is not true.[2]

Psychopathology of the Attackers

General Characteristics

As noted in the previous section, the parents in this study were not at all a homogenous group from the standpoint of their general descriptive characteristics. In respect to psychopathology they were equally heterogenous. They do not fall into any single one of our usual psychiatric diagnostic categories. On the contrary, they present the wide spread of emotional disorders seen in any clinic population—hysteria, hysterical psychosis, obsessive-compulsive neurosis, anxiety states, depression, schizoid personality traits, schizophrenia, character neurosis, and so on. It was not

[2] It would be hard to find a group more deprived and in more socioeconomic difficulty than the Spanish-American migrant agricultural workers. We spent some time running down rumors of child abuse in this group and were unable to document a single instance. Possibly some cases do occur, but we were unable to find them.

possible to make a simple diagnosis in most patients. They presented mixed pictures such as "obsessive-phobic neurosis with marked masochistic features and mild depression." A majority of the patients could be said to be depressed at some time. Psychosomatic illnesses such as asthma, headaches, migraine, colitis, dysmenorrhea, urticaria, and vomiting were significant in several patients. Sociopathic traits such as passing bad checks were quite rare. The diagnosis of sociopathy was entertained in one case but could not be firmly established. We would not agree with the concept that by definition anyone who abuses a child is a sociopath. No doubt sociopaths have attacked children many times, but certainly, sociopathy and child abuse are not closely related.

It is our impression that with few exceptions our patients had emotional problems of sufficient severity to be accepted for treatment had they presented themselves at a clinic or psychiatrist's office. As noted before, a few of our patients were picked up in the clinic or hospital during treatment undertaken for reasons other than child abuse. One patient had been treated for depression during adolescence and again for a mild postpartum psychosis a year before she abused her child and came into our study. Most of our patients had been living for years with a significant amount of emotional difficulty, feeling it was not worthwhile or not possible to look for help from anyone. They had not been able to engender in their environment any useful, sympathetic awareness of their difficulties.

Child abusers have been described as "immature," "impulse ridden," "dependent," "sado-masochistic," "egocentric," "narcissistic," and "demanding." Such adjectives are essentially appropriate when applied to those who abuse children, yet these qualities are so prevalent among people in general that they add little to specific understanding. Categorical psychiatric diagnoses contribute little more, and do not answer the crucial question of why a certain parent abuses children.

Instead of trying to associate child abuse with a specific type of psychiatric disorder or a commonly accepted character-type description, we have searched for a consistent behavior pattern which can exist in combination with, but quite independently of, other psychological disorders. Although we constantly dealt with the whole gamut of emotional turmoil, we persistently focused on the interaction between caretaker and infant. From direct observation of parents with children and the descriptions given by them of how they deal with their offspring, it is obvious that they expect and demand a great deal from their infants and children. Not only is the demand for performance great, but it is premature, clearly beyond the ability of the infant to comprehend what is wanted and to respond appropriately. Parents deal with the child as if he were much older than he really is. Observation of this interaction leads to a clear impression that the parent feels insecure and unsure of being loved, and looks to the child as a source of reassurance, comfort, and loving response. It is hardly an exaggeration to say the parent acts like a frightened, unloved child, looking to his own child as if he were an adult capable of providing comfort and love. This is the phenomenon described as "role reversal" by Morris and Gould (5). They define this "as a reversal of the dependency role, in which parents turn to their infants and small children for nurturing and protection." We see two basic elements involved—a high expectation and demand by the parent for the infant's performance and a corresponding parental disregard of the infant's own needs, limited abilities, and helplessness—a significant misperception of the infant by the parent. Kaufman (6) has described the same thing in terms of parental distortion of reality and misperception of the infant. He states that "the child is not perceived as a child, but some symbolic or delusional figure" and "may be perceived as the psychotic portion of the parent which the parent wishes to control or destroy." He further describes "other parents who are extremely infantile and wish to be babied themselves resent the dependency and needs of their child and express this resentment in hostile ways." Kaufman believes parents "project much of their difficulty onto their child and feel that the child is the cause of their troubles" and "they attempt to relieve their anxiety by attacking the child instead of facing their own problems." He conceives of this as "a type of schizophrenic process" because of the strong use of the mechanisms of denial and projection. While agreeing with Kaufman's phenomenological descriptions and his thought that there is an abnormal ego function, we do not believe this is necessarily a schizophrenic process. Our concepts of the particular type of ego function involved will be discussed later.

Examples of this high parental demand combined with disregard of the infant are the following:

> Henry J., in speaking of his sixteen month old son, Johnny, said, "He knows what I mean and understands it when I say 'come here.' If he doesn't come immediately, I go and give him a gentle tug on the ear to remind him of what he's supposed to do." In the hospital it was found that Johnny's ear was lacerated and partially torn away from his head.

> Kathy made this poignant statement: "I have never felt really loved all my life. When the baby was born, I thought he would love me; but when he cried all the time, it meant he didn't love me, so I hit him." Kenny, age three weeks, was hospitalized with bilateral subdural hematomas.

Implied in the above vignettes and clearly evident in the tone of voice of the parents as they told us these stories, is a curious sense of "rightness." We have often called it a "sense of righteousness" in the parents. From early in infancy the children of abusing parents are expected to show exemplary behavior and a respectful, submissive, thoughtful attitude toward adult authority and society. Common parental expressions were: "If you give in to kids, they'll be spoiled rotten." "You have to teach children to obey authority." "I don't want my kids to grow up to be delinquent." "Children have to be taught proper respect for their parents." To be sure, such ideas are extremely prevalent in our culture and are essentially acceptable ideals of child rearing. Parents feel quite justified in following such principles. The difference between the non-abusing and the abusing parent is that the latter implements such standards with exaggerated intensity, and most importantly, at an inappropriately early age. Axiomatic to the child beater are that infants and children exist primarily to satisfy parental needs, that children's and infants' needs are unimportant and should be disregarded, and that children who do not fulfill these requirements deserve punishment.

We believe there exists in parents who abuse children this specific pattern of child rearing, quite independently of their other personality traits. It is not an isolated, rare phenomenon but rather a variant form, extreme in its intensity, of a pattern of child rearing pervasive in human civilization all over the world. Reports of this same type of attack on infants and young children have come from England (7, 8), Canada (9), Australia (10), Norway (11), Sweden (12), Germany (13), Italy (14), Hungary (15), the Netherlands (16), South Africa (17), and Hawaii (18). While we know of no medical reports from oriental countries describing child abuse in the sense with which we have been dealing with it, we do not doubt that it occurs there also. We have heard from a friend who observed the following: A Chinese mother who had four children dealt with her two younger ones in very opposite ways. The youngest, who had originally been unwanted, turned out to be a very fat, delightful baby who conformed to all the standards of an ideal Chinese baby. He was much loved and well cared for. The older child, who had originally been wanted, was terribly skinny, less happy and less responsive. The mother thought of him as an "unrewarding baby" and often stuck pins and needles into him.

It is this pattern of caretaker-child interaction and style of child rearing with which we will be concerned in the following sections.

Background and Life History of the Parents

In describing the life histories of the parents in our study, we will concentrate on those elements which have the most direct connection with the problem of the parent-child relationship involved in abuse. It is not our purpose to trace development of other facets of the personality, such as the particular form of the Oedipal conflict and its resolution, the source of obsessive-compulsive traits, or psychosomatic illness, and so on. These follow the various patterns which are familiar from the study of patients in general and need not be elaborated here. To be sure, the vicissitudes of early experience in the lives of our patients carried genetic potential for the many variations of their character structures, but we will accent their importance as sources of the particular type of parent-child relationship described in the preceding section.

Without exception in our study group of abusing parents, there is a history of having been raised in the same style which they have recreated in the pattern of rearing their own children. Several had experienced severe abuse in the form of physical beatings from either mother or father; a few reported "never having had a hand laid on them." All had experienced, however, a sense of intense, pervasive, continuous demand from their parents. This demand was in the form of expectations of good, submissive behavior, prompt obedience, never making mistakes, sympathetic comforting of parental distress, and showing approval and help for parental actions. Such parental demands were felt to be excessive, not only in degree but, possibly more importantly, in their prematurity. Performance was expected before the child was able to fully comprehend what was expected or how to accomplish it. Accompanying the parental demand was a sense of constant parental criticism. Performance was pictured as erroneous, inadequate, inept, and ineffectual. No matter what the patient as a child tried to do, it was not enough, it was not right, it was at the wrong time, it bothered the parents, it would disgrace the parents in the eyes of the world, or it failed to enhance the parents' image in society. Inevitably, the growing child felt, with much reason, that he was unloved, that his own needs, desires, and capabilities were disregarded, unheard, unfulfilled, and even wrong. These factors seem to be essential determinants in the early life of the abusing parent; the excessive demand for performance with the criticism of inadequate performance and the disregard of the child as an individual with his own needs and desires. Everything was oriented toward the parent; the child was less important.

From another descriptive standpoint, all of our parents were deprived as infants and children. We are not concerned here with material deprivation. Some were raised in poverty with great material deprivation, others in average circumstances, and a few in the midst of material abundance and wealth. We are referring to deprivation of basic mothering—a lack of the deep sense of being cared for and cared about from the beginning of one's life. When describing this deprivation of mothering, we do not imply that our patients have lacked maternal attention. Usually, they have been the object of great attention. Their mothers have hovered over them, involving themselves in all areas of the patient's life throughout the years. But again, this has been in a pattern of demand, criticism, and disregard designed to suit the mother and leave the patient out.

Our very strong belief in the importance of "the lack of mothering" as a most basic factor in the genesis of parental abuse is based on several things. First, it is based on the recollections given by patients of their unrewarding experiences with their own mothers. They documented their ideas with many reported incidents from early childhood up to the present and felt this type of relationship had been there "all their lives." Even allowing for the inevitable distortions, exaggerations, and omissions in patients' stories of their lives, we could not avoid the great significance of this consistently reported pattern. In addition, we occasionally had the experience, both enlightening and distressing, of talking to the abusing parent and her mother together. On these occasions, it was possible to observe many of the interactions which our patient had previously described. Her mother would "take over," answer questions directed to the daughter, tell the daughter what to answer, indicate in many ways what she expected the daughter to do, and either overtly or implicitly criticize and belittle her, all without paying attention to what the daughter was thinking, feeling, or trying to do. From spouse and siblings we have had further corroboration of the abusing parent's life story.

Of great interest to us has been the scant but suggestive data concerning the childhood experience of some of the abusing parents' parents. From what our patients know of their own parents' lives, from what they (the grandparents of the abused child) themselves told us, and from bits of information from aunts and uncles, it appears that the grandparents, too, were subjected to a constellation of parental attitudes similar to that described above. We believe we have seen this style of child rearing or pattern of parent-child relationship existing in three successive generations. Unwittingly and unfortunately, it is transmitted from parent to child, generation after generation. To a large extent, it has been socially acceptable, although subrosa, and to some extent it is probably culture-bound.

The central issue involved concerns a breakdown in what we referred to earlier as "mothering"—a disruption of the maternal affectional system. In speaking of this we do not mean to sound as if we were joining the popular pastime of glibly blaming everybody's trouble on "bad mothers"; rather, we are trying to explore and understand the process by which the tragic handicaps of parents, resulting from their own unhappy childhood experiences, are unintentionally effective in recreating a similar handicap in their own children's ability to be good parents. We believe our observations are useful in the understanding of child abuse, and may also contribute to knowledge of early psychic development in infants and to general problems of child rearing.

The Mothering Function

We have described child abuse as a pattern of child rearing characterized by derailment of the normal mothering function. By "mothering function" we mean the process in which an adult takes care of an infant; that is, a theoretically mature, capable, self-sufficient person caring for a helpless, needy, dependent, immature individual. We call this function "mothering" because it usually is performed by a mother, although it can be done by others. There are basic ingredients in mothering which we can call "practical" or "mechanical." They consist of feeding, holding, clothing, and cleaning the infant, protecting it from harm, and providing motility for it. Along with these are the more subtle ingredients of tenderness, of awareness and consideration of the needs and desires of the infant, and of appropriate emotional interaction with it. These latter qualities which we subsume under the title of "motherliness" are a most important accompaniment of the mechanical ingredients. They provide the atmosphere in which the other functions are performed, and profoundly affect the response of the infant, its immediate well-being, and its subsequent development.

Physical abuse of infants is associated more with breakdown in motherliness than with deficits in the other aspects of mothering. The infants in our study were almost always well-fed, clean, and well-clothed, but the emotional attitudes of the one who was caring for the infant were fraught with constant tension and frequent disruptions. It is often during the mothering acts of feeding, cleaning, and comforting the infant that abuse occurs. This is because of difficulties in maintaining an attitude of motherliness, not because of inability or lack of desire on the part of the caretaker to perform the caretaking acts. This will be described in more detail later when the circumstances of the attack are described.

Breakdown and failure in the more mechanical aspects of mothering such as cleaning and feeding, produce the picture of the "neglected child" or the infant with "failure to thrive" (19, 20). The abusing parent and the neglecting parent have many common characteristics. Both need and demand a great deal from their infants, and are distressed when met by inadequate response, so it is not surprising that we occasionally see an infant or child who is both neglected and abused. Yet there is a striking difference in these two forms of caretaker-infant interaction. The neglecting parent responds to distressing disappointment by giving up and abandoning efforts to even mechanically care for the child. The abusing parent seems to have more investment in the active life of the child and moves in to punish it for its failure and to make it "shape up" and perform better. In the present article we are concerned only with patterns involved in abuse rather than neglect.

There is still a lack of firm knowledge about the origin and development of the components of human mothering behavior. We do not see in the human mother those automatic, efficient, caretaking behaviors characteristic of subprimate mammals with their offspring. Such patterns are standard for each species and are thought to be genetically determined spontaneous actions and response mechanisms. In the human, menstruation, ovulation, pregnancy, delivery, and lactation are inescapably genetically determined physiological processes, and there is undoubtedly in most women something in the nature of a drive or a wish to reach sexual maturity and bear children. Yet in the human being, these basic physiological processes and psychological drives are intensely modified and channeled by cultural influences and individual experience. Even in the most primitive societies which have been studied by anthropologists, sexual behavior, child bearing, and child rearing are profoundly affected by local tribal custom, taboos, and cultural sanctions. Recent studies of sample cultures over the world today reveal remarkable variations in infant care and child rearing (21).

In Western culture generally and in America particularly, the processes of childbirth and infant care and child rearing have changed profoundly during recent generations. The medical profession in its successful efforts to minimize maternal and infant mortality and illness has radically altered the patterns of how a mother delivers her baby and takes care of it. Pediatricians have developed useful, new suggestions and rules for ideal infant care and child rearing; yet these have changed from decade to decade. Educators, psychologists, psychiatrists, and sociologists have offered their many ideas of how infants and children should be raised. Baby-care books are consistent best sellers. Magazines, newspapers, radio, television, and government publications are filled with advice, admonition, and warnings about infant care. Baby food advertisements and promulgators of vitamin and mineral products have added to the confusion. In addition, most mothers get plenty of criticism and advice from their own mothers, other female relatives, neighbors, and friends. Add to this the demand from an irritable husband, "For heaven's sake, do something about that crying baby." In the face of such a barrage, it is surprising that any mother can keep her equilibrium and carry out with sensitivity and efficiency the demanding tasks of infant care. In addition to all the rewards and advantages that have come from our modern knowledge of improved infant care, there are occasional backfires, too. Not rarely have we seen mothers who in their valiant efforts to follow the best advice they can obtain, find that things are not working well with their infant and the infant does not respond the way the book says he should. Such mothers, possibly somewhat unsure of themselves to start with, become very doubtful of their own value and capabilities as a mother, and also doubt if their infant is really all right. The mother-infant relationship then becomes filled with tension, and troubles can become significant. We believe the mother is fortunate who, when there is disagreement between what the book says and what the baby says, decides in favor of the baby. In the ever-recurring debates of breast feeding versus bottle feeding, of demand feeding versus schedule feeding, of pacifiers or no pacifiers, of times and means of toilet training, and so on, it seems best if the mother and child can decide this between themselves rather than be caught by rigid rules. For the mother and child to do this, we believe the mother has to have an adequate amount of motherliness. Our culture sets high value on good mothering and provides abundant advice on all aspects of its practical implementation. We also greatly admire and strongly advocate motherliness, yet we seem to expect it to appear automatically and are vaguely bewildered and distressed when it does **not** exist.

Instead of assuming, as many do, that motherliness is intuitive behavior which is part of the native endowment of a woman, we shall try to explore its origins.

Motherliness

If we leave aside all the culturally channeled styles and mechanics of mothering, we come to a substrate of maternal behavior which must have its roots in physiological mechanisms and individual psychological experience. In her classical work, *Psychosexual Functions of Women*, Benedek (22) documented all the subtle interactions between hormonal levels, menstruation, pregnancy, lactation, and the woman's psychic state and her mothering behavior. Deutsch (23) in her equally classic studies, *The Psychology of Women*, portrays the psychological vicissitudes of the woman throughout life, and through motherhood in particular. Despite the validity of these studies, we consider them for the purpose of our present exploration of motherliness to be largely irrelevant for several reasons. Motherliness is not confined to biological mothers. It can appear full-fledged in adoptive mothers, foster mothers, matrons in foundling homes, and nurses. Children, even very young boys as well as girls, can demonstrate it with each other and with babies. Even men can show it, and we feel that it is a breakdown of motherliness in the man's attempts to do mothering which is crucial in his abuse of infants.

We agree with Josselyn (24), who in discussing motherliness writes that the ability to show tenderness, gentleness, and empathy, and to value a love object more than the self, "is not a prerogative of women alone; it is a human characteristic." We cannot, therefore, find the source of motherliness through the study of specifically female physiology and psychology alone. We must look further.

Recognition of the effect of early childhood experience on psychic development and the eventual personality patterns of the adult is basic to most of our present-day understanding of human psychology. Surprisingly little has been written, however, correlating such early experience with the specific facet of adult behavior subsumed under the title of motherliness. There are occasional tantalizing references to "identification with the mother" in the literature, but the idea has rarely been adequately developed. Benedek (25) approached the core of the problem when she described the upsurge of childhood memories occurring when the adult becomes a parent. These memories return in two forms; those of what it was like to be a child, and others of how one was parented. Much of such memory return would, of course, be unconscious, and probably many memories would be about vague feelings, moods, and atmospheres, as well as of clear, specific events. Inevitably, this recall of early childhood experience will profoundly influence both consciously and unconsciously the patterns of behavior of the new parent toward the baby. Early in our work we facetiously spoke of abusing parents as following a distortion of the golden rule, "Do unto others as you have been done unto." There is truth in this despite its superficiality. It is a common observation that people bring up their children to some extent in the same way that they, themselves, were brought up, often despite very conscious resolves to do differently.

Our observations suggest that the pattern of parenting practiced in adult life, particularly motherliness, probably has its roots in the earliest infantile experience. Abusing parents, as do all other parents, demonstrate their particular child rearing style at the time the baby is born or soon thereafter. A clear example of this is shown in the case of Bertie.

> Bertie had fractured the femur and skull of her first baby during its first three months of life. While under treatment a second unwanted pregnancy occurred, and she delivered another baby girl. Several hours after delivery the baby was brought to her for her first contact with it. Instead of holding the baby close to her body, cuddling and looking her over, she lay there with the baby sitting on her stomach at arm's length. The baby was quiet. Bertie said, "Now she's mad—look at her—she's really mad now."

This vignette of distorted "claiming" behavior is indicative of Bertie's derailed style of motherliness and indicates her deep feeling that the infant is unrewarding and troublesome.

Since we have seen the parenting style appear in three successive generations and its expression beginning in the neonatal period, we infer a connection between the two. This is consistent with Benedek's idea, referred to above, that memories of how one was parented surge up when a baby is born and influence one's parental behavior. How soon this has an effect on the baby is hard to say. Spitz (26) suggests there is a change from reflexive activity to learning beginning around the three-months period, at which time the rudiments of the reality principle are being established. Marquis (27) indicates learning in the form of a conditioned response can be established in a baby within two weeks after birth. We have seen babies respond accurately to rather unreasonable parental demand within the first six months, and by the ages of one and two, show exquisitely sensitive responses to parental needs. This is assumed to be learned behavior. We have also observed other non-abused children in a family show this same, unusually high degree of responsiveness to parental demand, indicating a basic style of parent-child interaction is present, which may or may not result in actual abuse.

Although sub-human primate behavior cannot be applied directly to the understanding of human behavior, some observations seem to show striking analogies to the phenomena seen in abusing and neglecting human parents. We refer particularly to the work of the Harlows (28) on monkeys:

> . . . four of our laboratory-raised females never had real mothers of their own, one being raised in a bare wire cage and three with cloth surrogates. The first week after the birth of the baby to the wire-cage-raised female, the mother sat fixedly at one side of the cage staring into space, almost unaware of her infant or of human beings, even when they barked at and threatened the baby. There was no sign of maternal responses, and when the infant approached and attempted contact, the mother rebuffed it, often with vigor.
> The next two unmothered mothers constantly rebuffed the approaches of their infants, but, in addition, frequently engaged in cruel and unprovoked attacks. They struck and beat their babies, mouthed them roughly, and pushed their faces into the wire-mesh floor. These attacks seemed to be exaggerated in the presence of human beings, and for this reason all formal testing was abandoned for three days for the third unmothered mother because we feared for the life of the infant. The fourth unmothered mother ignored and rejected her infant but did not exhibit excessive cruelty.

These observations do suggest that there may be some connection between the lack of early "being mothered" experience and deficits in later parental function. There are, however, some significant differences between the being mothered experience of Harlow's monkeys and that of abusing parents. The monkeys were raised not only without motherliness but without any positive or negative actions from their wire-cage or cloth mothers. Abusing parents have not had as infants nearly enough motherliness, but at the same time were exposed to very active caretaking behavior from their mothers coupled with demand and criticism. Their resultant behavioral deficit is in motherliness rather than in practical mothering. The infant monkeys are possibly more like the babies who developed hospitalism as a result of more totally deficient mothering as described by Spitz (29, 30). Robertson (31) described a milder form of the same condition developing in infants whose mothers were moderately indifferent, aloof, and uninvolved.

The Early Origin of Motherliness and Its Vicissitudes

In several papers (25, 32, 33, 34), Benedek has described the mutually rewarding symbiotic relationship between mother and infant and its crucial importance for the baby's immediate well-being and future development. In particular, she stresses the appearance in the infant of a fundamental sense of confidence that needs will be met, a phenomenon related primarily to the feeding situation but also to other aspects of being cared for. By using Benedek's formulations, we can see why abusing parents have been unable to develop an adequate ability in the sphere of motherliness. They did not have, as far as we can tell from our data, the experience in infancy of a fully satisfying symbiotic, confidence-producing relationship with their mothers.

It is recognized that around the age of three months an infant begins to change from the primary narcissistic state of undifferentiation to the first awareness of the self as separate from the object world; the I and the non-I are beginning to be established. The infantile experience of the outside world, the mother, is a mixture of pleasure-giving need satisfaction and of pain-producing frustration. These two images of the mother provide the material for the first primal identification, the pleasure-giving mother introjected as the first basis of the ego ideal and the pain-producing mother as the anlage of the archaic, punitive superego. This will be discussed more fully later in the section on aggression and the superego. For the moment, we are concentrating on the concept that the early identification with the image of an insufficiently caring mother is the basis of the diminished motherliness we find in the adult, both male and female. In the abusing parent there has been a marked imbalance between the two mother images with the frustrating mother being much more powerful than the empathic, caring mother. This early identification state is the fertile ground for reinforcement through many later similar experiences of the growing child. Examples of such reinforcing experiences are:

> In puberty, Amy tried to talk to her mother about how to dress and fix her hair so as to be attractive and popular. Mother said, "Forget about trying to be pretty. Just develop character."

> Penny wished desperately for ice skates and her mother finally gave her some hand-me-down ones which were too small and hurt her feet. When Penny complained, her

mother responded by feeling hurt and unappreciated. She scolded Penny and told her to wear the skates and be grateful.

Larry and his older brother were each to get five dollars for taking care of the dairy farm for a long weekend while their parents were away. The brother kept the entire ten dollars, giving Larry only fifteen cents for a soda. When Larry told his parents of this injustice, they said, "Forget it" and did nothing about it.

The identification of the abusing parent with diminished motherliness persists into adult life. It is accompanied by an equally persistent disbelief in the possibility of finding a safe, empathic, motherly relationship despite great yearning for it.

An example is Sally. After delivery her mother, on the advice of the pediatrician, instituted a rigid four-hour feeding schedule. Evidently this was not syntonic with Sally's own needs for time, and she cried a great deal. Her mother managed the constant crying by putting the baby in a room by herself, shutting the door, and leaving the house until feeding time returned. Sally, of course, cannot remember these events, but often heard about them in family talks, and they were corroborated during interviews we had with her mother. What she does recall is that at age three, shortly after her brother was born, her mother went to work and left her in the care of various people during the ensuing years, that she never had a close relationship with her mother during childhood and puberty, and could never talk to mother about things which mattered to her. It is not surprising that she has had many psychosomatic illnesses, asthma, migraine, various digestive disturbances, and musculoskeletal problems.

Toward her two adopted infants Sally showed rigid, controlling attitudes with demands to conform to her expectations in eating and in general behavior. Failure of the infant to respond properly was dealt with by severe physical punishment, although no fractures or serious injuries resulted. At one time when she was on a regimen of bed rest because of a ruptured lumbar intervertebral disc, plus great emotional enhancement of the symptom, she reported "getting out of bed only to punish the children."

Despite Sally's ability to relate many instances of the poor relationship with her mother, she had never been able to express criticism directly to her mother, nor could she countenance any expression of criticism of the mother from the psychiatrist. Once after having an interview with the mother, the psychiatrist spoke to Sally's husband, Bob, saying that he could "see how Sally might have felt it very difficult to get anything meaningful from her mother." Bob repeated this to Sally who responded by refusing to see the psychiatrist again for a period of four months. She felt she had just begun to have a good relationship with her mother and be able to talk to her, and the statement of the psychiatrist threatened the possibility of keeping this going.

Her intense need for mothering plus her basic hopeless disbelief in the possibility of such a relationship was apparent in another situation. While Sally was in the hospital for observation, the social worker began to build a relationship with her. At a crucial time in one interview, during which Sally was crying and the worker put a sympathetic hand on her shoulder, they were interrupted by the ward personnel demanding Sally come out and join in the routine group therapy scheduled at that time. She later described the situation as follows: "When Mrs. D. put her hand on my shoulder, I felt a sense of hope for the first time in my life, and then they ruined the whole thing." It took weeks to reestablish this shattered sense of rapport and trust.

Most people have residuals of the dual image of the mother with its resultant ambivalence. It is our impression that the patients in our study group, both men and women, have this ambivalence to an unusually high degree, with accent on the negative side. One patient, Penny, expressed it with rare clarity in a dream told in her fourth interview. "I was with mother. There was the usual feeling of tension. It was like we were in a motel and we had gone to bed in twin beds. I woke up. Something in white was standing over me very threatening. It was terrifying. I called to my mother for help. She answered, 'I am your mother,' and it turned out that she, herself, was the creature in white who was threatening me. I woke up screaming." Penny's associations elaborated but did not significantly alter the meaning which is so obvious in the manifest content of the dream: The one to whom one looks with a wish for help is the one who will attack. The dream was reported in relation to material about her anger toward her mother, her punitive anger toward her five-month-old son, and the distressing feeling that she was just as bad as her mother was. Since it appeared in the early stages of Penny's looking to us for help, it carried significant transference implications. In this brief vignette we see the interweaving of many of the patient's ideas: I have a bad mother; I hate my mother; I am like my mother; I am mean to my child; I do not believe I can ever get help.

Much of the preceding discussion of motherliness seems oriented toward women, but it applies equally to men. Male and female abusing parents are similar in their motherly qualities. In our view there is no essential difference in the origin of motherliness in men and women. In both sexes it involves a pre-gender identification in the infant's early life with the mother's behavior. In males later masculine strivings and identifications may allow persistence of motherliness or diminish it. In females the early motherly identification becomes woven into the normal psycho-sexual development leading to motherhood and identification with the child bearing woman. Most simply, we believe child-caring and child-bearing behaviors have separate and distinct origins.

Lack of Confidence

Benedek (32) described a sense of confidence which develops in the infant as a result of the recurrent experience of being adequately understood and cared for by the mother. Erikson (35) has written about the same phenomenon, calling it "Basic Trust." Confidence engendered in the infant and made firm by later experience involves belief that others can be looked to for help and oneself is worth helping. It is long-lasting and leads to an optimistic ability in adult life to maintain useful relationships with others, especially when in time of stress or need one needs comfort and aid. Abusing parents did not have this confidence-producing experience. As adults they feel it unrewarding to look to family, friends, or others for need-satisfying relationships. Although they may persistently return to seeking from their own parents some evidence of love, understanding, and assistance, they usually find again criticism and inappropriate response instead of what they want. They often speak of having "lots of good friends," but on closer examination these turn out to be friends only by title. Such relationships are rather distant, meager, superficial, and unfulfilling. Thus, the abusing parent tends to lead a life which is described as alienated, asocial, or isolated (3, 5, 36, 37). It is a persistence of the pattern of lack of confidence engendered early in childhood with the parents. Toward the rest of society, there is a transference of attitudes originally felt toward parents to all others looked to for help and understanding. The lack of confidence not only helps instigate this transference but also compounds the trouble by making it next to impossible for the abusing parent to express clearly to others his real needs and desires. Thus, the social environment, being unaware of what the patient really wants, continues to respond poorly, thereby perpetuating the cycle.

In addition to the more obvious forms of isolation from the environment and the inability to seek help from it, there are many minor but interesting evidences of these phenomena. We have noticed that many of our patients keep their blinds drawn in the house, even during bright, warm, sunny days when most people would enjoy observing the outdoors. Many of them have unlisted phone numbers, more frequently than does the general population and with less obvious reason. They seem to have more than normal difficulty in keeping their automobiles in good repair and in coping with break-downs of household appliances. We have jokingly remarked that if one goes down the street and sees a house with the blinds drawn in broad daylight, with two unrepaired cars in the driveway, and finds the people have an unlisted phone number, the chances are high that the inhabitants abuse their children.

Lack of confidence also plagues the marriage of the abusing parent. Many of our patients, just like many other neurotic people, have demonstrated an uncanny ability to become involved with and marry people who tend to accentuate rather than solve their problems. The spouse is too much like the patient and too much like the patient's parents. Despite many other admirable qualities and many abilities, the spouse is often needy, dependent, unable to express clearly his needs, and at the same time is demanding, critical, and unheeding of the patient. Meaningful communication between husband and wife is thus diminished. They have deep yearnings for understanding from each other, yet lack of basic trust leads them to be hesitant in expressing need, and satisfaction is rarely forthcoming. The marriage may be firmly held together by this mutual need, particularly because there is no confidence that anything better could be found elsewhere, but the marriage has become one more situation reinforcing the patient's sense of disappointment and hopelessness.

Lack of confidence originating in the inadequate mothering in infancy, reiterated in later life experiences to which the patient has made his own contributions, has left him with the conviction that his needs can never be met by parents, spouse, friends, or society in general. Yet there is still one hope left. When all the rest of the world has failed him, the abusing parent will look to the child in a last, desperate attempt to get comfort and care. An example of this is Kathy's statement quoted before that she had never felt loved by anyone in all of her life and looked to her child to fill this need.

Aggression and the Superego

Aggression released on infants is the most disturbing manifestation of the abusing parents' behavior and is a central issue in our problem. We shall try to trace the origin and development of aggression in our patients, not only because of the obviously aggressive act of abuse, but because we think the aggressive constellation diminishes adequate development of the motherliness which we consider so important. In the ensuing discussion, using direct observations of infant abuse and the infant's behavioral response, we draw conclusions concerning the psychological development of the infant. We also infer a similar psychological development has occurred in the abusing parent. The rationale for this broad inference comes from the historical data about our patients' early years, and all the indications that they were treated much the same way as they treat their own babies. We believe we see *in statu nascendi* in the results of the interaction between abusing parent and infant, the development of psychic processes which are evident in the adult but whose origin can be studied only in retrospect. Hence, we speak almost interchangeably of the observed development in the infant and our reconstruction of development of the adult patient.

We assume the universality of an innate aggressive drive with its potential for aggressive behavior quite comparable to the libidinal drive. The abusing patients we have seen do not show evidence of an unusually strong basic aggressive drive. They are not fundamentally "mean" people, nor do they seem significantly more or less action-oriented than average. Although their release of aggression against infants is overt and intense, they usually show significant inhibition of aggression in many areas of their lives. It is impossible to discuss the vicissitudes of aggression without, at the same time, discussing that structure of the human psyche which evaluates and directs the discharge of the aggressive drive, namely, the superego. We shall do this in the conceptual framework presented by Spitz (38) with whom we are in essential agreement.

Spitz believes the superego in the strict sense takes its final form at the time of the resolution of the Oedipal conflict, but previous to this time there are significant superego precursors and rudiments existing as early as the first year of life. He considers physical restraint to be the earliest rudiment, and says

> . . . among the primordia which will form up the supergo there are some to which we have paid little attention up to the present. They belong to the perceptual sector of tactile and visual impressions, such as restraining the child physically on the one hand, the facial expression, as well as the tone of voice which accompanies such prohibiting interference on the other. Similarly, imposing physical actions on the infant, whether he likes it or not, in dressing, diapering, bathing, feeding, burping him, etc., will inevitably leave memory traces in the nature of commands. These physical primordia of prohibitions and commands are not easily recognizable in the ultimate organization which is the superego.

We feel much more strongly than Spitz does about the significance of this early experience in the development of recognizable superego rudiments, probably because we have been working with situations in which these phenomena are much more blatant than in his studies. We have observed parents deal aggressively with their infants, beginning shortly after birth, in all areas of infant care. In the process of feeding they say angrily, "Now, eat," and also slap and yank at the infant to make it obey, or the infant's hands are slapped when he interferes with the spoon at the first time of solid food feeding. In the processes of diapering and bathing, the infant is told to "be quiet," to "lie still" in an angry tone accompanied by blows and yankings sufficient to cause bruises and fractures. The crying infant who does not respond to comforting may be severely shaken or hit on the head. These observations coupled with the fact that we see infants soon responding correctly to parental commands lead us inescapably to the idea that we are witnessing the genesis of superego rudiments. It seems obvious that the change in external behavior of the infant must be accompanied by some sort of primitive, intrapsychic change.

Spitz follows Anna Freud (39) in believing that the mechanism of identification with the aggressor is a preliminary phase in the development of the superego, and he places its appearance as a primordium of the superego in the beginning of the second year of life, associated with the child's acquisition of the semantic "No." We, too, feel the classic mechanism of identification with the aggressor is sufficiently complicated that it could not be accomplished before the second year. Something very similar to it seems, however, to appear earlier. Whether this should be described as a precursor or as something quite different is a questionable point. It may be that earlier it would be a more simple, direct identification with aggression rather than with an aggressor, as identification with an aggressor implies some degree of sophistication in object relationships. Such primordial identification with aggression beginning in the first few months of life is continuously reinforced by parental command and criticism, especially if accompanied by physical attack. In the second and third years of life, after object relations are well established, it develops into a true identification with the aggressor. Such identification is not necessarily a global one leading to indiscriminate aggressive discharge; in many of our patients we see a rather narrowly channeled specific identification with a "parent-against-child" aggressor.

It must not be forgotten that at the time the parent is making demands and attacks upon the infant, he is also frustrating some of the infant's most basic needs for comfort and empathy. Such frustrations are repetitive stimulations to the basic aggressive drive. Stimulation of the aggressive drive with its accompanying anger toward the frustrating caretaker, coupled with the parallel development of strict superego rudiments, inevitably leads to a strong sense of guilt. This guilt, largely unconscious, predominantly in relation to the mother, persists through the patient's life, and leads to turning much of the aggression inward toward the self. It accounts in the adult for the frequent periods of depression and contributes to the pervasive sense of inferiority and low self-esteem. When the parent misidentifies the infant as the embodiment of his own bad self, the full aggression of his punitive superego can be directed outward onto the child. By the third year of life our parents have had both the stimulation of aggressive drives and the establishment in the archaic superego of strict, punitive, commanding components. Their earliest memories often depict this period. Bertie, for example, recalls that before age three she would hear mother and father fighting, feel frightened, cry, and then be beaten for crying.

In subsequent years there is reinforcement of the same processes due to continued experience with critical, demanding, unempathic parents, as well as "moral instruction." By the latter we mean the education the child receives in regard to what is right and wrong, what is bad in the world and warrants attack. Lack of proper respect for authority has been pictured to our patients as a most reprehensible behavior and one which always warrants punishment. They were told this by their own parents and characteristically use it excessively as righteous justification for attitudes about their own offspring, supported by widely held cultural standards.

Aggression itself has been encouraged as well as depiction of channels for its release. Examples will clarify our meaning.

> Larry was taught by his father to use a gun by age eight and was forced to assume the task of shooting to death any animal on the farm which was born defective, became

crippled, was too old and decrepit, or in any other way unrewarding. These experiences were devastating to him when the animal involved was one of his own pets.

Dora, as a little girl running barefoot in the park, suddenly realized she had unknowingly stepped on something, and upon investigation found she had crushed a small frog. She was terribly upset, confessed her sin to the priest and could hardly be consoled. Yet she also told of having lifted a stone in the nearby woods and finding a snake under it. Upon being told by companions it was a poisonous snake she smashed it to death with a righteous sense of doing a good duty.[3]

These examples show the release of aggression in superego-approved channels—for instance, it is right to destroy bad things. In addition they reveal another factor which we have temporarily neglected, a sense of compassion for the innocent and helpless.

Abusive parents are not one hundred per cent so. Although we have focused primarily on the abusive elements of parental behavior, we also wish to emphasize the presence of love, tenderness, consideration, and desire to do well for infants. There is some ego ideal as well as a superego; the balance between the two is variable. An infant may be abused recurrently, but rarely constantly. Between episodes of abuse, parents may show fairly good amounts of motherly caretaking, while demand and criticism recede temporarily to a lower level. Similarly, some children in a family are rather well treated, with a minimum of punitiveness, although another child in the same family is abused. Probably the crux of the problem of distinguishing the non-abusing from the abusing parent lies in the fact that in the latter when there is significant environmental and intrapsychic stress, with a contest between ego ideal and superego, the punitive superego wins out.

Identity and Identifications

Erikson (41) defines identity as the sense a person has of being a unique, separate individual with a continuity of personal character and ability to maintain solidarity with social groups. We do not find such identity in the abusing parent. Instead, we see a rather loose collection of unintegrated, disparate concepts of the self. There are multiple identifications which remain separate and unamalgamated. Strong ambivalences remain unresolved. Our patients can feel like a confident parent and quickly change to being nothing but a helpless, ineffectual, inadequate child. They can be a kindly adult and shift suddenly to being a punitive adult. They know they are men and women but are not really sure of it. They have one firm concept of what they should be and another of what they actually are. Any sense of being reasonably good can be easily displaced by a conviction of badness. They are usually quite uncertain about allying with a group even if they join it. In the context of child abuse a most important defect is a lack of useful integration of the two experiences of being a child and being parented. This cannot be separated from the persistent, intense ambivalence about the mother.

Probably the most potent factor in the genesis of this lack of integration was the persistent demand and criticism our patients felt from their parents. Faced with constant expectations to do more and to be different, they never had the chance to find

---

[3] We have not found in our patients evidence of a childhood pattern of tormenting and cruelty to animals described by MacDonald (40) as being frequent in persons with homicidal tendencies.

out what they really were and develop any continuity or enjoy independent thought. Attempts to ally with other people more appealing than the parents were often stopped by denigration or outright prohibition.

A most explicit description of these problems of identification and identity was given by Bertie.

"I look in a mirror and hardly know if it's me. Sometimes I'm like my mother, sometimes like my grandmother. Sometimes I'm like my husband Jack's mother. Sometimes I'm like his grandmother. Jack wants me to be first like one and then the other. Everybody wants me to be somebody else." At another time, "when I'm alone, I'm more like grandmother than anyone else in the world. I'm quieter, more calm, peaceful, and more loving. I can be like her, the way I want to be, but when someone comes in and says, 'why don't I do this way or that way' or criticizes me, I'm all lost and confused. I try to become like everything they say. I hardly know who I am. I'm still so scared of mother that I get anxious if she has been angry at me. I'll pull the shades down and lock the door and keep the chain on. If she got mad enough and thought I said anything against her, she'd come out and beat me within an inch of my life."

The highlights of Bertie's history will help in understanding her statements. She was a first child. Her mother frequently berated her because the pregnancy had ruined the mother's figure, damaged her pelvic organs, and disrupted her marriage since the father began then to be unfaithful. From infancy into early childhood, the mother repeatedly attacked Bertie with her fists, razor strops, or wire coat hangers—and occasionally slapped her in adult life. There were many battles between the mother and father, and once in her early teens Bertie witnessed her mother shooting one of father's alleged paramours, the bullet going through the woman's housecoat, missing her body.

With her strict, pseudo-moralistic policeman father, she had a rather warm relationship which the mother constantly tried to disrupt by telling each how bad the other was. Bertie was her grandmother's favorite and she returned the love without hesitation. "She was the only woman I've never been afraid of." Mother tried unsuccessfully to break this attachment, too, by criticizing the grandmother and often preventing their getting together.

Bertie conceived on her honeymoon. She was dismayed and angry. She did not want the baby because it would ruin her youth, deny her freedom and happiness, and shatter her chances for a good marriage. Frequently during the pregnancy she would talk to Jack about how she was afraid he would spoil the baby, and wondering how soon she could start disciplining it. When her baby girl, Cindy, was a month old, she was found to have a broken leg from "getting her leg caught in between the slats and turning over in her crib." At age three months, she was brought to the hospital with a fractured skull and bilateral subdural hematomas, cause unknown. At this time we first met Bertie, the first patient in our study. After a few interviews on the pediatric ward, Bertie came to the office and we asked our secretary, a quite sophisticated woman, to record her impressions. She wrote, "Bertie is very feminine, sweet, pretty, poised, and completely unabashed at coming here. The one unusual thing about her appearance was her rather sexy, smoky, black hose and dressy shoes which would have been more appropriate for evening wear or a cocktail party. This was inconsistent with the rest of her outfit." And after detailing their conversation, concluded, "My general impression was that our conversation was a typical, Denver (or anywhere), housewifely chat. In all, I liked Bertie, and she reminded me of many typical American girls with whom I have played bridge, golf, and so on. It was very difficult for me to believe her capable of beating her child."

One week later, Bertie was admitted to the hospital in an hysterical, disoriented, confused state, cowering and saying over and over again, "Please don't let them beat me. Make them stop fighting. Take the guns away," and so on. She had made a suicidal attempt by taking a lot of pills, none of them dangerous. That morning Bertie had been faced with undeniable evidence that she had been stealing money and bits of apparel from her friends when on social visits, a fact which had been suspected but which she had denied (in the past her mother had been picked up twice for shoplifting, and the charges were dropped). She went to the bathroom, looked in the mirror and thought, "This is all true, even if I didn't know it. My husband will hate me and leave me. I'm as bad as my mother. I don't remember it, but I must have hurt my baby, too. I deserve to die." Then she took the pills and collapsed. The almost psychotic regressive state cleared completely in a few days.

Many months later Bertie had a recurrent dream of being in a fog and going to the cemetery where grandmother was buried, being tied to a tree, feeling scared, then feeling cold and numb as if she were in a tomb. Then she would suddenly find herself down in the grave with her grandmother, and her own mother was standing over the grave looking down at her gloating and evilly laughing. She would wake crying and shaking with terror.

Bertie has identified with her mother's aggression and stealing, also with her mother's belief that a baby will damage a mother's physical, emotional, and marital well-being. She has also identified with the strong disciplinary attitudes of both mother and father. In contrast is the yearning for love and the identification with the kindly grandmother for which she fears she will pay the price of being killed by mother. Further, there is the persistent feeling of being a trapped, frightened, naughty, helpless child who has to try to please everybody. Truly, she knows not who she is.

Of prime significance is Bertie's concern about her unborn baby. She expects it will be spoiled by the father, will need early discipline, and will ruin her life. She is, of course, describing the picture of herself as a child, and more specifically, her "bad" self. Seeing the baby who is attacked as another edition of one's own bad self is characteristic of the abusing parent. Not all parents express it as clearly as Bertie did, however, nor is it always easily detected before the baby is born. Investigation during pregnancy of the expectations parents have of their future baby are very revealing and have great predictive value as well as opening avenues for preventive therapy.

Penny had come to us for help with her distress over antagonism and rough actions with her baby boy. Two years later she became pregnant and conflicts about the coming baby arose. She felt she could manage quite well if it would be another boy. Although she would like to have a girl, she was very apprehensive about it. "If it's a girl, I'm likely to treat it the way mother treated me, and she'll be angry at me as much as I'm angry at mother. It will be a mess." (Cf. Bertie's "claiming" behavior, above.) Airing this conflict enabled Penny to work it through. She did beautifully with her second baby, which was, indeed, a girl.

Quite common descriptions of the infant by the parent are "he's just like me," "she's fussy like I was when I was a baby," or, "he got all his bad qualities from me." Thinking of the infant as being the equivalent of the parent's bad self has been described as a misperception or projection. Projection seems unlikely, as it involves denial, the mechanism being, "It is not I who am this way; it is he." We feel the mechanism is, "I am bad; he is bad just like me." This is an identification process, described by Fenichel (42) as "reverse identification."

The identifications with the "good" and "bad" mother residual from earliest life may become reinforced and overdetermined by the identifications which become stabilized with the resolution of Oedipal conflicts. At this time the identification with the parent of the same sex may be complicated by further identifications with the aggressor. Particularly if the aggressor is of the opposite sex, some further confusion about sexual identity may result. Attempts by our patients in later childhood and adolescence to find other models and new identifications have had only partial success, owing to the persistent demand from their parents to adhere strictly to parental expectations and not look elsewhere. Allegiance to new ideas in differing peer groups is limited, and the old fixations persist.

Secondary Factors Involved in Abuse

Contributions Made by Other Elements of Parental Psychopathology

Up to now we have concentrated on those basic psychological factors essential to the pattern of abuse. There are other factors which are not essential ingredients but are potent accessories in instigating abuse and in determining which infant is selected for attack. Three such factors are intense unresolved sibling rivalry, an obsessive-compulsive character structure, and unresolved Oedipal conflicts with excessive guilt. Following is a clear example of sibling rivalry precipitating abuse.

> Naomi was a fourth child raised largely by baby sitters until age six and then by a grandmother whom she felt did not love her. She did not think either mother or father really cared for her, especially mother. An older sister was the only person she loved or felt loved by. A three-year-older brother was the family favorite, and she felt her life was ruined by being neglected while he got everything. She hated and envied her father, brother, husband, and all men. A belligerent sense of rightness in her behavior thinly covered deep feelings of being inadequate and worthless as a mother. Her first child, a girl, was raised strictly and became very submissive, obedient, and cooperative. However, Naomi said, "I'd beat her, too, if she rebelled or got angry at me."
>
> An unwanted pregnancy produced a boy two years later. Naomi said, "He came too soon after the girl and cheated her out of her childhood. I weaned him at two and a half months because nursing him upset her. I hate him; the mere sight of his genitals upsets me. I don't have time for him; I wish he'd never been born or that I could give him away to someone who'd love him. I want to hit him, hurt him, shake him, get him out of the way." She also said she saw all her own undesirable qualities in him. Naomi did slap, bruise, and rough up her baby boy, and by age two he had had three head wounds requiring stitches.

Obviously Naomi's sibling rivalry abetted by her envious anger toward males was important in the release of attack on her baby boy. Yet it is equally clear from her story that she had the underlying attitude of demand and criticism characteristic of the abusing parent. Only the fortunate accidents of sex, time of birth, and ability to respond correctly had spared her first child from attack.

Obsessive-compulsive personality traits often channel parental expectations and disapproval of infant behavior in specific ways. The conflicts over dirt and messiness lead to excessive early demand for the baby to eat without slopping and smearing food around and to control excretory functions too soon. Inability of the infant to comply will arouse parental ire. The inevitable tendency of older infants to strew toys around and to get fresh clothing dirty will also cause trouble if the parent is overly concerned with neatness and cleanliness. We postulate that the infant's behavior stimulates the parent's unconscious and threatens a breakthrough of his own unacceptable impulses to be messy. Defensive control must be instituted by aggressive repression in the parent and by aggressive action against similar bad behavior in the baby.

The role of unresolved Oedipal conflict is harder to assess. In the case of Bertie given above, it is easy to see the difficulty and guilt she has over her own Oedipal problems and how she views her baby daughter as a rival for her husband's affections. Further evidence in this direction came from frequent dreams which Bertie had of a sexy brunette who seduced her husband away from her. She always identified this woman as looking exactly the way her baby, Cindy, would look when she grew up. Such clear-cut Oedipal material was not frequently seen in our patients. More often what appeared superficially as Oedipal rivalry turned out on deeper investigation of unconscious motivation not to be entirely so. The mother who is angry at the baby girl having a good time with the father, and the father who is aggressive toward the little boy who is happily involved with mother are really angry at the child because it is getting what is seen as the motherly attention which they so deeply yearn for and missed out on in their own childhood. Thus it is more in the sphere of a sibling rivalry rather than an Oedipal problem.

It is our impression that few of our patients experienced a true, fully involved Oedipal situation. Most of their conflicts and fixations are pregenital. As boys, instead of close involvement with fantasies of warm sexuality with mother, they were caught by their ambivalence toward her and could only remain distant from her, yearning for basic motherliness. As girls, they turned to fathers with slight stirrings of sexual love overshadowed by a hope that father would supply the mothering which had been lacking.[4] Naturally no two patients were alike; some had gone farther than others. Those with hysterical personalities had obviously been unable to resolve an intense Oedipal situation, and those with a more generally healthy personality structure had developed farther and more successfully, despite pre-Oedipal fixations.

Zilboorg (43) in discussing parent–child antagonism accents the part played by Oedipal conflicts. He is describing older children, and we would agree that abuse of children over three or four, especially beginning at that time, is profoundly influenced by parental concern over sexuality and competitiveness. We are in complete accord with Zilboorg's statement that

> . . . the stronger the parents' "conscience," that is, the stronger their inhibitions, the greater will be their hostility against the child's freedom. To put it in technical terms: to the unconscious of the parents the child plays the role of the Id; the parents follow it vicariously for a time and then hurl upon it with all the force of their Super Ego; they project onto the child their own Id and then punish it to gratify the demands of their uncompromising Super Ego.

In the context of abuse of infants, however, we are more involved with the earliest pregenital determinants rather than Oedipal residues.

---

[4] Two of our patients had had overt incestuous relationships with their fathers. They described it more as satisfaction of dependent needs for love and comfort than as having real genital sexual meaning. One had been mildly depressed and the other psychotically so.

Contributions of the Non-Abusing Parent

Usually only one parent actually attacks the infant. The other parent almost invariably contributes, however, to the abusive behavior either by openly accepting it or by more subtly abetting it, consciously or unconsciously. An example of this is the strong support given each other by parents in their protestations of innocence, although it is clear both knew injurious abuse was occurring. Even though one parent openly accuses the other and righteously documents the other's abusive behavior when it has come to the attention of authorities, on investigation it is obvious that he or she has previously condoned it.

More direct instigation of abuse occurs when a spouse expresses opinions that the infant is being spoiled and needs more discipline or should be punished to break excessive willfulness and be brought under control. Similarly, one parent feeling overwhelmed and frustrated may turn the infant over to the other with admonitions to do something more drastic to stop the baby's annoying behavior. The non-abusing parent may show undue attention and interest toward an infant which stimulates feelings in the spouse of envy, abandonment, and anger leading to attack on the baby.

A husband's direct criticism of his wife's baby-caring ability, pointing out her errors and inadequacies, can trigger her attack on the child. Such husbands seem aware, at least on an unconscious level, that this will happen; yet they do it repeatedly.

Behavior which in any way signifies rejection or desertion is a potent stimulus to the attacker. If the abusing parent's own needs are neglected or rebuffed, there is an immediate turning to the infant with increased demand, and attack is likely. One woman told her husband she was uneasy about being alone with her previously injured baby and asked him to stay with her. He ignored her request and left the house. Shortly afterwards the baby was hit, resulting in a subdural hematoma. Less overt desertions can have a similar effect.

The various actions of the non-abusing parent become quite understandable when it is discovered that he or she had much the same life experience as the abuser and has developed a similar set of attitudes about parent-child relationships. Present in lesser intensity are the same feelings of unheeded yearnings for care, inferiority and hopelessness, coupled with the basic tenet that children should satisfy parental need. Thus, unknowingly, the marriage has become almost a collusion for the raising of children in a specific way. One parent is the active perpetrator; the other is a behind-the-scenes cooperator. Such parental tendencies become obvious when under treatment an abusing parent becomes gentler and the previously non-abusing parent starts being abusive. In a sense the infant becomes the scapegoat for inter-parental conflicts. Inability to solve their frustrated dependencies and antagonisms with each other leads them to turn for comfort to the child who is then attacked for failure to assuage the needs. It is obvious that treatment is often needed for the spouse, as well as for the overtly abusing parent.

The Contribution Made by the Attacked Child

There is no doubt that the infant, innocently and unwittingly, may contribute to the attack which is unleashed upon him. An infant born as the result of a premaritally conceived pregnancy or who comes as an accident too soon after the birth of a previous child, may be quite unwelcome to the parents and start life under the cloud of being unrewarding and unsatisfying to the parents. Such infants may be perceived as public reminders of sexual transgression or as extra, unwanted burdens rather than need-satisfying objects. An infant may also be seen as "uncooperative" or unsatisfying by having been born a girl when the parents wanted a boy or vice versa. Babies are born with quite different behavioral patterns. Some parents are disappointed when they have a very placid child instead of a hoped-for, more reactive, responsive baby. Other parents are equally distressed by having an active, somewhat aggressive baby who makes up his own mind about things when they had hoped for a very placid, compliant infant. A potent source of difficulty is the situation in which babies are born with some degree, major or minor, of congenital defect, therefore requiring much more medical as well as general attention. Often such infants are fussy, crying, and difficult to comfort and are limited in their ability to respond as a normal, happy baby should. Intercurrent illness may produce a similar picture. Babies born prematurely require much more care and offer less response soon enough to satisfy the parents' needs. A case which illustrates several of these points is as follows.

> Jerry and Connie had their first baby, a boy, as the result of a pregnancy which was instrumental in leading them to get married. Unfortunately, this otherwise quite healthy little boy was born with a congenital stricture of the bladder neck which required two long hospitalizations with surgery during the first six months of his life. Not surprisingly, he was a fussy, whiney, difficult to care for baby, requiring much more than average care and offering less happy, rewarding behavioral response to his parents. When he was eight months old, his father returned home late from an unusually hard day at work and found his wife terribly upset and irritable because of conflicts arising with his mother. His wife, in an effort to assuage her own turmoil, left the baby with Jerry and went to visit her own mother. Jerry, tired, feeling quite needy, deserted by Connie, was faced with caring for a crying baby. After several attempts to comfort and feed the baby, he became out of patience, angry, and struck the baby, fracturing its skull. There were no serious consequences, fortunately, from this injury. Jerry came under our care some three years later because of his worry over the fact that he was still very punitive toward Willie and often spanked him and slapped him to an unnecessary degree. By this time, a second boy, Benny, had been born and was now nine months old. Jerry spoke of his attitude toward Benny being extremely different, and when asked why responded with, "Well, Benny's just the kind of a kid I like. Whenever I want to wrestle with him, he wrestles. He does everything that I want him to do."

Thus, it is obvious that characteristics presented by the infant, such as sex, time of birth, health status, and behavior are factors in instigating child abuse. An interesting presentation of the role of the child is that of Milowe and Lourie (44) with its accompanying discussion. Often stated in support of the idea that it is somehow "all the infant's fault" is the fact that occasionally battered children have been attacked and injured again in the foster home where they have been placed for protection. We have not had the opportunity to study such an event nor have we seen any report of an adequately thorough study; but our other experience leads to doubt the assumption that only the child is at fault.

Despite the contributions which infants make toward the disappointments and burdens of their parents, they can hardly be used as an excuse or adequate cause for child abuse. They are part of the inevitable hazards all of us face in being human and in being parents. The essence of the problem is again the excessively high demands which parents impose upon infants, disregarding the inability of the infants to meet them.

Circumstances of the Attack

Most abusing parents have difficulty in describing just what happened at the time the infant was injured. To some extent, this is due to their reluctance to reveal anything for which they may be criticized. Sometimes it is due to a more or less unconscious defensive forgetting or amnesia. Both of these factors are usually diminished under therapy. More universal and impossible to eliminate is a vague "haziness" about the actual attack, although events immediately preceding and following the attack may be recalled with clarity. We have not considered this haziness to be either a real cognitive slip nor a psychological repression, but rather the normal vagueness everyone feels when trying to describe in detail an extremely intense emotional storm. By using all other information we have about the patient's psychological patterns, plus his description of events before, during, and after the attack, as well as associative material, we have developed an understanding of the circumstances of the attack in which we have reasonable confidence.

The parent approaches each task of infant care with three incongruous attitudes: first, a healthy desire to do something good for the infant; second, a deep, hidden yearning for the infant to respond in such a way as to fill the emptiness in the patient's life and bolster his low self-esteem; and third, a harsh, authoritative demand for the infant's correct response, supported by a sense of parental rightness. If the caring task goes reasonably well and the infant's response is reasonably adequate, no attack occurs and no harm is done except for the stimulation of aggression and accompanying strict superego development in the infant. But if anything interferes with the success of the parental care or enhances the parent's feelings of being unloved and inferior, the harsh, authoritative attitude surges up and attack is likely to occur. The infant's part in this disturbance is accomplished by persistent, unassuaged crying, by failing to respond physically or emotionally in accordance with parental needs, or by actively interfering through obstructive physical activity. At times the parent may be feeling especially inferior, unloved, needy, and angry, and, therefore, unusually vulnerable because some important figure such as the spouse or a relative has just criticized or deserted him or because some other facet of his life has become unmanageable.

On a deeper psychological level, the events begin with the parent's identification of the infant for whom he is caring as a need-gratifying object equivalent to a parent who will replace the lacks in the abusing parent's own being-parented experience. Since the parent's past tells him that the ones to whom he looked for love were also the ones who attacked him, the infant is also perceived as a critical parental figure. Quite often abusing parents tell us, "When the baby cries like that it sounds just like mother (or father) yelling at me, and I can't stand it." The perception of being criticized stirs up the parent's feelings of being inferior. It also increases the frustration of his need for love, and anger mounts. At this time there seems to be a strong sense of guilt, a feeling of helplessness and panic becomes overwhelming, and the haziness is most marked.

Suddenly a shift in identifications occurs. The superego identification with the parent's own punitive parent takes over. The infant is perceived as the parent's own bad childhood self. The built-up aggression is redirected outwardly and the infant is hit with full superego approval.

This sudden shift in identifications is admittedly difficult to document. Our patients cannot clearly describe all that happened in the midst of such intense emotional turmoil. We interpret it as regression under severe stress to an early period of superego development when identification with the aggressor established a strict, punitive superego with more effective strength than the gentler ego ideal. In such a regressive state the stronger, punitive superego inevitably comes to the fore.

Following the attack, some parents may maintain a strict, righteous attitude, express no sense of guilt about the aggression, insist they have done nothing wrong, and are very resentful toward anyone who tries to interfere with their affairs. On the other hand, some parents are filled with remorse, weep, and quickly seek medical help if the child has been seriously hurt.

It has not been possible in all patients to obtain a clear story of what they actually did to the child at the time a serious injury occurred, even though abuse is admitted. They insist they did nothing differently than usual. In some cases this may be a defensive forgetting. In others we think it is probably a true statement. They have been hitting or yanking the child routinely and are not aware of the extra force used at the time of fracture.

The following condensed case histories, when added to the fragments already quoted, will illustrate the main streams of the patients' lives related to the ultimate abusive behavior.

> Amy, twenty-six, is the wife of a successful junior executive engineer. She requested help for feelings of depression, fear she was ruining her marriage, and worry over being angry and unloving with her baby boy. She was born and raised in a well-to-do family in a large city on the west coast. Her parents were brilliant, active intellectuals who apparently had minimal involvement in the earliest years of their children's lives. She and her younger sister and brother were cared for by governesses, about whom Amy has vague fragmentary memories. One was very warm, kind, and loving. She recalls another who was demanding, stern, and mean and who roughly washed Amy's long hair as a punishment and held her nose to make her eat. We suspect, without adequate documentation, that the governesses raised the infants as much to meet the high behavior standards of the parents as to meet the variable needs and whims of their charges.
>
> As a child Amy had more interaction with her mother, but she could not feel close or really understood by either parent. Both parents had compulsive traits of wanting everything in perfect order and tasks done "at once." Her father was quite aloof, uninterested in children because they could not talk to him on any worthwhile level. When Amy was about thirteen, both mother and father had psychotherapy. Since then, her father has been warmer and has some liking for small children, but he still maintains a pattern of wanting to be the center of the stage and have people pay attention primarily to him, not only in the family but in all social situations. In recent years Amy has felt closer to her mother and has felt that they could talk more frankly and openly with each other. During her childhood, Amy felt inept, awkward, ugly, unable to be liked by other people, and somewhat dull intellectually. Even though she made good grades in school, they never seemed good enough to gain approval. (Her I.Q. is in the upper normal range.)

Although not physically punished or overtly severely criticized, Amy felt great lack of approval and developed a deep sense of inferiority, inability to please, and worthlessness; she thought of herself as almost "retarded." In college she was capable but not outstanding, and after graduation she worked for a while, gaining a significant amount of self-respect and self-assurance. She had become a quite attractive, adequately popular girl and had made a good marriage. She and her husband are well-liked, active members of their social set.

Of her first-born child, Lisa, now age two and a half and doing well, Amy says, "I did not like her too well at first and didn't feel close to her until she was several months old and more responsive." By the time Lisa was a year old, with much maternal encouragement, she was walking and beginning to talk and Amy began to think much more highly of her, and for the most part, they get along well with each other. However, if Lisa has tantrums or does not behave well, whines or cries too much, Amy occasionally still shakes her and spanks her rather violently. Their second child, Billy, was born not quite a year and a half after Lisa. He was delivered by caesarian section, one month premature. He did not suck well at first and feeding was a problem. Also, Amy was sick for a while after delivery. She never felt warm or close or really loved him and had even less patience with him than with Lisa. His "whining" drove her "crazy" and made her hate him. Because of his crying and lack of adequate response, she would grow impatient with him and leave him or punish him roughly. She spent little time cuddling or playing with him, and he became, as a result, somewhat less responsive and did not thrive as well as he might have. When he was seven months old, during a routine check-up, the pediatrician unfortunately said to Amy, "Maybe you have a retarded child here." Amy immediately felt intense aversion to Billy, hated the sight of him, couldn't pick him up or feed him easily, and began more serious physical abuse that evening. She felt depressed, angry, and irritable. Billy also seemed to stop progress. However, when checked by another pediatrician, he was said to be quite normal. Amy felt reassured but not convinced. She became aware that Billy was responsive and alert if she felt all right and loving toward him, but he acted "stupid" if she were depressed or angry at him. This awareness of her influence on him served only to enhance her feelings of worthlessness and guilt. At times when he was unresponsive or seemed to be behaving in a "retarded" way, and especially if he cried too much or whined, she roughed him up, shook him, spanked him very severely, and choked him violently. No bones had been broken, but there were bruises. Amy described alternating between feelings of anger at Billy because he was "retarded" and feeling very guilty because she had "squashed him" by her own attitudes and behavior.

Amy described being inadequately prepared for and overwhelmed by the tasks of motherhood. This was enhanced by her feeling that she was trying to accomplish the mothering tasks without the help that her mother had had in bringing up her children. Further difficulty arose because her husband, although overtly quite sympathetic with her difficulties and expressing wishes of helping her, would also withdraw from her in times of crisis and imply a good deal of criticism of the way she dealt with the children. She also felt that there had been no one to whom she could really turn to air her troubles and get comfort and help without too much admonition and criticism. Further, Amy had a cousin who was retarded and she felt devastated by fantasies of the burden of bringing up a retarded child.

This case shows the identification of the abusing parent with her own parents' attitudes toward children, the premature, high expectation and need of responsive performance on the part of the infant, and the inability to cope with lack of good response. Most clearly, it shows the parental misperception of the infant as the embodiment of those bad behavioral traits (being "retarded") for which the parent herself was criticized as a young child. During treatment Amy's depressive feelings and sense of worthlessness were ameliorated. She began to interact more happily with her children, and they responded well to her change in behavior. Billy, particularly, began to thrive, grew rapidly, and became a happier, more rewarding baby. Amy and her husband began to communicate a little more effectively and her aggressive behavior toward her children almost completely disappeared. After six months treatment had to be terminated because of her husband's transfer to another city. We had the good fortune to see her and the children four years later. Amy was doing very well and the two children were active, happy, bright youngsters. Wisely, we believe, they have had no more children. The improvement that occurred in this situation is partly due to our therapeutic intervention, but we would guess that it is also due to the passage of time which enabled the children to grow up and inevitably become more behaviorally and conversationally rewarding to their mother.

Larry, age twenty-seven, is a quiet, shy, unassuming, little man who works as a welder's assistant. Since childhood, he has been plagued by a deep sense of inferiority, unworthiness, and unsureness of himself in his work and in all human relations. There is also a deep resentment, usually very restrained, against a world which he feels is unfair.

He was brought up on a dairy farm, the third of five children. The oldest, a sister, is ten years his senior. He has never been able to find out the truth about her from his parents or other relatives but thinks all the evidence indicates she is a half-sister and an illegitimate child of his mother's before her marriage. Some resentment against his mother is based on this situation. His two younger sisters he felt were bothersome and annoying during their childhood. His brother, two years older, took advantage of him, and his parents always took the brother's side, allowing him to do many things for which Larry was criticized or punished. This brother was quite wild, and while on leave from the navy, he was in a serious auto accident. Larry said, "Too bad he wasn't killed," but then found his brother had been killed. Overwhelmed by guilt and grief, Larry took leave from the army to take his brother's body home for burial.

Larry's parents were deeply religious. He imagined his mother became fanatically so following her illegitimate pregnancy. She was against smoking, alcohol, coffee, tea, and most of the usual forms of amusement. Even after his marriage, his mother told his wife not to make coffee for him. Larry felt she was always much more strict with him than with his siblings. She forced him to attend Sunday school and frequent church services, much against his will. She berated him for minor misdeeds and constantly nagged and criticized him to the point where he felt everything he did was wrong, and that he could never do right in her eyes. He occasionally rebelled by smoking or drinking. Larry's father drank moderately but became a teetotaler after his son's death. He often had outbursts of temper and once beat Larry with a piece of two-by-four lumber for a minor misdeed. Larry does not recall either mother or father spanking as a routine, but there were constant verbal attacks and criticism. He felt that neither of his parents, particularly his mother, really listened to him or understood his unhappiness and his need for comfort and consideration.[5]

While he was in the army, Larry and Becky planned to marry. She was to come to where he was stationed, and they were to be married at Christmas time. He waited all day at the bus station, but she never appeared. Sad and hopeless, he got drunk. Months later, a buddy told him she had married somebody else the first of January. He saw her again a year later when home on leave. She had been divorced; so they made up and got married. She had a child, Jimmy, by her first marriage.

[5] See previous references to Larry above.

Larry has been dependent on Becky and feared losing her. Seeing Jimmy reminds him of her previous desertion. He feels she favors Jimmy; he is critical of Jimmy and occasionally spanks him. Becky has threatened to leave Larry over his aversion to Jimmy. During their five years of marriage they have been in financial straits, and at such times Becky and Larry have gone to their respective family homes for help until he could find a new job. Becky resented these episodes and criticized Larry for being an inadequately capable and providing husband.

They have had three more children of their own. Mary, age four, is liked very much by both parents, although Larry is more irritated by her than by their next child, David, age two and a half. David is "a very fine, active, alert, well-mannered little boy." He is quite responsive and both parents like him and are good with him. Maggie, four and a half months old, was thought by both parents to be "a bit different" from birth. She seemed to look bluer and cried less strongly than their other babies and was also rather fussy. Becky is fond of Maggie and gives her good mothering. Larry is irritated by her, much as he is by Mary, and more than by David, but he does not dislike her as much as he does Jimmy.

Maggie was admitted to the hospital with symptoms and signs of bilateral subdural hematoma. She had been alone with her father when he noticed a sudden limpness, unconsciousness, and lack of breathing. He gave mouth-to-mouth respiration, and she was brought to hospital by ambulance. There was a history of a similar episode a month before when Maggie was three and a half months old; when alone with her father she had become limp, followed by vomiting. Medical care was not sought until a week later. Following this, there was a question of increasing head size. No fractures of skull or long bones were revealed by X ray. Two craniotomies were done for the relief of Maggie's subdural hematomas. During the month she was in hospital, we had frequent interviews with the parents. We were impressed by Becky's warmth, responsiveness, and concern over Maggie's welfare. Larry, however, maintained a more uneasy, aloof, evasive attitude, although he was superficially cooperative. What had happened to Maggie was not clearly established, but it seemed obvious she was the victim of trauma. We thought Larry was likely to have been the abuser, despite his maintenance of silence and innocence. We felt we had adequate, although meager, rapport with Larry and Becky and allowed them to take Maggie home with the adamant provision that she never be left alone with Larry.

A week later Larry called urgently for an appointment. Filled with shame, guilt, and anxiety he poured out his story. President Kennedy had been assassinated two days before. Larry was shocked, then flooded with feelings of sympathy for Kennedy and his family, anger at the assassin, grief over the unfair, unnecessary loss of an admired figure, and a sense of communal guilt. In this emotional turmoil he had a few beers at a tavern, went home and confessed to Becky what he had done to Maggie, and then phoned us. The circumstances of the attack were as follows: Larry's boss told him that his job was over. The construction contract had been suddenly cancelled and there was no more work. Feeling discouraged, hopeless, and ignored, Larry went home, shamefacedly told Becky he had lost his job, and asked her if she wanted to go with the children to her family. Saying nothing, Becky walked out of the house leaving Larry alone with Maggie. The baby began to cry. Larry tried to comfort her, but she kept on crying so he looked for her bottle. He could not find the bottle anywhere; the persistent crying and his feelings of frustration, helplessness, and ineffectuality became overwhelming. In a semi-confused "blurry" state he shook Maggie severely and then hit her on the head. Suddenly aware of what he had done, he started mouth-to-mouth resuscitation; then Becky came home and Maggie was brought to the hospital.

Recurrent in Larry's life are the themes of feeling disregarded and deserted and of being helplessly ineffectual in his attempts to meet expectations. These concepts of himself as worthless and incapable express the incorporation into his superego of the attitudes of his parents toward him during childhood; they have been enhanced by his later reality experiences of failure. He has further strong identifications with the aggressive parental attitudes of criticizing and attacking the weak, the helpless, and the maimed.

The attack on Maggie occurred when several of Larry's vulnerabilities were activated at the same time. He had experienced a lack of being considered and a feeling of failure in losing his job, his wife "deserted" him again with implications of criticism, he felt helpless to cope with the crying demands of the baby, and his own deep yearnings for love and care could not be spoken. Frustration and anger mounted, and the baby was struck. Larry said that in the "blurry" state he had a fleeting queer feeling that he had hit himself.

Later we found similar circumstances were present when Maggie had been less severely injured a month before. Becky had started working evenings to supplement Larry's inadequate income. She would depart soon after he came home from his job, leaving him alone to fix supper, wash the dishes, and put the children to bed. He found the tasks difficult and was upset by the children's crying, particularly Maggie's. One evening, feeling overwhelmed, helpless, and unable to seek help, he attacked.

Larry's relationship to Becky was highly influenced by his unconscious tendency to identify her with his mother. This transference was facilitated by the reality facts that Becky had a child by a previous liaison, urged Larry to be more involved with the church, took Jimmy's side while disregarding Larry, frequently criticized Larry for failure to meet her expectations, and had several times deserted him, both emotionally and physically. Most basic and potent was Larry's urgent dependent need to find in Becky the motherliness he had never known. Constantly, despite disappointment, he yearningly looked to her to satisfy the unmet needs of all his yesterdays. When she failed him, there were only the children to look to for responses which would make him feel better.

Psychological Testing[6]

Psychological testing of child-abusing parents has provided several interesting findings which support impressions gained from clinical observations. First, there is no evidence of a significant relationship between intelligence as measured by intelligence tests and abuse. The I.Q.'s obtained by the patients seen for testing range between 73 and 130, with most of the patients falling into the average range (90–110). The cognitive styles of these people tend to be more along the lines of action-orientation as opposed to the dependence on thought and delay of impulse gratification. This is not true, however, for all of our patients. Second, the test results indicate no one basic personality structure, in the usual nosological sense, possessed by the patients. A few patients show existing ego pathology of psychotic proportions. Others show apparent overall ego strength. Personality patterns featuring hysterical trends are evident in a number.

[6] This section was written in collaboration with Richard Waite, Ph.D., associate professor of clinical psychology and director, child section, department of psychology, University of Colorado School of Medicine. We are very grateful for his help.

Obsessive-compulsive patterns predominate in others. However, these "patterns" reflect to a large extent the defenses and other ego mechanisms which predominate in the patient's overall functioning.

Among those patients who were given the entire psychological test battery,[7] common underlying conflicts are apparent. The test reports specifically mention strong oral-dependent needs as significant intrapsychic areas of difficulty for every patient tested. In four-fifths of the patients unresolved identity conflicts were cited as major determinants of their behavior, and in nearly as many, depressive trends and/or noteworthy feelings of worthlessness were noted. Almost as common were evidences of suspiciousness, distrust, and feeling victimized, but in only one case were they significant enough to be classified as truly paranoid. It is emphasized that these problem areas appeared in people of widely differing personality constellations; people whose test behavior and surface attitudes were extremely varied. All of the patients defended against the conscious experience of depressive affect with efforts varying in complexity and effectiveness. Some utilized strong and resilient character defenses, others employed classically neurotic constellations of defenses. Nevertheless, the test results clearly indicated the underlying presence of the depressive elements. A review of the nature of the depression in these cases indicates that while frequently superego pressures and guilt contributed to the depressive feelings, in all but one case the depression is basically of the anaclitic type.

The following comments, abstracted from the test reports, indicate the kind of depression and oral longings found in these patients.

> "An intense and long-lasting fear of abandonment or loss of care and protection." "A long-standing sense of having been rejected." "Strong, ongoing, unsatiated dependency needs." "She may well wish that somebody would take her away from her cares and responsibilities and treat her more as a beloved little girl."

The identity problems noted in the test reports indicate developmental failures to establish successful syntheses of identity fragments. The test results suggested that frequently these patients consciously doubt not only their adequacy as wives and mothers, husbands and fathers, but they also actively wish to be something else. Some of the patients appear to have retained, as one important aspect of their identity struggles, part-identifications as little girls or boys, a finding directly related to the prevalence of unsatiated oral-receptive longings.

The hypothesis that these patients have failed to achieve a synthesis of identity fragments gains further support from an inspection of their Rorschach protocols. Responses traditionally classified as reflecting inadequately confirmed identities are present. They emphasize such activities and orientations as role playing, performing, and disguising. For example, one patient's percepts included a child playing Indian, people in a ballet, and kids at Halloween. Another saw modern dancers and a cross between a rat and a cat. A third patient saw seals performing, and a fourth saw a mask and a dress with no one in it.

The scanty direct references to children appearing in the test reports describe them as "fussy," "demanding," "bothersome," "whiney," "good when asleep," or "bad

---

[7] The test battery always included the Wechsler Adult Intelligence Scale, Rorschach, Thematic Apperception Test, and usually the addition of the Sentence Completion Test and Figure Drawing.

little children who are sorry for what they've done." Notably lacking in the reports are references to good nurturing mothers, in contrast to frequent descriptions of punitive, depriving, and prohibiting mothers. Not rarely fathers are over-idealized as more gratifying. Superego pressures are usually described as intense, more often as an identification with the mother than the father.

Material obtained in the course of interviews and therapy of patients stimulated the hypothesis that these patients have particular problems in coping with their own mothers and their internal representations of their mothers. Test data from seven women was examined to ascertain whether or not it would support such a hypothesis. There is no question but what the patients' test responses, particularly to the TAT cards, suggests such difficulties. This did not emerge clearly, however, as a distinct conflicted problem area in the test responses—that is, an independent rater comparing these responses with those obtained from other psychiatric patients probably would not be struck by a difference between the two groups along this dimension. Certainly their responses to card VII of the Rorschach, which is frequently cited as a card which stimulates perceptual responses reflective of fantasies about maternal figures, indicated no untoward disruptions. Their reaction times to this card were no different from their reaction times to the rest of the test cards, and the content of their responses was varied and not unusual. It was noted that in their responses to Picasso's "La Vie," one of the TAT cards, five out of six of the patients saw a mother, usually taking the young couple's child away, or the woman back, which may or may not reflect problems with mother, since we do not know how frequently such responses occur in other patients. This is probably the most disruptive card for these patients, with their reaction times tending to be significantly longer than to other cards in the test, and several of them having extreme difficulties in making up a story. Several other factors could contribute to the disruption, however, including the presentation of nude figures in this picture and the card's potential for stimulating conscious fantasies related to taking care of children, fantasies which in spite of their battering experiences would be disturbing to them. Finally, the patients' responses to card XII-F of the TAT were looked at closely, since this card depicts an old woman frequently seen as a witch-like figure, standing directly behind a pleasant looking young woman. Three out of six patients could not tell a story to this card, and the remaining three patients had a great deal of difficulty. Here again, however, caution in citing this finding as support for the hypothesis is indicated, since we do not have comparison data.

Finally, the patients' responses to the comprehension sub-test of the intelligence test were studied to ascertain whether or not specific questions gave them more trouble than others—that is, we looked for the items on which the patient failed to score at the level one would expect from the rest of their responses on this sub-test. Three such items clearly emerged as being difficult for this group of patients. The first of these is "Why should people stay away from bad company?" Six out of seven patients scored lower than one would expect on this item. Interpretation of this finding is difficult, since there are several possibilities. Perhaps the finding simply reflects the patient's guilt feelings resulting from their maladaptive maternal behavior, or it may well reflect feelings of being influenced by others. The second item causing disruptions in cognitive organization is "What does the saying mean, strike while the iron is hot?"

Here, five out of seven of the patients scored lower than expected. The aggressive significance of this item is probably the most important factor in causing the disruption. The third item is "Why are child labor laws needed?" Here again, five out of seven patients failed to do as well as expected. In this item, with its direct reference to children and their exploitation, it is the patient's belief in the child's usefulness in serving the needs of adults that is probably the primary determinant of the lowered efficiency of cognition.

Comparative studies between these patients and other psychiatric patients are again indicated in regard to the comprehension sub-test. To establish the significance of these findings one should determine whether or not patients in general have problems with these three items.

In summary, the test findings provide some support for the hypothesis that child-abusing parents have fairly oral conflicts, underlying feelings of depression and worthlessness, and have failed to establish age-appropriate ego identities. Their support of other hypotheses remains open to question at this point. Moreover, the test results indicate significant diversity in personality structure among these patients in the complexity of defenses and ego-adaptive mechanisms available to them. They indicate that child-abusing behavior is not common to one or two diagnostic entities and that this behavior can occur in people having relatively resilient and adaptive egos.

Treatment

Notwithstanding its difficulties, psychotherapy of the patients in our study group has been very rewarding, both for them and for us. There were treatment failures, sometimes due to uncontrollable external circumstances such as the patient moving away, going to the penitentiary, or living too far away for contact, and sometimes due to a combination of the severity of the psychiatric problem and our own lack of knowledge. In the great majority of patients treatment was successful, highly so in some, moderately so in others. Criteria of success were multiple. Of primary importance was a change in the style of parent-child interaction to a degree which eliminated the danger of physical harm to the child and lessened the chance of serious emotional damage. Accompanying the change in parenting style, and in fact a necessary precursor of it, was a change in the patient's general psychic functioning evidenced by signs of better handling of intrapsychic conflict, and also by improvement in the marital relationship, in other interpersonal relationships, and in dealing with the various problems of daily living. Treatment was oriented to the patient as a human being, not toward a person pigeonholed as one who abuses children. As noted before, our patients had all the variety of psychological states encountered in any practice, and therapy was in many ways the application of techniques ordinarily used. However, the symptom of child abuse related as it is to the dynamics described in previous sections gives rise to certain problems which call for special attention in therapy.

Probably the first difficulty met by the therapist is the management of his own feelings about a parent who has hurt a small baby. Most people react with disbelief and denial, or on the other hand, with horror and a surge of anger toward the abuser. It helps to gain a more useful, neutral position to realize from the very first that not only has an infant been hurt but that the parent, too, is a hurt child himself. We were fortunate in that our research goals led us to a broad interest in the patient's whole life rather than attempts to cure a symptom. The more the therapist can mobilize the same curiosity he has about other patients, the better he will do with the abusing parent. Aggressive acts toward infants are a symptom of deep conflict and can best be treated by investigation of the total personality, rather than by belaboring the symptom. In this sense, therapy of these patients is quite similar to treatment of patients with such symptoms as impotence, frigidity, or hand-washing compulsions. Thinking of the abusing parent in this framework is quite helpful in ameliorating those less useful emotions which arise in the therapist when first faced with the problem.

Another difficulty present on first contact and for some time thereafter is the attitude the patient has about getting help and his view of the therapist. He may be a bit belligerent and say he doesn't need treatment, doesn't want treatment, and considers the whole project an imposition. He has not done anything wrong, stupid people are making an unwarranted fuss over nothing, and the therapist is wasting his time. On the other hand, a patient may be meek, mild, and submissive, and express a desire to cooperate in any way. There are, of course, many gradations and mixtures of these two polar attitudes. Patients can respond in either of these gross ways to the experience of having had abuse discovered and having been talked to in an accusatory, punitive manner by physicians, social workers, law enforcement investigators, or others. Those who come voluntarily seeking help are more likely to show the cooperative, submissive attitude and express belief in the usefulness of treatment.

It is important not to accept these first attitudes at face value, but to use them as first clues to what will be needed to develop the therapeutic alliance vital for ongoing, successful treatment. These are people whose early life experience taught them the not-yet-forgotten lesson that those to whom one looks for help are those who will attack one and that to look for help is hopeless. They have learned that a modicum of safety lies in self-negation and in submissively trying to do what others expect. Simultaneously they have the belief that a very good way to deal with trouble is to attack it with strong aggression. With this potpourri and without enough of that quality we call basic trust or confidence, it is no wonder they approach treatment tentatively, dubiously, and with a variety of overt attitudes.

This situation is not as bad as it looks. The patient comes to the psychiatrist in a severe crisis of distress over his behavior, distress created by his own internal conflicts or by the reaction of the environment. He feels attacked, either by his own conscience or by society. As an inevitable corollary, he will have intensified yearnings for love and protection, and this opens a useful avenue for the therapist to make contact. We learned not to be dismayed by a patient's first negative, rejecting attitudes, particularly if he or she had been heckled and threatened by others. It is easy to say to the patient, "It sounds as if you have been having a perfectly dreadful time. Let's see what we can do about it." Such simple statements of sympathy give the patient at least a faint idea he has been listened to without being criticized. The therapist is then to some extent "on the side of the angels," offering asylum and protection from the threatening world. Sympathetic listening is equally important for the cooperative or voluntary patient. Their distrust of treatment is very strong, although well camouflaged.

It is a commonplace that psychiatric patients enjoy the time and attention of the therapist and the privilege of being listened to. We are convinced abusing parents need this more and respond to it better than any other patients we have seen. Being listened to helps build the needed sense of confidence and lays the foundation for developing a sense of self-respect and identity. An important part of the patient's improvement is directly related to this, involving identification with the therapist. We know we are well on the road to success when a patient says something to the effect, "You know, doctor, I'm listening to my baby the way you listen to me. He is a real person to me now and it's lots of fun."

In addition to listening, the therapist must also ask questions. If it is not already known which parent has attacked the infant, questioning about it is often fruitless and puts the therapist in the role of unwelcome accuser. When the seriously injured infant is in the hospital, the necessary information usually appears spontaneously before discharge. In the case of non-hospitalized milder injuries, it usually becomes obvious who has hurt the child without direct questioning or confrontation. The therapist can well ask the patient about his present and past life and how he was raised as a child. This leads naturally and unobtrusively into how he deals with his own offspring. Any direct question carrying a sense of accusation is best avoided. To ask, "Do you get angry when the baby cries?" is likely to stimulate denial or evasion. But to ask, "Does it almost push you beyond your strength sometimes when the baby cries so much?" may well produce much pertinent material including the feelings of anger and frustration.

Although protection of the infant is a main goal, direct interest in the infant should be avoided by the therapist, paradoxical as this may seem. Attention should be focused almost exclusively on the parent. The rationale for this lies in the fact that paying attention to the baby leaves the parent back in the old nightmarish feeling of nobody listening to his needs, thereby reinforcing his hopelessness and lack of trust. Probably our most basic tenet in treatment has been to get the parent to look to us to find out how to get his needs filled, rather than to the infant for satisfaction. If this can be accomplished to even a moderate degree, there is less demand on the baby, less parental frustration, and the baby is essentially safe. A clue to this element of safety is the patient phoning between appointments to speak of loneliness, frustration, and increasing tension, a turning to the therapist instead of the baby for response.

Closely related is the therapeutic goal of changing the patient's isolated way of life. After a good alliance has been established with the therapist, the patient can be encouraged to seek more outside social contacts with friends or neighbors. This can be done best by helping the patient recognize his own desires for contact and amelio-rating his fears of it, rather than by direct advice or admonition. The more involvement there is with others, the less the baby is used to supply parental comfort. Patients often require encouragement to do such a simple thing as get baby sitters so that they can occasionally have freedom for other activities. This must be handled carefully because of the tendency of parents to feel "left out" if attention is paid to the baby. One mother told it succinctly: "When my mother comes to help me with Billy and she picks him up, I feel she has not only taken Billy away from me, but that Billy is also taking mother away from me. I feel angry at both of them." She added that even when wanting help with her baby, for another person to take over meant she herself was being criticized as a no-good mother. Such complex feelings underscore the necessity of paying primary attention to parental need.

A frequent problem in therapy is the requests patients make for advice. Out of their life-long obligation to do what others want they ask many questions about what to do and the proper way to do it. Giving such advice is useless; the patient will follow it submissively in a way that makes it not work, or if in a healthier mood he will disregard it. To use a standard psychiatric gambit such as, "Why do you ask?" is equally fruitless. It puts the patient on a spot; he feels rejected and can only come up with a lame remark, "Well, I want to do the right thing." No ground has been gained. A more useful approach is to mention several ways of doing something, including one's own point of view, and counter this by suggesting the patient can follow any method or devise another which suits him better. Usually patients do well with this encouragement, gaining confidence and self-respect. The same principle applies to the question of "setting limits" or controls. Abusing parents have already been overburdened by controls to which they responded poorly. Rather than ordering them to stop certain behaviors it is more productive of change to ask, "Do you suppose you could think of another way to do it so as to bring out more of what you want?"

The patients in our study group were exquisitely sensitive to desertion and rejection in any form. We noted earlier that feeling rejected by spouse, parent, or other meaningful figure is a potent factor in precipitating a specific abusing act. Such symptomatic acting out also occurs in reaction to the therapist. Early in our work we made the mistake of all three therapists being out of town at the same time for a few days. Some patients responded by reinstituting mild abusive behavior toward their infants. Since then, we have always had at least one member of the group available for patients to contact if need arises. As a rule, it is worthwhile to let patients know when one is leaving town and returning, even though the absence will not interfere with scheduled appointments. Giving such information seems to help the development of the patient's trust and confidence. Telephone contacts can be tricky. Patients inevitably phone at inconvenient or impossible times and feel rejected if dealt with brusquely. If one can take the time to say, "I can talk to you for a minute now if it's very urgent, but if you can wait a couple of hours, I'll have freedom to talk more leisurely. Is that possible for you?" Patients usually respond well. After a few experiences of this sort they become more like average patients who leave a request with the secretary to call when convenient. Again, the time and attention are priceless gifts to these patients.

Termination of treatment can arouse once more the feelings of being deserted and rejected, and not rarely there will be a mild transient recurrence of tendencies to demand too much and be too aggressive toward the infant. This affords an opportunity for the therapist to make more precise interpretations and for the patient to gain more definitive insight as the conflict is worked through. We suspect some of the patients' acting out was because they knew we were interested in the problem of abuse and the obvious way to maintain our interest was to do some abusing. Because of our research interest, we let patients know we would be glad to hear from them again, even after therapy had been tapered off and technically terminated. While writing this section, our first patient, Bertie, was feeling a bit lonely and made her roughly semi-annual phone call to us. Her two daughters are thriving in school and kindergarten. She occasionally has to mollify her husband who thinks she is too lenient with the girls and wants to use a strap on them for discipline. On the whole, she is managing adequately well. We had seen her husband, too, but because his work made contacts extremely difficult, his treatment ended prematurely.

Treatment of the non-abusing spouse is indicated whenever a significant contribution or provocation of abuse is made by him. We mentioned earlier that our patients tend to marry someone who is rather like themselves in background and basic character structure. Hence, when an abusing mother under treatment begins to be more tolerant and considerate of the infant, the father may then pick up the role of abuser, although often in a milder form. Further improvement by the wife may enable her to meet more of her husband's needs so that he will no longer turn to the child for satisfaction, but therapy of both patients is highly desirable if it can be accomplished. Unresolved sibling rivalry leading to parental competition for the child's affection may be a productive area for therapy in the non-abusing spouse. We believe our general principles of treatment apply equally to both spouses since their psychodynamics related to abuse are similar.

By far, the most difficult task in therapy is to help patients establish a better relationship with their own parents, particularly their mothers. We feel that until some sense of peace and useful rapport is felt with the mother, the patient's own ability to be motherly remains hampered. The patient's recurrent sense of disappointment with the mother, the fear of her, and the intense ambivalence about her make the task seem almost impossible. Only after a strong therapeutic alliance has developed with increased confidence in the therapist, should any attempt be made to lead the patient toward finding the good qualities of the mother. Even then it must be done cautiously and skillfully. Gradually, with luck, a patient can find her own way of maintaining equilibrium during contacts with her mother and even find means of pleasing the mother so as to bring responses of real love and approval. Whatever amount of relationship and new identification can be made with the "good" mother will be directly reflected in the release of the patient's own motherliness. Although the patient's rapprochement with the mother might be handled in an exclusively psychotherapeutic situation, we used the additional help of a sensitive woman social worker in nearly all cases. Following an initial period of variable length of being rejected and tested, she was trusted by most of the women patients and became the usable object of their pent-up longings to be mothered. She was an empathic, non-critical, non-controlling, available substitute mother, thus providing a new experience for the patient and a new object for identification. The therapeutic significance of this relationship was often tremendous. In addition to its own intrinsic value, it facilitated and speeded up therapy with the psychiatrist. A good relationship with the social worker was many times a first step in the patient's break out of restricting isolation into broader social contacts. Often it was the patient's bridge toward remodelling the relationship with her own mother.

The social worker was involved very early in some cases, interviewing patients just before or after the first psychiatric contact. The psychiatrist and social worker then continued contacts, the former in office interviews, the latter predominantly in home visits until the case was terminated. This pattern worked well. It gave the patient opportunity to deal with two people of different sex who were allied in an effort to be of use to the patient. It also provided alternatives for the patient. If in trouble with the psychiatrist the patient could turn to the social worker, and vice versa, thereby airing troubles more freely and lessening the sense of hopelessness. This byplay back and forth between the man and the woman therapists had a special meaning for many patients because of specific childhood experiences. They had felt disillusioned and disappointed when they looked to their mothers for satisfaction of dependent needs. Turning then to fathers for this satisfaction they overidealized them, partly because the fathers did provide a modicum of satisfaction, but more because the father relationship was less fraught with primitive ambivalence and fear. But fathers could not provide enough of what they wanted, and they were disappointed again. Sometimes they had asked their fathers why they had trouble with mother and were answered with lack of understanding and no help. In therapy the turning from one "parental" figure to the other was reenacted and reevaluated with beneficial understanding. We have thought this lack of real confidence in either men or women has helped create the impression in both male psychiatrists and female social workers that abusing parents are almost untreatable.

In some cases the social worker was not involved until after many weeks of contact with the psychiatrist. Bringing her in could then be complicated. One patient, when asked if she would like to have the social worker visit her at home, responded by looking surprised and a little annoyed, hesitated a bit, then acquiesced. Much later, after she had found the social worker to be "one of the best things that ever happened to me," she told us what had gone on. "When you asked me if I would see Mrs. D., I thought: 'How stupid can Dr. S. be? I've just been telling him how afraid I am of women and how I hate them. Then he shoves another one down my throat, but I guess he knows what he's doing, so I'll go along with it.'" This incident illustrates the patient's mixture of suppression of anger about not being listened to, her willingness to submit quickly to the desires of others, and just enough confidence in the therapist to carry through a rough spot in therapy.

The social worker provides invaluable help when the decision must be made about whether or not an infant may safely be left in the care of parents who have injured it, may be left at home provided some other reliable person is constantly there to provide protection, or must be placed in a foster home in custody of juvenile court or child protective agency. Her evaluation of the situation derived from interviews and observation of parent-child interactions in the home is crucially valuable material for use in decision making. Hence, it is usually advisable for a social worker to be involved in care of the patient from the beginning.

Under the present universal system of legal requirement of reporting of injuries to children due to other than accidental means, many segments of our society become involved—law enforcement officials, child protective agencies, probation officers, juvenile courts, prosecutors, social workers, pediatricians, roentgenologists, and psychiatrists. Determining the best means to insure a better future for the abused child and his family, therefore, requires the cooperative effort of many people. It is the task of the physician to determine if injury has occurred, its severity, and whether or not it can be accounted for by purely accidental means. If non-accidental causes can be reasonably suspected, he must report to designated authorities. He will also instigate, hopefully, psychiatric evaluation of the parent or other caretaker. Social workers of the child protective agency, the law enforcement investigator, and the psychiatrist must then share their information and decide if the situation warrants filing a dependency petition and asking for foster home placement of the child. The juvenile court will then need information from all concerned to make a logical decision of dependency, take custody temporarily from the parents, and order placement of the child. Data given to the judge must include justifiable statements that the child has been significantly and unnecessarily injured, that the danger of repeated injury is high, that the home situation is significantly underprotective, and that the caretakers are unlikely to change their behavior in the immediate future. The psychiatrist and social worker can use their special skills in determining the degree of disruption and pathology in the family, marriage, and social situation, and the amenability of the parents to therapeutic intervention while the injured child is in hospital. The child can then be discharged to foster home care or his own home with some degree of confidence. In doubtful cases, the court may take temporary custody of the child but permit the parents to keep it at home under probation which requires continued contact with social worker or psychiatrist and favorable reports from them. In determining the amenability of parents to therapy, it is necessary to remain alert for and to recognize the difference between a usable therapeutic alliance and the ability of abusing parents to readily submit to authority and to rules while retaining great hidden antagonism. Presence of a valid, ongoing alliance with the therapist, be it psychiatrist or social worker, makes leaving the child in the environment where injury occurred a relatively safe procedure. Most parents deeply resent and fight any effort to take their child away from them, and those faced with the task of forcing the separation may feel uneasy and reluctant to do it. We have found much can be accomplished if the social worker, psychiatrist, or other physician who discusses separation with the parents does it without punitive accusation or direct criticism of the parents' behavior, but rather with empathy and consideration. In many cases parents then feel willing, even partly comfortable, about separation as it temporarily relieves them of the burden of helplessly trying to cope with an unmanageable situation.

Too often in the past, severe abuse of children has been managed by separating the child from the parent and placing it in a foster home, and the problem is then considered to be solved. While separation is useful and often an absolutely necessary intervention, it does not in any way deal with the basic issues involved. Sooner or later will arise the question of whether the child can be returned to parental custody. Also, the abusing parents already have or may have in the future other children who can be mistreated. Therefore, effort must be directed not only to handling the immediate situation so as to protect an infant from further abuse, but also toward investigating the total pattern of parent-child interaction in a family and instituting remedial measures. In a similar vein, we are very doubtful of any value in "treating" an abusing parent in the context of criminal law with determination of guilt and the imposition of punishment. If the prosecutor fails to get a conviction, which can easily happen, the parent feels exonerated in his behavior and goes on his way and is highly resistant to treatment. On the other hand, conviction followed by punishment does nothing to really change the parent's character structure and behavior; rather, it is one more reinforcing repetition of the experience of being disregarded, attacked, and commanded to do better—the very things which led him to be an abuser in the first place. As one of our patients put it, "As soon as I get out of the penitentiary, we're going to get out of this state to where we aren't known. Then we'll have some kids and raise them the way we want to."

Summary

Our treatment of those who abuse infants has been directed toward improving the basic pattern of child rearing. It is based upon the hypotheses derived from the study of the psychology of the abusing parents in our study group. We were able to establish useful contact with all but a few of the sixty families, and of this treated group well over three-fourths showed significant improvement. Some changed a great deal, some only moderately, some are still in therapy. We considered it improvement when dangerously severe physical attack of the infant was eliminated and milder physical attack in the form of disciplinary punishment was either eliminated or reduced to a non-injurious minimum. Of equal significance was a reduction in demand upon and criticism of children accompanied by increased recognition of a child as an individual with age-appropriate needs and behavior. Further signs of improvement in the parents were increased abilities to relate to a wider social milieu for pleasurable satisfaction and source of help in time of need rather than looking to their children for such responses. We did not always try nor did we always succeed in making any change in all of the psychological conflicts and character problems of our patients. These were dealt with only as much as the patient wished or as far as we thought necessary in relation to our primary therapeutic goal. Our philosophy of the value of treatment is twofold; first, it deals in the most humanitarian and constructive way we know with a tragic facet of people's lives; second, therapeutic intervention in a process which seems to pass from one generation to the next will hopefully produce changes in patterns of child rearing toward the lessening of unhappiness and tragedy.

Acknowledgment

This study was supported by The Children's Bureau of the Department of Health, Education, and Welfare, Project No. 12:HS, Project 218.

References

1. Kempe, C. H., Silverman, F. N., Steele, B. F., Droegemueller, W., and Silver, H. K. 1962. The battered-child syndrome. *J. Am. Med. Assoc.* 181:17–24.
2. Adelson, Lester. 1961. Slaughter of the innocents. *New Engl. J. Med.* 264:1345–49.
3. Young, L. 1964. *Wednesday's children: A study of child neglect and abuse.* New York: McGraw-Hill.
4. Greengard, Joseph. 1964. The battered child syndrome. *Med. Sci.* 15:82–91.

5. Morris, M. G., and Gould, R. W. 1963. Role reversal: A concept in dealing with the neglected/battered child syndrome. In *The neglected-battered child syndrome*, pp. 29–49. New York: Child Welfare League of America.

6. Kaufman, I. 1962. Psychiatric implications of physical abuse of children in *Protecting the battered child*, pp. 17–22. Denver: Children's Division, American Humane Association.

7. Roaf, R. 1965. Child care in general practice: Trauma in childhood. *Brit. Med. J.* 5449:1541–43.

8. Turner, E. 1964. Battered baby syndrome. *Brit. Med. J.* 5378:308.

9. Cochrane, W. 1965. The battered child syndrome. *Can. J. Public Health* 56:193–96.

10. Storey, B. 1964. The battered child. *Med. J. Australia* 2:789–91.

11. Gjerdrum, K. 1964. The battered child syndrome. *Tidsskr. Norske Laegeforen.* 84:1609–12.

12. Frick, A. 1964. Mistreated small children. *Svenska Lakartidn.* 61:3004–12.

13. Trube-Becker, E. 1964. On child abuse. *Med. Klin.* 59:1649–53.

14. Ferracuti, F., Fontaneu, M., Legramante, A., and Zilli, E. 1965. La sindrome de bambino maltratto. *Quaderni Crimino. Clin.*

15. Antoni, P. 1965. The tormented child syndrome. *Orv. Hetilap.* 106:1934–37.

16. Kuipers, F., *et al.* 1964. Child abuse. *Ned. Tÿdschr Geneesk.* 108:2399–406.

17. Krige, H. N. 1966. The abused child complex and its characteristic X-ray findings. *S. African Med. J.* 40:490–93.

18. Patterson, P. H., *et al.* 1966. Child abuse in Hawaii. *Hawaii Med. J.* 25:395–97.

19. Leonard, M., Rhymes, J., and Solnit, A. 1966. Failure to thrive in infants. *Am. J. Diseases Children* 111:600–612.

20. Barbero, G., Morris, M., and Reford, M. 1963. Malidentification of mother, baby, father relationships expressed in infant failure to thrive. In *The neglected-battered child syndrome*. New York: Child Welfare League of America.

21. Whiting, Beatrice B. Ed. 1963. *Six cultures: Studies of child rearing*. New York and London: John Wiley and Sons.

22. Benedek, T. 1952. *Psychosexual functions in women*. New York: Ronald Press.

23. Deutsch, Helene. 1945. *The psychology of women*. Vol. II. *Motherhood*. New York: Grune & Stratton.

24. Josselyn, I. 1956. Cultural forces, motherliness and fatherliness. *Am. J. Orthopsychiat.* 26:264–71.

25. Benedek, T. 1959. Parenthood as a developmental phase. A contribution to the libido theory. *J. Am. Psychoanal. Assoc.* 7:389–417.

26. Spitz, R. 1950. Relevancy of direct infant observation. *Psychoanal. Study of the Child* 5:66–73.

27. Marquis, D. P. 1931. Can conditioned responses be established in the newborn infant? *J. Genet. Psychol.* 39:479–92.

28. Harlow, H. F., and Harlow, M. K. 1962. The effect of rearing conditions on behavior. *Bull. Menninger Clin.* 26:213–24.

29. Spitz, R. 1945. Hospitalism. *Psychoanal. Study of the Child* 1:53–74.

30. ———. 1946. Hospitalism: A follow-up report. *Psychoanal. Study of the Child* 2:113–17.

31. Robertson, J. 1962. Mothering as an influence on early development. *Psychoanal. Study of the Child* 17:245–64.
32. Benedek, T. 1938. Adaptation to reality in early infancy. *Psychoanal. Quart.* 7:200–215.
33. ———. 1949. The psychosomatic implications of the primary unit: Mother-child. *Am. J. Orthopsychiat.* 19:642–54.
34. ———. 1956. Psychobiological aspects of mothering. *Am. J. Orthopsychiat.* 26:272–78.
35. Erikson, E. 1950. *Childhood and society.* New York: W. W. Norton.
36. Nurse, S. 1964. Familial patterns of parents who abuse their children. *Smith College Studies in Social Work* 35:11–25.
37. Merrill, E. 1962. Physical abuse of children—An agency study. In *Protecting the battered child,* pp. 1–15. Denver: Children's Division, The American Humane Association.
38. Spitz, R. 1958. On the genesis of super-ego components. *Psychoanal. Study of the Child* 13:375–403.
39. Freud, Anna. 1946. *The ego and the mechanisms of defense.* New York: International Universities Press.
40. MacDonald, J. 1963. The threat to kill. *Am. J. Psychiat.* 120:125–30.
41. Erikson, E. 1956. The problem of ego identity. *J. Am. Psychoanal. Assoc.* 4:56–121.
42. Fenichel, O. 1945. *The psychoanalytic theory of neurosis.* New York: W. W. Norton.
43. Zilboorg, G. 1932. Sidelights on parent-child antagonism. *Am. J. Orthopsychiat.* 2:35–43.
44. Milowe, I., and Lourie, R. 1964. The child's role in the battered child syndrome. *J. Pediat.* 65:1079–81.

6 | The Role of the Social Worker

Elizabeth Davoren

5080 Paradise Drive
Tiburon, California 94920

The role of a social worker in the violent, often frightening world of the battered child most frequently has been, and will probably continue to be, the role of "curing." The beginning of the "cure," and at times the only cure of this situation, may be removing the attacked child from his dangerous environment. Those who have done the beating, usually the child's parent or parents, hopefully will be amenable to help so that their other children, if they have them, or the children they may have in the future will not be in danger. The most desirable goal for treatment, of course, is that the child who has been selected for abuse will have it made safe for him to live in his own home.

I was introduced to the study of child abuse by Brandt Steele, who called one day to ask if I would like to visit a couple of mothers who had severely abused their children and find out as much as possible about them and their home situation. At home with my own baby, I was contemplating at least temporary retirement from social work. The opportunity to work occasionally and flexibly seemed a good one, and I looked forward to a research project that I could join with the detachment of a researcher and part-time work that would allow time and energy to be spent on other things. As I write this, four years have passed. The detached, part-time research I undertook became a way of life without my even realizing it, and as I emerge from this "way of life," I welcome the chance to share what I have learned along with Dr. Steele and Dr. Pollock as we attempted to answer the question: What causes anyone to beat a child severely, perhaps killing or maiming him for life?

To answer this question, first we had to ask and answer some others: What are

Mrs. Davoren was the psychiatric social worker who worked with Drs. Steele and Pollock from the onset of their study. She is now a consultant to several social service agencies in California.

people like who severely beat children? How do they appear to others, and how do they appear to themselves? What are their lives like? What, if anything, makes them different from other human beings? How could we go about improving the lot of the adults and children who lived in the remarkably volatile and dangerous situation that led to child abuse? We learned early in our work that the best way to remove the danger of abuse to a child at home was to substitute ourselves as an always-available source of satisfaction to the adults who were threatening the child. That is why our research project turned into a way of life. The people who were slowly and reluctantly becoming our patients were encouraged to call us at any time they felt a need to, and we tried to meet what requests they made whenever it was humanly possible to do so. Because we made ourselves so available, we were able to learn what child beaters were like on a 24-hour-a-day basis—about their personalities and life habits, what situations in their lives were likely to produce crises, how they responded to crises, how they responded to minor provocation, and what kind of minor provocation could turn into a major one from their point of view.

My behavior as an observer-turned-therapist was influenced greatly by the needs of the people with whom we worked. Therefore, although descriptions of our people are presented elsewhere, I should like to describe the characteristics of the patient group that influenced me. Most notable about our people was how much like everyone else they seem to be. To the even not-so-casual observer (at this moment I am thinking of the adoption worker), they are like any cross section of the American population. They are rich, poor, highly intelligent, of low intelligence, educated, uneducated, clean, dirty. They worship in various religions or none at all. Occupations cover a wide range from prestige-associated, high-paying jobs to no job at all. They have many children, or they have only one child. Their relationship to the abused child is one in which they are responsible for the care of the child, and as such they may be parents, foster parents, or even baby sitters. A fair proportion of those we knew were adoptive parents who succeeded in agency adoptions at a time when the demand for children was much greater than the supply. Despite these tremendous differences in their way of life, the child beaters that we came to know did have common characteristics which we believe they share with others who severely beat their children. If knowledge of these characteristics is used intuitively and not as scientific certainty, it can help in discovery and diagnosis and be invaluable in pointing direction in therapy.

The most outstanding characteristic the child beaters share is their attitude toward their children. Understanding this attitude and what it means helps one to make sense of the behavior of these people. The severe beater of children is not capable of seeing the infant or child as an immature human being without capacity for adult perception and behavior patterns. When a mother on our study said, "I taught him not to reach for a spoon when he was three weeks old and he never has," she was seeing a three-week-old infant as being capable of coordinated and controlled hand movements, capable of understanding that her slapping his hands meant he was not to reach for a spoon while she was feeding him, because she did not want the inconvenience of trying to feed a baby with waving arms. Three years later I was having luncheon one day with this mother who by then had her second child. Her seven-month-old daughter was sitting in her high chair, eating with us, holding her hands upright in the air parallel to her body as she ate quickly and well from the spoon that her mother was offering her.

On the same day I visited another mother from our study who had her second child, a seven-month-old daughter, too, and saw the same rigid arm-holding performed. I thought of my seven-month-old son at home, wrestling for the spoon, the cup, the dish, anything within reach, so that the surrounding space, as well as the feeder, was food covered. I envied these young mothers their easy, clean meals. It was probably inevitable, however, that the curiosity of their children was being nipped in the bud by what, for these mothers, was essential child behavior.

Even more than the high expectations of muscular coordination and understanding of orders are the emotional demands on the abused child by the parents. This child, who may be only a few days old, is to provide a climate of warmth and acceptance, and a love for the parent above all things. The parents must be made to feel wanted and competent by the child. The abused child is responsible for creating an atmosphere that allows the parent to have a feeling of comfort and security that he has never had before. It was not unusual for an abusing parent to say: "Nobody has ever loved me. I thought my baby would. When he cries, I feel he doesn't care." It simply did not occur to them that the baby might be crying because he needed something.

The thing that amazed me during my observations in home visits was how responsive most of the abused babies I saw were to this need for comforting. I remember watching an eighteen month old soothe her mother, who was in a high state of anxiety and tears. First she put down the bottle she was sucking. Then she moved about in such a way that she could approach, then touch, and eventually calm her mother down (something I had not been able to begin to do). When she sensed her mother was comfortable again, she walked across the floor, lay down, picked up her bottle, and started sucking it again.

Not only must the child be sensitive to his parents' needs, but he must also obey instantly. One mother had a full day of hysterics because her son did not keep his coat on while he was outdoors. Above all things, the parents must feel in control of the child and not diminished by the child's lack of responsiveness to them. Children are considered sources of gratification for their battering parents. Although they may be well-tended, care takes place without the parents having any feeling for adaptation to the child and the child's wants.

Examples of parental control without sensitivity were evident in the toilet training experiences we observed in our families. For instance, during home visits I watched one of our study mothers go through a series of maneuvers that would allow her to maintain control over her two-and-one-half-year-old son's bowel movements. Phase one consisted of her insisting that he ask her to accompany him to the bathroom. When this pattern was well established, she began belittling him whenever he told her he had to go. "Baby, can't you go to the bathroom yourself? Won't you ever learn, stupid?" He then tried handling bathroom attendance himself, but sometimes failed to get undressed in time. He was severely beaten and reprimanded whenever he had an accident. He was also told, "You just stand there and go in your pants, Mr. Smartypants—that will teach you." He became constipated. Laxatives and enemas were employed, accompanied by beatings for accidents of his overstimulated bowels.

He became more constipated. More laxatives along with increased punishment and bribes finally produced the desired result—complete maternal satisfaction with the amount, time, and place of production of bowel movements. This one example serves to demonstrate not only how keen parental need for personal satisfaction from the child's behavior is, but also what impossible goals are set for the children's past, present, and future.

The significance of what has been said about abusive parental attitudes toward abused children and its relationship to treatment becomes evident when one realizes that *these parents treat their children as they were treated as children.* They had the impossible expected of them, with their needs always secondary to their own parents' needs. They were not recognized as distinct human beings with needs, wishes, and desires of their own. And so they have come to believe that children are born to provide for parents and to solve their problems. And because no child can do this, these parents grow up feeling that they have lived lives of failure and that they are now completely incompetent. Their sense of worthlessness is overwhelming and foremost. Their parents have so dominated them, maneuvered them, and manipulated them that they are afraid to do for themselves. It is not that they look to others to help them; they look to others to criticize them, to outrank them, to show their superiority to them, and to leave them feeling more helpless than ever. For whatever they do, they will never make the mark and attain parental approval.

What does all this add up to? When the child beater is discovered by doctor, neighbor, court, or others and someone in the social, medical, or legal fields is in the position of having to do something, it soon becomes apparent that these are extremely difficult people to reach. The person discovered harming his child fears punishment whether or not the agency pursuing him is punitive. He fears punishment because he views his environment as hostile and punitive. He feels somewhat uncomfortable about hurting his child because he senses environmental disapproval, and also, part of his own being disapproves of what he has done. One mother who feared she would choke her child to death expressed her own feelings about her behavior this way, "Although I love him very much, my nervousness leads me to do things which I often disapprove of at the time, and if I don't disapprove of my actions at the time, I frequently disapprove of them later." She went on to say, "Many times after I beat him he would lie in his crib and cry himself to sleep. I would sit next to the crib and cry and wish I could beat myself." At the time she was talking this way, she had no memory of what provoked her attacks on her child.

Usually the child beater feels quite justified in his abusive behavior. One young man, father of two seriously injured children, told of endless unprovoked punishments by his own father, such as having his head held in the toilet. He explained that it was the way he was brought up and that his parents only wanted him to be well-behaved— they didn't want him to get into any trouble. Yet here he was in prison and for, of all things, the disciplining of his children, whom he was trying to make into well-behaved adults who would not get into trouble. It is hard for such a patient to understand why he is in trouble. What he perceives is that he is being hunted and about to be trapped. That someone might be offering "help" makes the situation even more dangerous.

Help in the true sense was never forthcoming while our patients were growing up.

Gifts and favors from parents—which have been many—have been gifts that the parents needed to give, not what our child beaters needed to receive. Gifts of clothing that didn't fit or furniture that our patients felt ugly or favors accompanied by angry complaints were hard to be grateful for. Yet their parents expected a great deal of gratitude. When taking something they really didn't want in order to please their parents, they felt diminished by the gift and its giver. It's a complicated situation that puts a great deal of demand on the gift receiver. Help? With this background of help, who needs it? And who wants it?

Although a number of our patients were adept at mouthing what they thought we would like them to say and although they found it useful to go through the motions of asking for help, we learned that when help with continuity was offered, it was turned down. This has been the experience of others. For instance, Leontine Young (1), who read many records, writes: "With the parents of the severe abuse group reaction to casework help, including the use of authority was different. There was no evidence in the records that the parents made any relationship with any of the caseworkers. Suspicious, secretive, hostile, they did not discuss anything personal if they could avoid it."

You will usually find the person you want to help responds to your offer with one of two behavior patterns that are familiar to him—flight or submission. If one is offering help in a hospital setting to those who use flight as a defense, the availability of the prospective patient diminishes with each new move to make an appointment, even though the appointment is offered entirely at the patient's convenience. Therapy deteriorates into a footrace down the corridor as therapist tries to prove to the potential therapee that he only wants to help him, not hurt him, and, furthermore, that he is quite capable of helping. If home visiting is the modus operandi, make an appointment with the patient who uses flight as a defense, and you guarantee his absence. Fail to let him know when you are coming, and he somehow fathoms you are coming. If he gets caught at home when you arrive, he hides and doesn't let you know he's there. I have traveled seventy miles to find a woman who "never leaves the house"—gone. I have visited twice weekly for six months at a stretch to leave notes to the parent absenting himself. This sounds pretty tedious, I know, but I should like to add that once those who are fleeing from you stop doing so and are willing to meet with you, you have someone you can really work with. If you do not pursue with persistence, you have no one at all.

A different group, those who submit rather than take flight, allow your presence in their lives from the time you first meet. You may be treated with surly indifference, angry attack, or even fake friendliness. You are no trusted ally, but you are there. I was delighted with the first study patient I saw because she was talkative, and an interview with someone who talks is always easier, or so I thought. After I left the interview, I knew that I had learned very little about the patient from what she said. As I got to know her better, I realized that she used talking to assault people and distance herself from them. It soon becomes evident that this sort of patient is a very self-defeating person. Therefore, if the patient defeats you in the process of defeating himself, remember that he has had lots of practice doing himself in.

Yet another reaction was produced by a third group who were referred to us probably because of our unique research situation. These were parents who asked for help, fearful of the severity with which they were treating their children. At first they seemed open and available for some kind of assistance. But on getting to know them, we learned that they managed to exclude all pertinent data from their discussions or that they gave a great deal of material based on perceptual distortion, or that they lied outright. Very often with this group, as with the submissive group, although you have a dialogue, it tends to be meaningless. Eventually, ways of working around these difficult behaviors were discovered. But before I discuss our work, it might be useful to describe some other characteristics that greatly affected therapy.

Another characteristic shared by abusive parents is that they have very meager relationships with other people. Deeply suspicious of the motives of others and feeling that they will be taken advantage of, they cannot look to family, friends, or neighbors for warmth and understanding. This makes them overtly antagonistic to others. We were faced with this rather forcefully whenever child beaters were hospitalized in our psychopathic hospital. Within a very short time after their arrival, the entire ward, if not the entire hospital, was in an uproar—doctors, nurses, patients, everybody.

Frequently committees of ward personnel would be formed so that "consistent care" would be insured for this difficult patient. The consistent care was usually punitive and reflected the dislike our patients had aroused from those who wanted to like them and help them. In their own homes, many of our patients lived behind closed blinds, closing out everyone else and closing in themselves. There were a surprising number of unlisted telephones. Most of the people we saw managed some sort of relationship with their parents at a tremendous threat to whatever small amount of personal integrity they had managed to muster over the years. Their parents inevitably failed them in crisis and could rarely sense when they were needed; if they did sense it, the abuser's parents ran off in the opposite direction. One young mother, whose baby was hospitalized with subdural hematomas after she had beaten him when he was twenty days old, had been able to arrange with our intervention to have her baby at home for a few hours' visit when he was about three months old. She had not seen her baby since he had left the hospital for foster care, and more important to her than seeing her baby was the fact that her mother should share this visit with her. Her mother arrived very late, and during the time she was there focused her entire attention as well as the attention of others present on herself. Another mother who had broken her stepson's leg, and we believe would have battered her fourth child, her own baby girl, had we not been working with her, gave a party for her parents when she and her husband managed to achieve more financial stability than they had in their entire marriage. Their marriage, in fact, had been a series of financial catastrophes from which her parents rescued them, much to their disadvantage, for it kept her husband from taking the responsibility that he was quite capable of handling. The party was particularly important because it represented an achievement on their own terms. The guests of honor, her parents, never did show up nor did they explain their absence. This illustrates, too, how the parents of our patients tended to denigrate success and emphasize failure in our patients. Because the likeable things about them have not been responded to while they were growing up, these patients do not know how to be likeable nor do they find it easy to like others.

This characteristic of not liking others plays a large role in the marital relationship and may have specific bearing on incidents of abuse. With a great deal of alienation from all facets of life and human companionship, these people are forced to rely almost totally on their marriage and each other. They cannot risk open hostility with each other, and parents who cannot deal directly with each other about the annoyance they may feel for fear of losing what mutually inadequate support they maintain, can and do take out annoyance on the picked-upon child with the full approval of the non-abusing parent. The devotion these parents feel toward one another is accompanied by a great deal of jealousy directed toward anyone of the same sex, regardless of age, who pays attention to their spouses. I remember during one home visit finally being able to reach a father who had been alternately distant and openly antagonistic. Pleasure with this success was brief. The mother went to the bassinet, picked up her urine-soaked, fly-covered baby girl and placed herself quite deliberately between her husband and me, as we sat there on the couch talking. Her message to leave her husband alone was very clear. Another mother refused to see me for over a year after I showed some sympathy toward her husband for his difficult early life in an orphanage. The force behind this jealousy was doubled by the keen competition between the battering parents for mothering and the threat of a rival for the husband's affection. This threat was surmounted in situations when either the husband was given considerably less attention, or our service had become so valuable that the discomfort of the jealousy was more bearable than separation from the worker.

One of the first and foremost therapeutic tools I found was the cultivation of a genuine liking for the patient with whom I wished to work. If you have read the foregoing account of patient characteristics, you might ask, "How do you genuinely like someone who isn't holding still long enough for you to get to know him, who often doesn't like you and is vocal about letting you know it, who is brutal to children, and who isn't very likeable to begin with?" It's not easy. On the contrary, it *is* easy—when going to call on someone like this—to feel unwanted, put off, and a bit uncertain about the whole thing—for in fact, you *are* unwanted, put off, and uncertain. The first rule I make for myself is to ignore the rebuff. It is not a personal attack, anyway, but an attack on the world at large. Be aware before you go that your patient is probably not going to be appealing and be prepared to look earnestly for something, anything, to like about him, no matter how small it is. You use a good deal of yourself in an exercise of this kind. You need to learn to use yourself wisely, by capitalizing on whatever you have in common with the people you see so that you can make your contacts with them genuine and warm. It is very helpful if you can reduce your expectations of patient performance. Our patients had already had too much expected of them. It was easy to see that any demand, no matter how slight, made by anyone in their environment was regarded with unyielding animosity. We, as social workers, frequently expect something from the people we see without being aware of it. We expect to be able to help them, or we expect some kind of response. It is not easy to go in with a total, giving attitude without expecting something in return. These expectations should be diminished because they only serve to infuriate the people with whom you want to work, and your expectations will be doomed to disappointment anyway. At the same time that you are trying not to make even the simplest demand on your patient, it is essential to view him as a person with some capacity and not go along with his low esteem of himself.

Because of the over-domination that child abusers experienced during their lives from infancy on, it is important that a helping person should not take over for the patient. These people are very easy to dominate and often unwittingly encourage domination. They ask for rules and it is easy to put words in their mouths. When they reflect your teachings by mouthing them, you can feel a great success, but such success is empty and misleading. Several things can happen when you become directive or "set limits," as it is often described. If the patient is in a reasonably healthy mood, he will tell you what to do with your "limits." If he is what you expect him to be—an easily dominated human being—he will meet your demands, hate you for them, and take his hatred out on the abused child, if the child is available. If he is in a thoroughly dominatable stage of life, he will do exactly as you wish. You will feel you have accomplished your goal, but that the whole situation would fall apart the minute you step out of it. Our patients had to test over and over again to see whether we would take over, and when they eventually found out that we were willing to behave like trusted friends and not managers they were overjoyed and proud of themselves because someone viewed them as competent.

It is helpful to let the patient know who you are and what you are about. In subtle fashion try to find out what he needs to know about you, and let him know these answers. You need to be willing to share yourself with these patients. They want a great deal from you, but cannot ask for it. In my case what they wanted to know most often was how I felt about my children and how I treated them. I tried to answer their questions as honestly as I could, mentioning mistakes as well as things I did easily for my children. Most patients did not want a detailed explanation of my behavior with my children. They wanted to know their names and ages, what they were like, and if my working meant that I was deserting my children. Usually the people you work with do not want a dossier or a lot of information about you. I think they usually want to learn that you have a degree of competence, but that it is not going to result in your showing them up or lording it over them or feeling superior to them. Eventually, when they get to know you well enough they want to know that you can be fallible and can accept failure without submitting to it as a way of life.

It is essential for the worker to give total interest to the patient. This is not always easy, particularly when the patient is giving back a great deal of misinformation. But complete interest in what another human being has to say is one thing that can be done in a minimum amount of time. Attention is one gift these patients appreciate receiving, and it is a true gift because it eventually can be used for the patient's very own, by turning it to his own advantage as he learns to pay attention to others, particularly his children. I found that it really was essential not to have the child the focal point of one's home visit, even though the child's safety is the reason for contact. The children I have known in our study have been friendly and easy to pay attention to. When I was being ignored or angrily assaulted or regaled with an impossible-to-follow account of the patient's woes, it was difficult to avoid the temptation to play with the children. Such attention to the children can be very threatening, however, to a parent who views your playing with the child as your method of showing him you can handle his child better than he can and thinks that this is your way of trying to belittle him. He also begins to feel frozen out by both you and the child and returns to that horrible nightmare feeling of being unwanted. It is much more useful in the long run to invest your attention in the parents of the beaten children and take care of their needs so that they, in turn, are free enough to take care of their children's needs.

Of the rules I made for myself the one with no exception was that to be useful one must always be open to changing preconceived notions and be wary of inflexibility.

The comforts of seeing patients in hospital interviewing rooms are many and hard to relinquish. You are on familiar ground. The hospital is full of people who know you, talk with you, and welcome your presence. The patient, usually furious with most of the people he has seen in the hospital, for one reason or another or no reason at all, will almost welcome your attempts at being friendly. On the other hand, home visits involve driving long distances to find nobody at home. Home visits are having the door shut in your face on cold, windy days. Home visits are attempting to make others comfortable enough in their own homes to tolerate your presence. Home visits are attempting to get some semblance of a dialogue going above a blaring television set. (Most patients, no matter how poor, had a television set to stare into when they wished to ignore me.) Home visits are also having people yell at their kids, bake bread, clean the bathroom, tend to a hundred other pressing chores so that they can shut you out. But home visits are gold mines of useful information. While attempting to include yourself, you can do lots of observing. Especially, you can see how each parent relates to each child, and how each child relates to him. Although you are regarded as an enemy and a spy, it is surprising how little attempt, if any, is made to change or cover up in any way the adult's behavior with his children. A number of times our people have told their children that just because I was there, they were not going to escape punishment, and so you see such incidents as a mother forcing her children to stand in the sun on a day when it is 103° in the shade, ostensibly because she wants them outside the house and that is the only area where she can watch them from the window.

Probably the hardest single thing I have ever had to do is watch sadistic child handling. We have all watched mothers and fathers beat children or use some other drastic form of punishment in public. It is easy to duck behind the cornflakes or move yourself away from strangers in a grocery store. But when you are working with parent and child, and when you are stuck in a witnessing position, there is no way out. Early in our research I tried to stop parents when they seemed to me extraordinarily cruel toward their children, and although the child had a greater measure of protection while I was there, he was more likely to be assaulted when I wasn't. So, when one mother handled her three year old's terror of separation from her by twisting his arm and hitting him so hard he fell, I kept quiet as he screamed and she said, "I don't know what he's crying about; I barely hit him." I knew that this young woman, deserted by her mother when she was only three, has never been allowed separation anxiety; therefore, she could not tolerate it in her child. My real efforts at protection would be to help her tolerate her own feelings enough to allow them conscious acceptance. This, by the way, has worked. A note received from this young mother is as follows: "If the baby cries, she cries—and for the first time since my four-year-old was born I enjoy the kids. The baby is a character. You have to laugh instead of doing what should be done—spanking." The mother's sense of the need for punishment has remained, but her behavior has changed.

I have tried intervening in quiet ways, interpretive ways, in the "I'm concerned about you" way as well as authoritatively. It never worked; in fact, it made it more difficult to reach the parent and exposed the child to further abuse. I think every worker will have to try for himself, because it is hard to believe that protecting a child when you cannot continue such protection beyond the moment may be the cruelest thing you can do for him.

Some of the agencies dealing with abusive parents are in the position of having to report them to some enforcement agency, such as the police, and then the agency needs to take on treatment after reporting. Although they often did not show it at first, our people were extremely resentful of those who "told on them," and they regarded the reporters as villains and lifelong enemies. We were in the fortunate position of being rescuers, at least during early contacts with our patients. We could side with them against the world and understand them, rather than be part of that misunderstanding world. I think it is very useful to have one person make the report about a family and another person do the treatment. If this is not possible, it will take more skill and stamina on the part of the therapist to make an ally out of an enemy.

An example that shows a reaction typical of a number of our patients is as follows: Two baby boys from one family had been hospitalized repeatedly for treatment of subdural hematomas. When the family's health insurance benefits were used up, the younger child still in hospital was transferred to the university hospital. The family then was referred to our research team by staff members who were not satisfied with the explanation of the cause of both boys' injuries. Our attempts to see this family were refused each time with new excuses about being busy. They failed to keep a late Sunday night appointment they had reluctantly made when they ran out of excuses. We finally gave up, for we had no way to force an office interview or home visit upon them, and they simply did not visit the hospital. Then an unusual thing happened. A couple of the father's relatives reported the mother to the district attorney's office. They said she had cruelly mistreated a three year old daughter. All children were removed from the home and the court pressured the accused family into seeing us. This was no joyous get-together, but these parents gradually allowed us a place, although very small at times, in their lives. Nor do they keep us out now that their children are back, as they have every one else involved in what has been for them an extremely painful situation. They have fled from every one of the father's relatives, refusing to see or talk with them, probably forever. The welfare department, attorneys, judge, personnel in our hospital, and other hospitals are heartily hated by these people. Even though we were openly suspicious, we managed to get something going between us. We were not substantial rescuers in this situation, because we had to say often that we could not in good conscience support the return of their children. However, we had not been the ones who had told either.

It is true that some parents are relieved to have their child protected, even when that protection is from their own abuse. But these feelings of relief are accompanied by a great deal of ambivalence. One must remember that to these people, children primarily represent a source of gratification. Sometimes the relationship has deteriorated to the point where the child is someone to take things out on, rather than a provider of good things for the parent. But being the scapegoat is a function, and an important one, too.

When you take that child away, no matter how much grief you may be saving everyone, you are representing a depriving parent—someone who is taking something away, someone who says that the patient about to be treated has no rights (which he actually believes himself). It is much easier to get to know the patient as a "treater"—the one who is going to help him get his child back after removal, the one who allies with his having things rather than with taking things away from him.

The question of what signs were there of improvement in the people with whom we worked requires an answer to: What do you mean by improvement? With our people improvement meant that the children were out of danger of being severely hurt, or, with the children in more benign situations, that they were less likely to be physically punished and abused emotionally. A change for the better that could be counted on, that would not be easily reversed, was usually preceded or accompanied by a marked improvement in the family's economic stability—no matter how economically successful the family had been originally. In each instance of such improvement, the bread-winner not only received more money for his work, but also found himself in a job situation that was much more to his liking than his previous job. If this was a result of treatment, and we surmise it was in most if not all instances, it was usually not a result of direct work with the father. It may be that as the mother made less demands on him, the father was able to release some of his energy to improve life, and she also was able to go along with this improvement. The activities of our patients became more useful to them, and they developed a capacity for fun-seeking. They stopped doing things that brought them more anguish than satisfaction. One mother, for instance, turned from exasperating committee work to what was for her very creative—ceramics; another took swimming classes and art lessons instead of sitting around with her mother and listening to her complain; another turned from preoccupation with psychosomatic illness and pill-taking and sleeping all the time to jelly making, vegetable growing, and projects with her children. Some of the mothers were able to establish much more meaningful relationships with their own mothers by using their newfound strengths to reject what they did not like and look for what they could enjoy about their mothers. Their mothers, in turn, began to enjoy, rather than control them. Regarding their mothers as someone they could really like—even though they would continue to be disappointed in what their mothers did to them or did not do for them —was a most important step.

Most of the mothers in our study talked with me quite openly about my giving them the mothering they had never had before. That they could use me as a mother, whether or not they talked about it, was an important step. But until they could feel some comfort about their own mothers, they continued to have personal doubts about their ability to take good care of their children. As a further prelude to acceptance of themselves came more compassion for their mothers, and/or mothers-in-law, or whatever sort of mothering women existed in their lives. This compassion was very different from the excuses made by some of our people in their early contacts. Early there were some who felt it essential to protect the illusions they had about their parents. One of our patients who was very protective of her mother's image and very careful not to complain, slipped one day when telling about her own responsibility for her younger twin brothers and said, "If mother only could have come home from work just once and said something nice instead of always being critical . . . ." She quickly covered up by saying she did not mean what she said and went on to talk about her mother's good qualities. She could not develop compassion for her mother because she could not look at her mother critically without feeling too attacked herself.

A giant gain in the lives of our patients as they improved was a new capacity for friendship. With some patients a first step was that I was treated as a friend. I was invited to lunch, given presents, called by my first name. I was asked more personal questions about my life. It is helpful if you can accept this kind of relationship with ease. Its intensity will not last long. The patients will have other friends who are more available than you are and who do not threaten to improve them. Eventually the social worker is dumped as a friend and reserved for emergencies as a therapist—as a friendly therapist.

Another early sign that the patient feels better about himself is that he takes a delight in your having a relationship with his child. There are no threats to parenting and prestige in the household if you and the children enjoy each other. At about this same time, the children tend to be less well-behaved and, of course, less disciplined. They still tend to be more inhibited and less rambunctious than the usual child in our culture.

The experience of our small research group with treatment cannot be duplicated by the agencies dealing with child abuse throughout the country. Large case loads preclude some of the individual attention that we were able to give, and few will have the inclination to make themselves available twenty-four hours a day to a group of very demanding patients. The purpose of our performance was to learn by gaining intensive knowledge of our patients' day-by-day living—their behavior in crisis and their reaction to their minute-by-minute environment. I believe what we learned can be adapted so that others can produce results with this type of patient without making the investment of time and effort that we did. For example, most of our work was done with the threatened child or children in the home. At times the abused child was kept in his own home because we felt it was feasible with our surveillance and the involvement of family and friends. We also tended to feel at first that removing the child might make work with the parents all but impossible and that it would jar existing relationships within the family in such a way that they would be permanently damaged. Although we did not continue to feel separation was undesirable, many of the people with whom we worked had no intention of relinquishing their children, even for a very brief time, and with meager court evidence their wishes were decisive. An advantage of leaving the child home was that disruption in the life of the child and the parents was not necessary. A disadvantage, of course, was that there was danger to the child unless a great deal of attention was paid to the situation. Where there is potential danger to the child, unless there is a very responsible relative who can oversee the situation, it will save time and energy for the therapist to have the child removed until he can feel reasonably sure the child will be safe. We used relatives to help where continuous observation was necessary to save the child's life and where no other solution would have been acceptable to the family. These were situations where for lack of evidence no court could have intervened.

There is the factor of the child's removal being viewed punitively by the abusing parent, and if you have to do the removing, you become part of that punitive world.

However, there are advantages. When parents no longer short-circuit their feelings toward each other through the child, they are forced to face some of these feelings rather directly. Without exception in my experience, when a parent has discussed the temporary or permanent removal of a beaten child, he or she has said to me, "If he goes, I will lose my husband" or "I will lose my wife." My interpretation of this is that the child is such an integral part of the marriage that it cannot be visualized without the child. Interestingly, one of the reasons expressed by a number of patients who wanted their child back was that they were concerned about what others would think of them for not having all their children at home. Their major concern was for how their lives looked rather than how they themselves felt. Usually, when a child is removed from the home, parents have a strong drive to have him returned. This can become an enormously motivating factor for therapy.

There has always been a shortage of trained, experienced social workers. Agency supervisors would quite rightly want to use the most experienced therapist possible to work with patients as difficult to work with as abusive parents are. It is true that the patients in our study reacted to the very young, inexperienced, and uncertain workers with considerable discomfort. Feeling so unsure themselves, our patients could not tolerate much unsureness in others. However, for the therapist's temperament to be suited to the needs of these patients could go a long way toward substituting for experience. Characteristics in a worker that I think would be useful for work with abusive parents are:

> A person with few, if any, managerial tendencies.
> Someone who is willing to put himself out for patients, but who does not go around sacrificing himself much to everyone's discomfort.
> Someone who has a fair number of satisfactions in his life besides his job so that he won't be looking to the patients to provide these satisfactions.
> Someone with a strong working knowledge of child behavior that can be shared with abusive parents at appropriate times.

There are excellent books that document what can be expected of infants and older children. Rene Spitz's writings are particularly helpful in giving understanding of the resources of infants (2–6). Children's Bureau Pamphlets (7–9), the Arnold Gesell and Frances Ilg books (10, 11), Benjamin Spock's writings (12), and the pediatric handbook by Drs. Silver and Kempe (13) give a substantial grasp of what the baby and growing child are like. A. S. Neill's (14, 15) keen respect for children and his ability to view them without moralizing about their behavior has allowed him some unusual insights about natural child behavior. Konrad Lorenz's (16) understanding of aggression relates loosely, but usefully, to human as well as animal interaction on all levels. Marian Morris (17) gives excellent clues for observation of mother–baby interaction. This is obviously no survey of available writings on important data on the baby and growing child, but it does represent what I found personally useful over a period of years of work with children. My own children have been of similar ages to the children with whom we worked on the battered child study, and I learned a great deal from them. In addition to reading, if the worker is not around children in his everyday life it would be helpful for him to spend some time with children of the same ages as those he is helping.

It would be helpful to have workers, who are particularly good listeners, who can observe as well as listen, and who will not need to draw strength for themselves by feeling superior to the people with whom they work.

We usually had two therapists constantly available to each patient, one psychiatrist and the caseworker. Having more than one person available for the patient to turn to is a saving for everyone involved. It saves wear and tear on both therapist and patient alike. It is particularly helpful for a patient who is learning to handle his anger with adults for the first time in an overt fashion to have more than one person to turn to. Some agencies may be able to provide more than one helper on their own staff, but if this is not possible there may be visiting nurses, doctors, teachers, or others in the community who can be enlisted to involve themselves with one or more patients.

Turnover in agency personnel often does not allow long-term casework with one person. If the change in workers brings with it a keen interest on the part of the new worker and a willingness to pursue the patient anew to help, a change will not necessarily be detrimental to the work that is being attempted.

What alternative is there for the amount of time that we spent with some of our patients? Deep, penetrating attention can go a long way in fulfilling needs for large amounts of attention. As the patients in our study got to know us and trust us, they had to know that we were willing to put ourselves out for them. Putting oneself out does not necessarily mean taking the calls around the clock as we did or racing out to the patient's home at a moment's notice. But the patient will know when you interrupt an interview or take a call at home from him from time to time in order to alleviate his anxiety. I saw one of the mothers on our study for three years, putting up with every inconvenience that one human being could cause another. These inconveniences included calls on every holiday with demands that I do something about a large variety of medical conditions despite the availability of two doctors to her at all times on our own staff, as well as many other doctors whom she could easily reach. She frequently called threatening to kill her children, and although this was not likely, it was not impossible, either. No matter how much time was spent, it never seemed to be enough. One time after I had moved away, however, I came back to visit her, and her feeling that I was doing this on my own time without its being my job made the visit something she could really use for her own.

I have tried the technique of providing food for patients only in a very limited way. This technique can be effective, I believe, but it must be done with sensitivity. For instance, I took one mother to a restaurant from time to time where she ordered tea. Had I offered her candy as I did a few other patients, she might have liked it, but she despised herself for her obesity, and it would have put her in an intolerable position to offer her fattening food. The key when giving or doing anything for these patients is that it must be done with unusual awareness of their needs, likes, wishes.

Probably the most unnerving experience any social worker could have would be to do a thorough, careful adoptive study and later discover the adoptive parents to be child batterers. What can adoption agencies do to avoid placement with potentially abusive parents? This is a hard question to answer. We were helpless when a judge awarded final adoption papers on a year-old child who had had 17 mysterious leg fractures. The family had refused all contact with us and we had no way of pressing it. All we could do was support the welfare agency to recommend against adoption, but obviously this was not enough. We did not have the opportunity to go over any agency's complete adoptive study of the parent who subsequently battered a child. Usually these records were not available to outsiders, and there were so many pressing demands on our time that we could not pursue some of the detailed study we should like to have made. Agency personnel willingly talked with us of their studies and their impressions and also sent summaries of their studies. From one such summary, a quote about the adoptive father—"He felt his parents were not overly demonstrative toward their children, but had a feeling for training them to be industrious and responsible Christians." For parents to have such an attitude toward their children is probably not unusual, but when the major feeling that comes through about an individual's upbringing is its sternness, this is at least a clue to the adoptive worker for very careful investigation.

In the adoptive study it would probably be very useful to go into a detailed investigation of the mothering that potential adoptive parents themselves have received. If innocuous questions that provoke significant answers could be developed in the area of "what have you learned about mothering?" it would be useful in all adoptive work. Infants and older children are usually placed for probationary periods of six months to a year before adoption becomes final. During this time an adoption worker can watch for any serious injuries. It might be helpful to have babies given their first year of medical care by the agency's pediatrician. The children could be carefully observed this way for growth development and injuries. I think it is very important for adoptions to be done in a climate of warmth and acceptance of potential adoptive parents, and it is not easy to be warm and suspicious at the same time. That is why it is exceptionally hard to answer the question of how to protect children and yet do adoptions in such a way that potential parents can be helped to feel warmth and love in all directions rather than feel like insects on a pin.

Our work with battering parents demanded a great deal from us, and at times not only failed to improve the family's situation but seemed to make things even worse for everybody. We frequently felt like "battered therapists." The babies were safer, but in the beginning we were not even sure of that. We often did not know what we were doing and why. We only knew we had to do something. We made mistakes, painful ones that lost us some of our patients and their progress for long periods of time. But when our patients began to make the kind of changes that would have lasting effects in their lives and their children's, it was exciting and unbelievably rewarding.

Not long ago when I revisited Denver and spent time with some of our patients, one of them called our secretary to ask if she would secretly find out what flower I liked best. Our patient had a basket of daisies sent to where I was staying with this line that she found in a book of quotations: "He is our friend who loves more than admires us."

References

1. Young, Leontine. 1964. *Wednesday's children: A study of child neglect and abuse.* New York: McGraw-Hill.

2. Spitz, Rene A. 1949. The role of ecological factors in emotional development in infancy. *Child Develop.* 20 (no. 3, Sept.).

3. ———. 1951. Purposive grasping. *J. Personality* 1 (no. 2, April).

4. ———. 1955. The primal cavity. *Psychoanalytic Study of the Child* 10.

5. ———. 1958. On the genesis of superego components. *Psychoanalytic Study of the Child* 13.

6. ———. 1959. *The genetic field theory of ego formation.* New York: International Universities Press.

7. Children's Bureau. 1955. *Infant care*, publication no. 8. Washington: United States Department of Health, Education, and Welfare.

8. ———. 1945 (revised). *Your child from one to six*, publication no. 30. Washington: Social Security Administration.

9. ———. 1949. *Your child from six to twelve*, publication no. 324. Washington: Social Security Administration.

10. Gesell, Arnold, and Ilg, Frances L. 1943. *Infant and child in the culture of today.* New York: Harper and Bros.

11. ———. 1946. *The child from five to ten.* New York: Harper and Bros.

12. Spock, Benjamin. 1946. *The pocket book of baby and child care.* New York: Pocket Books.

13. Silver, Henry K., Kempe, C. Henry, and Kempe, Ruth S. 1958 and 1960. *Healthy babies, happy parents.* New York: McGraw-Hill.

14. Neill, A. S. 1960. *Summerhill: A radical approach to child rearing.* New York: Hart.

15. ———. 1966. *Freedom—Not license.* New York: Hart.

16. Lorenz, Konrad. 1966. *On aggression.* New York: Harcourt, Brace & World.

17. Morris, Marian 1966. Psychological miscarriage: An end to mother love. *Transaction* (Jan.-Feb.).

PART 4

Legal Aspects

7 | The Law and Abused Children

Monrad G. Paulsen

Dean, School of Law
University of Virginia
Charlottesville, Virginia 22901

Law as well as medicine is concerned with child abuse. Legislators have formulated a set of social responses to such cases, designed to prevent repetition of the incident, to protect the victim's siblings, and to deter others who might be tempted to harm their children.

The Responses of the Law to Child Abuse[1]

A physician who comes to suspect that he is treating a battered child has an obvious interest in understanding the main outline of the law's attempt to protect children from abuse. Of primary significance are four sets of legal provisions:

  1. Provisions of the criminal law, which can be invoked to punish persons who have inflicted harm upon children.
  2. Juvenile court acts, which universally provide that when there is evidence of abuse, parents or other caretakers may be found to have "neglected" a child. After an adjudication of neglect the juvenile court may institute protective supervision of the child or order his removal from the home.
  3. Legislation, in many states, which authorizes or establishes "protective services" for abused and neglected children as a part of a comprehensive program of public child welfare services.

Mr. Paulsen was professor of law at Columbia and was director, Columbia Study of Child-Abuse Reporting Laws. He now is Dean and John B. Minor Professor of Law, University of Virginia School of Law.
  [1] This portion of the chapter is a revised version of a piece already published by the author: *The Legal Protections Against Child Abuse*, CHILDREN 42 (March–April 1966).

4. Child abuse reporting laws, now existing in every state, encourage the reporting of suspected child abuse so that the other provisions for the protection of children can be called into play.

The Criminal Law

The child abuse problem does not require new criminal legislation. Murder, mayhem, assault, and battery, even when committed by parents, are punishable crimes in every state criminal code. Furthermore, existing criminal laws expressly forbid "cruelty to children" in those very words, or in a similar phrase. State legislatures often forget these facts, however, when the public, stirred up by newspaper reports of sensational cases, demands new, but unnecessary, punitive laws.

In any event, criminal sanctions are a poor means of preventing child abuse. Day-to-day family life, charged with the most intimate emotions, is not likely to be an area of life easily ruled by the threat of fines or imprisonment. A criminal proceeding may punish an offender who deserves punishment, but it may also divide rather than unite a family. The criminal law can destroy a child's family relationship; it cannot preserve or rebuild it. The most severe cases of child abuse may call for prosecution, but the prosecutors often are not able to arrange for the care a child needs.

A criminal prosecution is a clumsy affair. The proceedings take a great deal of time —for the prosecutor to prepare his case, for postponements to serve the convenience of the defense, the judge, or the witnesses. Convictions are not easy to obtain because guilt is hard to prove, particularly in child abuse cases, since the abuse usually takes place in the absence of witnesses who will testify. The case against a defendant must be proved beyond a reasonable doubt.

The public prosecutor exercises a very great discretion in the prosecution of criminal cases. Not all parents who have assaulted their child will be tried on criminal charges. In any given case the prosecutor may very well judge that the matter is best handled in a juvenile court or a family court should there be one. Perhaps the biggest difficulty which the prosecutor faces if he decides that the parent should be dealt with by an agency other than the criminal court is the fact that the prosecutor is an elected official who may feel the need to respond to public pressure in a highly publicized and sensational case.

The beginning of a prosecution is likely to be the end of a chance to improve a child's home situation. Parents are nearly always resentful of the proceeding. The hostility engendered makes casework with the child's family all but impossible if the offending parent is still in the home.

All in all, criminal sanctions can do little to help a child. The major problems concern his care and custody.

The Juvenile Court

In every state statutory provisions give juvenile courts power over "neglected" children. And in every state, irrespective of the particular legislative language of the juvenile court act, a parent's physical mistreatment of a child is legally a form of "neglect." The neglect provisions, however, vary. Some of the states focus on the behavior of the caretaker; a neglected child is one whose parents "subjected him to cruelty or depravity." Other states stress the child's surroundings: "A neglected child is one who is not provided with a home or suitable place of abode, or whose home is unfit for him by reason of neglect, cruelty or depravity of either of his parents . . . ." Some states simply draw attention to the child himself; a neglected child is one "who is subject to cruel and inhuman treatment and shows the effect of being physically mistreated."

The differences in statutory language are important. The words tell us precisely what evidence is necessary to make out a case of neglect. For example, in states which define neglect in terms of the misconduct of parents, a neglect case can be proved only by adducing evidence of parental involvement. In these states neglect adjudications are not possible in some cases because the injuries cannot be tied to the conduct of the parents. Although juvenile courts in most states only require proof by a preponderance of the evidence and not proof beyond a reasonable doubt, this standard must be met by legally sufficient evidence. Situations about which objective items of proof cannot be produced cannot be remedied in court.

In many instances, however, the judges are overly timid in how they view the evidence. Adjudications of neglect can properly rest on circumstantial evidence. Inferences of parental fault can properly be drawn—for example, from the young age of the victim, the number and nature of the injuries, the place where they were incurred, the unconvincing parental explanations, and the fact that the parents were the injured child's custodians and hence in proximity to him most of the time. Not every legal remedy need rest on the testimony of an eyewitness.

A recent opinion of Judge Harold A. Felix of the Family Court of the State of New York is especially significant because he permitted circumstantial evidence to put a burden of "satisfactory explanation" on the child's parents. In denying a motion to dismiss a neglect petition, Judge Felix wrote that the

> . . . proceeding . . . was initiated undoubtedly by a consensus of view, medical and social agency, that the child Freddie, only a month old, presented a case of a battered child syndrome. Proof of abuse by a parent or parents is difficult because such actions ordinarily occur in the privacy of the home without outside witnesses. Objective study of the problem of the battered child which has become an increasingly critical one has pointed up a number of propositions, among them, that usually it is only one child in the family who is the victim; that parents tend to protect each other and resist outside inquiry and interference; and that the adult who has injured a child tends to repeat such action and suffers no remorse for his conduct.
>
> Therefore in this type of proceedings affecting a battered child syndrome, I am borrowing from the evidentiary law of negligence the principle of "res ipsa loquitur" and accepting the proposition that the condition of the child speaks for itself, thus permitting an inference of neglect to be drawn from proof of the child's age and condition, and that the latter is such as in the ordinary course of things does not happen if the parent who has the responsibility and control of an infant is protective and non-abusive. And without satisfactory explanation I would be constrained to make a finding of fact of neglect on the part of a parent or parents and thus afford the court the opportunity to inquiry [*sic*] into any mental, physical, or emotional inadequacies of the parents and/or to enlist any guidance or counseling the parents might need. This is the court's responsibility to the child.[2]

Statutes which define neglect in terms of a child's environment do not present the same difficulty of proof as do those which address themselves to the parents' conduct.

[2] In the Matter of S, 259 N.Y.S. 2d 16Y (Fam. Ct. 1965).

The fact that several injuries have occurred under inadequately explained circumstances can suffice to show that a child's "environment is injurious to his welfare."

Juvenile court judges have a wide range of powers designed to give the highest practicable degree of flexibility in making dispositional decisions. A judge may warn parents or counsel them. He may order medical or psychiatric treatment for the child or the parents. He may place the child under protective supervision in his own home. He may remove the child from his parents, should that extreme step be necessary. The judge also has ample power to act quickly in emergencies, but, unfortunately, a fast judicial response to emergencies may not, in fact, take place because a juvenile court judge may not be readily available.

Another important point is to see the relationship between this wide range of powers and the evidence required to establish a case of neglect. Proof of neglect really involves answering two questions: What really happened, and are the "facts" to be characterized as "neglect?" What a judge is likely to characterize as "neglect" will, I believe, depend upon the action which he feels called upon to take.

The point to be grasped in Judge Felix's opinion is that he was not contemplating removal of the infant when he entered his judgment. Juvenile court judges surely are affected by a sense that the action taken by the court order must be related to the seriousness of parental unfitness as demonstrated by the evidence. A severe spanking by a mother, harassed by the problems of everyday living, might sustain a neglect adjudication if the court were to make the adjudication to expedite further inquiry or to supply social services through the probation staff. It would hardly sustain the judgment if the court were to take the child away from home for any but the briefest period.

If the parents are represented by a lawyer in neglect proceedings it may be expected that proof of physical abuse will be more difficult, simply because the evidence will be probed and tested by the challenging questioning of an attorney. This questioning, with its aggressive stance, is frequently distasteful to physicians. It seems like a poor way to "get at the truth," yet it is based upon the faith that a tribunal will approximate truth (as close as any system allows), if the interested parties produce the evidence which they find favorable to their claims and the opposing side tests the strength of the case by adversary methods such as cross-examination. While a lawyer for parents may well counsel parents against asserting every legal right because to do so may disadvantage a child, the parents undoubtedly have the right to insist that their position under the law be firmly asserted. If the lawyer decides that he cannot conscientiously advocate his client's position, he should step aside. Even parents who abuse their children are entitled to the right of counsel to represent their interests as they see it—not counsel out of sympathy with their point of view.

The full use of juvenile court powers can keep a child in his home and still offer protection by providing official intervention into family life. The United States Children's Bureau has warned that protective supervision "should not be allowed to degenerate into mere watchfulness" but should be "a purposeful activity directed toward the improvement of the child's situation through the use of established casework techniques and the utilization of other community resources."[3]

[3] U.S. Department of Health, Education, and Welfare, Social Security Administration, Children's Bureau: Standards for Specialized Courts Dealing with Children. C.B. publication, No. 346, 1954.

We should not forget, however, that many families will resent such official intervention. Court ordered protective supervision contains an important element of authority. Therefore, orders of protective supervision should be periodically reviewed by the juvenile court with a view to termination if the intervention is no longer necessary. Indeed, the New York Family Court Act limits the duration of an order of supervision in a neglect case to a period of one year unless "the court finds at the conclusion of that period that exceptional circumstances require an extension thereof for an additional year."[4]

The problem of the juvenile court judges in abuse cases, of course, is to balance the interests of the parents against the likelihood of new harm to the child. No task is more difficult than predicting the recurrence of behavior which can endanger a child. The "balancing of interests" is made more difficult for a judge who is considering whether to take a child from his parents when the degree of parental involvement in the child's injury is not perfectly clear.

Nevertheless, leaving in his home a child who bears the marks of unusual injuries which seem to have been intentionally inflicted is taking a chance with the child's life. Not all doubts should be resolved in favor of parents. Those who seek a court order to remove a child from a dangerous situation should not have to disprove every plausible explanation for the child's wounds. Temporary removal is not the same as a permanent change of custody. Parents who accept and profit by protective intervention can and do regain custody of their children when new evidence suggests that they are able to care for them properly. Parents have a right to their children, but their children have a right to live.

Protective Services

In many states, the law has provided for "protective services" as a part of public programs of comprehensive child welfare services. In addition, the states have granted charters to voluntary agencies to carry out protective services.

Protective services aim at effecting constructive change within the family in which there has been child neglect or abuse so that the child's environment may be improved. A key point is that the offer of services is made as a result of a complaint or referral from someone in the community and not usually at the request of one or both of the child's parents. Some of the parents most in need of assistance would never seek such help voluntarily.

Child protective services are offered without a court order although they may, in some instances, be identical with the services provided in protective supervision ordered by the court.

The Children's Bureau has proposed that a state or local welfare department be required to:

> Investigate complaints of neglect, abuse, or abandonment of children and youth by parents, guardians, custodians, or persons serving in loco parentis; and on the basis of the findings of such investigation, offer social services to such parents, guardians, custodians, or persons serving in loco parentis in relation to the problem, or bring the

---

[4] New York Family Court Act, Sec. 354.

situation to the attention of a law enforcement agency, an appropriate court, or another community agency.[5]

Thus, under proper child protective legislation, a welfare department would be *required* to "investigate" and to "offer social services" to families in cases of alleged child abuse. But the duty does not stop there. The offer of service may be refused. If so, the welfare department can "bring the situation to the attention" of others, including a juvenile court.

In some states, the laws require that protective services be established; in others, the services are merely authorized, leaving the final decision to local units of government. In any case, if the public welfare agency is to provide protective services to investigate complaints and serve abused and neglected children, the legislature must not only mandate or authorize these services but must also provide appropriations to make them a reality.

The "reaching out" with protective services, whether by a public welfare department or a voluntary agency, presents a problem which the good motives of the agency ought not to obscure. If help is offered when it is not wanted, the offer may contain an element of coercion. There is a danger of overreaching when the agency deals with the most vulnerable members of the community who may easily be cowed by apparent authority. The extent to which the offering of protective services should be reviewed by some judicial or administrative agency is beyond the scope of this chapter. Here, it is appropriate merely to note the problem. The privacy of a family ought not to be upset lightly.

Reporting Laws

Whatever protection the criminal law, the juvenile court, or child protective services can offer to children, it can be offered only in respect to known instances of abuse or neglect. Bringing suspected cases to the attention of community authorities has been inhibited by many factors. Children, generally, cannot or do not speak out. Neighbors and friends hesitate to make accusations. An abusive father or mother, facile with explanations, often escapes discovery because of the common assumption, "Certainly these respectable people couldn't do such a terrible thing to their children." The statutes which encourage the reporting of suspected cases are an integral part of the law's attempt to protect children.

The Main Characteristics of Child-Abuse–Reporting Legislation

Child abuse reporting laws are now in effect in every American state, in the District of Columbia, and in the Virgin Islands.[6] These statutes seek to facilitate the discovery of

[5] U.S. Department of Health, Education, and Welfare, Social Security Administration, Children's Bureau: Proposals for Drafting Principles and Suggested Language for Legislation on Public Child Welfare and Youth Services (1957). (Multilithed.)

[6] See also Paulsen, *The Legal Framework for Child Protection*, 66 Colum. L. Rev. 679 (1966); and Paulsen, *Child Abuse Reporting Laws: The Shape of the Legislation*, 67 Colum. L. Rev. (1967). The legislative background is discussed in Paulsen, Parker, and Adelman, *Child Abuse Reporting Laws: Some Legislative History*, 34 Geo. Wash. L. Rev. 482 (1966). For an earlier analysis of the professional

instances of suspected child abuse by requiring (or expressly permitting)[7] physicians and others to report their suspicions in appropriate cases. To encourage compliance with the statute, the reporter is given a certain degree of immunity from the legal liability which might flow from making a report. After the making of a report, the statutes all contemplate that appropriate action will be taken by some agency, public or voluntary; hopefully, the steps taken subsequent to the report diminish the prospect of further injury to the child and his siblings.

State legislatures were offered four legislative models. These formulations have been suggested by the United States Children's Bureau,[8] the Council of State Governments,[9] the American Humane Association,[10] and the American Medical Association.[11] By far the most influential model has been that of the Children's Bureau.

Who Should Make Reports

The Legislative Models

The model legislation offered by the Children's Bureau placed a primary duty to report on physicians, including osteopaths, interns, and residents, although staff physicians would merely be required to "notify" the hospital administration which would in turn honor the reporting requirement. The advisory committee to the Children's Committee of the American Humane Association suggested that the reporting requirement extend to "hospital personnel coming into contact with children. This Council of State Governments recommended that registered nurses—examining, attending or treating . . . a child in the absence of a physician" be required to report while the official position of the American Medical Association insisted that reporting be encouraged on the part of "any registered nurse, any visiting nurse, any school teacher or any social worker acting in his or her official capacity."

The Children's Bureau limited the reporting requirement to doctors for a number of reasons. First, the Bureau embraced the view that abused children most frequently come to public attention when a caretaker seeks medical assistance for a child. In particular, reporting by physicians was perceived as a protection of the very young who could neither run away from abuse nor talk and reveal the abuser. Second, the proposed legislation sought to uncover those cases of child injury which a physician—

literature and the legislative issues see McCoid, *The Battered Child and Other Assaults upon the Family* (Pt. 1), 50 MINN. L. REV. 1 (1965). The research supporting these publications was made possible through a grant by the U.S. Department of Health, Education, and Welfare, Child Research and Demonstration Grants Program No. R-194.

[7] See the laws of New Mexico, North Carolina, and Texas. A "permissive" statute extends to the reporter immunity from any legal liability for reporting. A mandatory law not only gives immunity but requires reporting.

[8] U.S. Department of Health, Education and Welfare, Welfare Administration, Children's Bureau: The Abused Child—Principles and Suggested Language for Legislation on Reporting of the Physically Abused Child (1963). (Hereafter: Children's Bureau, Principles for Legislation.)

[9] The American Humane Association, Children's Division: Guidelines for Legislation To Protect the Battered Child. Denver, Colo. (1963). (Hereafter AHA Guidelines.)

[10] Council of State Governments: Program of Suggested State Legislation. Chicago, Ill. (1965). (Hereafter: Council, Program of Legislation.)

[11] American Medical Association: Physical Abuse of Children—Suggested Legislation. Chicago, Ill. (1965). (Mimeographed.) (Hereafter: AMA, Suggested Legislation.)

because of his special skill and training—might come to suspect as instances of child abuse. In many cases, only the diagnostic ability of a physician is a sensitive enough instrument to sort out discrepancies between a child's physical state and the caretaker's explanation of the event. Because the proposal was aimed at requiring physicians to report professional insights gained during a medical examination, the notion that others should be required to report was beside the point. Furthermore, it was felt that physicians had failed to report in the past for reasons which did not deter other groups such as teachers and social workers who, in fact, seemed to have brought to public attention those instances of suspected abuse which they recognized. It was feared that a good many physicians felt that reporting was either mere "meddling" or a violation of a "professional confidence." The legislative reporting requirement was designed to overcome inaction based on either opinion, as well as on the reluctance of physicians to "become involved" in proceedings which end in court and require their appearance as a witness. It is likely that some physicians were also deterred by a fear of civil liability should they report, a fear which can be diminished by enacting a statutory immunity from liability.[12]

In short, the purpose of the Bureau's draft was to bring to light the cases hidden to all but the expert, to pinpoint a physician's professional duty to protect children by reporting, and to establish that a doctor ought not, by remaining silent, assist those who mistreat children. There was also the concern that a broadly based mandatory reporting duty might overwhelm social welfare agencies with reports requiring at least a threshold investigation—a point not wholly consistent with the observation that other groups have been reporting suspected cases.

The proposal that nurses should make reports is obviously not designed to uncover those cases which only a physician's skill can uncover. The suggestion is out of character in the sense that nurses generally take only such responsibility as an attending physician delegates. It is perhaps for this reason that the Council of State Governments limited the reporting duty to nurses acting in the absence of a physician.

The American Medical Association position agreed against limiting reporting to physicians, in part, on the ground if doctors alone were to report, parents and other custodians of children would fail to bring their children in for needed medical care. While this point would seem to argue against any reporting by physicians, AMA representatives felt that a broader list of reporters might blunt the impact of publicity which otherwise might stress the reporting role of physicians and hence deter parents from bringing a child to a hospital. Limiting the class of reporters was also seen as a sign of an incomplete plan for dealing with the question of child abuse. Thus, an editorial in the *Journal of the American Medical Association* warned that "it is unwise to draft and adopt statutes which fail to come to grips with the entire problem."

Recently, a study published by the American Humane Association has embraced the view, contrary to the views of the advisers to the Association's Children's Committee, that reporting should become a duty of all persons. "If we accept the concept," the study asserts, "that casefinding is a universal obligation of all responsible citizens

---

[12] "In the child-abuse situation, there not only is a fear of liability, but also a fear of the loss of valuable time, and perhaps the expression of a determination not to get involved with the police or legal authorities." H. Foster, *Lawmen, Medicine and Good Samaritans*, 52 A.B.A.J. 223, 226 (1966).

and all community agencies . . . the translation of that obligation into legislation is truly appropriate."[13]

Although such a moral duty may be admitted, a reporting statute's proper function is neither to enlarge the potential for casefinding, nor to articulate a moral duty, but to spur reporting and, hence, actual casefinding. Arguably, physicians encounter the great bulk of the most serious child abuse cases, yet fail to report many of them. If physicians can be persuaded to report the cases which come to their attention, a most important gain will have been made. The legislation therefore should focus upon the physician's duty, moral and professional, to report and should assist in establishing practical programs to encourage reporting—for instance, educational programs directed to physicians and the setting up of simple administrative ways of handling reports. A duty laid upon "any person" is not likely to appear as a direction to a physician's conscience. The medical doctor who sees a suspected case of child abuse faces professional problems not encountered by "any person." The law should assist him in resolving the questions in such a way that he will cooperate with those social and legal agencies which seek to assure the protection of children against mistreatment.

The Legislation in the States

In all the states having child abuse legislation, medical doctors are covered by reporting laws, either by express terms referring to them or because they are obviously in the class "any person."

The statutes of several states,[14] the Virgin Islands, and the District of Columbia essentially embrace the position of the Children's Bureau draft and limit the reporting duty (or limit the encouragement to reporting which a grant of immunity from legal liability can provide) to persons giving some form of "medical" or "health" care—from physicians, surgeons, residents and interns, osteopaths, and chiropractors, to hospitals or hospital administrators. In these states the list of reporters reflects the state's judgment about the kind of training required to practice the art of healing. Illinois, for example, requires podiatrists and Christian Science practitioners to report; Washington permits reporting by "chiropodists," Iowa by "optometrists." In twelve states dentists are expressly called upon to report cases.

The list of reporters is often extended to engage in activities auxiliary to the practitioners of the healing arts. Twenty-one states list varying classes of nurses; five list pharmacists and two expressly include "laboratory technicians."

A review of the legislation indicates that many lawmakers have failed to find persuasive reason for limiting the reporting duty to those who might discover cases in the course of a health examination. Like the AMA draft, a number of states expressly have required (or encouraged) reporting by teachers or school administrators and by welfare or social workers. South Dakota and Maryland list law enforcement officers and Arkansas, coroners. Attorneys and clergymen must report in Nevada, and clergymen are named in the law of New Mexico as well.

[13] Children's Division, American Humane Ass'n., Child Abuse Legislation 17 (1966).
[14] Arizona, Colorado, Delaware, Florida, Idaho, Illinois, Louisiana, Maine, Massachusetts, Michigan, New Jersey, Oregon, Rhode Island, South Carolina, Vermont.

Many states [15] have made the duty to report universal by requiring disclosure by any person who possesses knowledge of a child abuse. In Arkansas, Iowa, and Maryland a statutory list of professionals *must* report, but any person *may* provide information, an arrangement which extends immunity against legal liability to a volunteer who reports in good faith. A 1966 amendment to the California reporting law neither requires nor expressly authorizes reporting by the director of a county welfare department, but extends immunity from civil or criminal liability should he do so.

The case for confining mandatory reporting to physicians is a strong one. The mandate speaks to the problems which doctors face in particular and which are likely to inhibit reporting. The rest of us are not bound by similar concerns about professional responsibility. Some of us might fail to speak, however, for fear of facing a successful tort action based on libel, slander, or an invasion of the right to privacy. Therefore, there is much to commend a scheme which requires physicians to report, but clothes every reporter who acts in good faith with immunity from civil and criminal liability. While generally we should not wish to encourage the "snooping" neighbor to report his acquaintances to public officials, the possibility of ending a child's agony ought to allow an exception in this case. In fact, without legislation, it is likely that a "good faith" report of apparent criminal conduct to officials is privileged.

Should Reporting Be Permissive or Mandatory?

The legislatures in a very few states having child abuse reporting laws do not require reporting but encourage it by the device or providing immunity from legal liability for calling suspected cases to the attention of an authorized report receiver.

Some physicians have objected to mandatory reporting on the ground that it would deprive them of making the judgment not to report in a given case where sound medical reasons existed for that decision. Indeed, the 1963 version of the California reporting law expressly authorized this use of a physician's discretion: "The physician and surgeon shall not be required to report as provided herein if in his opinion it would not be consistent with the health, care or treatment of the minor."

However, the case for mandatory reporting rests upon the judgment that the decision to report is not properly a medical matter; it is a matter of social policy. It is thought better, on balance, that all cases of reasonably suspected child abuse should be investigated by a welfare agency carrying the function of protecting children, by the juvenile court authorities, or by the police.

Mandatory reporting, it must be remembered, does give support to physicians whose patients criticize them for alerting the authority. In February, 1966, the Committee on Infant and Pre-School Child of The American Academy of Pediatrics supported mandatory reporting largely on such a ground. "The widespread dissemination of the fact that the physician is legally mandated to report a case of suspected child abuse should also remove, or at least reduce, the parents' resentment." [16] Furthermore, without mandatory reporting, the chances for an accurate statistical picture of the phenomenon of child abuse is greatly lessened.

[15] E.g., Indiana, Nebraska, Tennessee, Utah, and Alabama.

[16] Committee on Infant and Pre-School Child, American Academy of Pediatrics, *Maltreatment of Children, the Physically Abused Child*, 37 PEDIATRICS 377, 380 (1966).

Do reporting laws deter parents from seeking medical aid because they fear involvement in a case of suspected abuse? Clearly the reporting laws will have an impact different from those requiring that a gunshot wound be reported. In the latter case victims will come to physicians for help because their own lives are at stake. Parents are not presented with danger to their own persons. While we do not know (and probably can never know) how many parents fail to take children to hospitals because they fear reporting, it obviously does occur. In the case of a mother suspected of child abuse, the Supreme Court of California has written, "defendant indicated to the police that she had not called the doctor because she feared that he might report her."[17]

On balance, mandatory reporting provides a considerable social gain. It will spur some reporting. It protects physicians and reminds them of their professional obligation to assist children in trouble. The number of parents who are willing to risk the life of their child by not seeking medical help is likely to be small. Many of those who inflict deliberate injury in moments of tension, high passion, or psychological imbalance will respond to a child's obvious need in later, calmer times. Perhaps most important of all, the reporting laws have encouraged reporting by providing an easy, well publicized way of doing it and by encouraging educational projects among physicians in respect to the nature and extent of the problem.

Over half of the mandatory reporting statutes carry penal sanctions for failure to report. Penalties expressed in child abuse laws themselves run the gamut from Vermont's "not more than $25.00" to the Virgin Islands' "not exceeding $500.00 . . . not exceeding one year or both." In California, Florida, Nevada, and Oklahoma the penal sanction is not set forth in the reporting laws themselves. Since the laws are found in the respective penal codes, they are subject to general provisions setting the penalties for all offenses in the code for which no penalty has been provided.

Some physicians object to these penal sanctions on the ground that the integrity of professional people ought not to be impugned by the suggestion that criminal measures are required to insure that they do their duty. Furthermore, doctors who examine children ought not to be subject to the risk of a criminal prosecution. The latter argument carries little force. Prosecutors will be reluctant to act, especially since conviction will be difficult. Most of the statutes impose a penalty only for "knowing" and "willful" violations. There is, indeed, little reason for placing a criminal punishment in the law except that its presence may strengthen the point that parents will find a physician's action in reporting more palatable if it is required by law.

What Are the Reportable Injuries?

The Nature of the Injury

Physicians (and others) who are required or encouraged to report ought not to be asked to play detective. A physician can often make a reasonable guess that the injuries suffered were not caused by unavoidable accident but it is beyond his professional competence to determine who inflicted injuries on a child. In making the judgment that

---

[17] People v. Forbes, 44 Cal. Reptr. 753, 755, 402 P. 2d 825, 827 (1966). A Virginia statute passed at the same time as the reporting law makes it a misdemeanor for anyone to "knowingly (fail or refuse) to secure prompt and adequate medical attention" for a child.

the injury was no accident, a child's age, his general state of health, the character of the injury suffered, evidence of prior fractures at varying stages of healing, and a disproportionate amount of soft-tissue injury are all items of evidence which a physician can compare with the family's account of how the child was hurt.

Some of the states have followed the formulation of the Children's Bureau in asking physicians to report "serious physical injury or injuries inflicted upon him other than by accidental means by a parent or other person responsible for his care."

Several points should be noted respecting this language. Only "serious" injuries are to be reported. While a "minor" injury may signal a pathological family situation, in most cases it will not. To invoke the investigative and child-protective machinery in such instances would be uneconomic. The formulation seeks only the reporting of "physical" as opposed to "emotional" harm. The day may come when emotional abuse can be documented readily by any physician who examines a child, but that time is not yet.

Unhappily, the language does require a reporting physician to make a judgment respecting the identity of the wrongdoer. Undoubtedly these phrases were put into the law so that doctors would not report intentional injuries inflicted by someone outside the family. Presumably, responsible parents will provide sufficient child protection in such cases. This point can be met by a proviso, however, which would permit a doctor to omit reporting if he has formed the opinion the injury was inflicted (without parental neglect or complicity) by someone other than a caretaker. He would not have to perform a detective's role in every case.

Perhaps the most satisfactory language in the actual legislation is found in Arizona and North Dakota where, following the principle of the Guidelines, reports are to be made of injuries "not explainable by the available medical history as being accidental in nature." One difficulty with this formulation is that some "accidental" injuries ought to be reported. If caretakers are so inattentive that a child is regularly placed in a situation of great risk to his safety, there is an obvious case for public intervention to improve the situation.

The overwhelming number of statutes do not define the terms "abuse" and "neglect." There is no need to be overly technical on the part of a physician who is puzzled whether to report a case. A physician's commonsense definition will do. His task is simply to report *suspected* cases. Any drastic action such as removing the child from the custody of parents or punishing parents will be decided upon by others.

Curiously, none of the reporting laws asks for a report on a child who has been killed through abusive conduct, except perhaps by implication, in Arkansas where coroners must report. While death ends the possibility of protecting the particular child, an investigation of the circumstances and the family may bring assistance to the remaining children. Furthermore, an adequate statistical record requires the inclusion of such occurrences. The lack in the statutory texts has been remedied in some places by a practice of reporting deaths.

Several states encourage the reporting of malnutrition cases. Indeed, it would not strain the typical statutory language to include malnutrition as a form of serious physical abuse or neglect. There is little reason not to require the reporting of children who are suffering from severe malnutrition. It is perfectly true that there are a great many possible reasons why a youngster does not flourish on a food intake completely adequate for a normal child, yet physicians must frequently form the opinion that a state of malnutrition is the result of parental inattention. When such cases occur, there is as great a need for social intervention as in the case of physical brutality. In *Biddle* v. *Commonwealth*,[18] a three-month-old baby died from malnutrition and dehydration because of his mother's failure to feed him, a failure related to marital difficulties with her husband. She fed the child only at times when she and her husband "got along well together." Had the youngster been brought to the hospital in time, and had the attending physician formed the opinion that his physical state suggested lack of nourishment for which there was no adequate explanation except failure to follow a proper feeding regimen, a report to an agency capable of giving the child protection might well have saved a life and a family.

The Reporter's State of Mind

So far we have discussed the nature of the injury to be reported. A further question is how certain the reporter should be before he is required or encouraged by a permissive statute to report. Here a curious statutory lapse is apparent. Generally the laws require (or permit) reporting if the physician has "reasonable grounds" or "reasonable cause" to "believe" or "suspect" that a reportable injury has occurred. But they do not speak to the question whether the physician (or other person) is mandated to report only if he actually believes or holds the opinion that such grounds or cause exist. Under the existing statutes, taken literally, a physician may be *required* to report a case in respect to which reasonable grounds to believe (or "suspect") abuse may be present, but the doctor does not, himself, hold that opinion. In theory then, some of the statutes which carry criminal actions for failure to report impose strict liability. Surely no one would be prosecuted for failure to comply with the literal command of the law, but the point should be put right if only as a matter of drafting aesthetics.

To summarize, in the writer's view, a physician should be required to report if he *forms the opinion* that he has reasonable grounds to suspect that a child's injury was not the result of unavoidable accident—provided that the physician need not report if he has formed the opinion that the injury was inflicted by someone other than a caretaker. Again, the proviso is added because normally a parent, rather than a representative of the community, can be relied upon to afford adequate protection against the aggressive acts of third persons.

The Religious Exemption

The statute of some states and the legislation applicable to the District of Columbia provide that a child should not be reported because injuries or illnesses are being treated by spiritual means or prayer. In the District of Columbia hearings on child abuse reporting the formal position of the Christian Scientist was spelled out by representatives who urged that any child receiving treatment by the practices of Christian Science should not be "considered to have suffered physical harm due to neglect."

[18] 206 Va. 14, 141 S.E.2d 710 (1964).

J. Buroughs Stokes, the manager of the Christian Science Committee on Publication in Washington, D.C., made his denomination's point as follows:

> Christian Scientists, as you may know, rely exclusively on prayer or spiritual means for healing. This method of healing has been practiced for nearly 100 years and is without legal restrictions in any state in the Union, including the District of Columbia. Christian Science parents, when their children get sick, do not neglect them and are just as desirous as other parents to see them well again. In this, they provide a system of health care which they have found to be most efficacious and successful and which is a recognized alternative to medical treatment.[19]

In a society which prides itself on religious freedom, the exemption is bound to be troublesome. Most of us have little faith in spiritual healing, but for those who do, the conviction may be at the center of their lives. Generally, we permit parents to provide for their children in the light of conscience, interfering only when a parent's indifference or brutality indicates that the trust has been misplaced. Many who seek religious healing will be among those most devoted to their children. On the other hand, we know that some religious healers are quacks, and some parents who limit their response to injury and illness to spiritual means are seriously stricken with mental illness. The statutes reflect a compromise between these competing considerations by requiring that the attempt to heal be in "good faith," or by means of "Christian Science," or by the teachings of a "well-recognized religion." The exemptions do go too far. Physicians should be required to report cases of harm related to situations of attempted healing by religious means if they form the opinion that life is in danger. This would reflect policy judgments made in other areas of the law.

The Statutory Plan for Handling Reports

In almost all the states reporters are instructed to make an immediate oral statement followed by a written report. Aside from a handful of states, the statutes outline the contents of a report generally asking that it include the name and address of the child, the name and address of the parents, the nature and extent of the injuries, the evidence of prior injuries and the extent thereof, and any information which might help to identify the perpetrator.

What is actually done when a report is received is the all-important question, since the purpose of the child abuse reporting laws is to trigger constructive action so that a child's life may be lived in safety.

Three aspects of the reporting laws influence what will happen after a report is made. First, the method of handling cases will depend, to some extent, upon which agency receives the report under the statute—a law enforcement agency, the prosecutor, the Department of Social Welfare, or the juvenile court.

Secondly, the law may contain a declaration of purpose which, while not technically binding on anyone, may be of great importance in shaping the actual course of practice. There are three general types of purpose clauses found in the legislation. The first, exemplified by the law of Delaware, merely states that the purpose is to "protect" children; a second type found in the Arkansas statute states the purpose to be "causing

---

[19] Hearings on H.R. 3394, H.R. 3411, and H.R. 3814 Before Subcommittee No. 3 of the House Committee on the District of Columbia, 89th Cong. 1st Sess. 36 (1965).

the protective services of the state to be brought to bear" in the effort to protect children; the third, similar to a Colorado formulation, speaks of an aim to invoke "protective services" in order that we may "prevent further abuses, safeguard and enhance the welfare of such children, and preserve family life wherever possible."

Finally, the reporting law may contain explicit legislative directions respecting the action to be taken.

In some states the primary tasks of receiving a child abuse report, of investigating the circumstances which prompted it, and of taking appropriate action in response, are expressly placed upon a public or voluntary child welfare agency. In other instances, reporting laws place primary responsibility for action on a welfare agency but also contemplate a role for law enforcement. For example, the law enforcement authority may be the report recipient although the statute directs the law enforcement agency to forward the report to the welfare agency or the law enforcement agency may be given the duties of investigation. Sometimes both law enforcement and welfare agencies are given responsibility for investigating the case. In a great many states reports are to be made to the police or the local sheriff.

In five states principal responsibility for handling cases of alleged child abuse is placed on local prosecutors. The principal decisions about handling a child abuse report are to be made by juvenile courts under the statutes of seven states, and in nine a reporting physician (or other person) is given a choice between two or more agencies which wield different powers and carry on different functions (for example, the prosecutor and a welfare agency). In Oregon, all reports are received by the "appropriate medical investigator."

The point to be underscored is that reported cases may be handled quite differently depending upon the normal role and function of the report receiver. For example, many social workers (and others) believe that all reports should be made to the public or voluntary child welfare service which carries the child protective function in the community. A report of the American Humane Association has set forth the reasons:

> Of all the possible investigative agencies in a community to which reports of child abuse cases might be made, the Child Protective agency is best qualified to focus on the problem of "what happens to children" in these circumstances. This involves a professional and skilled evaluation of the continuing hazards and dangers to child victims of abuse and whether removal from parental custody is indicated. Where removal of children is considered necessary such action will be commenced in the appropriate court. Where removal is not seen to be necessary the community would be assured that services are extended to parents to help remove the causes of their abusive behavior and to help them assume more responsible parent roles.
>
> In making this position statement the committee is fully aware of and recognizes the responsibility of the police and other law enforcement agencies in assessing the community's action against the parents; and the decisive role played by the Juvenile Court, particularly when immediate protection and removal of custody are made necessary by the risk of continuing hazard to children.[20]

A chief reason for selecting the police as the report receiver is pointed out in a commentary accompanying the published text of the model law of the Children's Bureau, "At present, law enforcement constitutes the only chain of services which is

---

[20] A.H.A., *Guidelines* 10.

sure to exist in every community and within reach of any medical personnel given responsibility for this reporting." The commentary goes on to recognize that discretion is placed in the police to determine the steps to be taken after a report is filed.

> Upon receipt of such a report, the law enforcement official may follow any of several measures to assure care and protection of the child. He may make the investigation himself and place the child in protective care for which provision has already been made. Or he may refer the child's case to a voluntary or public social agency given this responsibility by law. Such an agency would make the investigation and take responsibility for the immediate care of the child, if necessary.[21]

Several objections have been made to the use of police as report receivers. An investigation by police is likely to appear oriented toward punishment rather than "invoking the protective social services." Further, the appearance of a police officer may so terrify parents that their cooperation in improving a child's environment is lost forever.

In the second place, the person who makes the investigation will have to make a series of decisions. Should the case be sent to juvenile court? Should the child be removed from home? Should he remain in the hospital? What is the best tack to take in handling this set of family problems? These are not decisions which should be made by policemen. The issues call for skill and experience in working with families in difficulty. Captain Carl Hamm of the Youth Aid Bureau of the Milwaukee Police Department has made the point:

> While the police officer is the first on the scene and trained to prepare a case for court, he is not trained to make the decision as to whether or not the child or children should be removed from the home; what services are necessary to sustain the family; nor is he empowered to command the necessary services to keep the family together.[22]

In contrast, some observers favor reporting to the police on the grounds that child abuse frequently does involve a violation of the criminal law whether we like it or not and that law enforcement officials are charged with specific responsibility in respect to such a matter. Further, it is said the police are, in practice, far more understanding of the human problems involved in child abuse cases than is ordinarily recognized. Finally, these observers point to the scarcity of trained welfare workers and argue that they should not be diverted from their proper task to perform police-type investigation for which they are untrained and which can only destroy the desired rapport with their clients.

It should be pointed out the Children's Bureau now favors reporting to welfare agencies in those places where protective services are adequate.

Those states which have provided for reporting to the juvenile court have yielded to still a different set of considerations. Planning for a family in which the pathology of child abuse has appeared requires the efficient use of authority, they would point out. Decisions about the child should not be taken in several separate places lest the

[21] Children's Bureau, Principles for Legislation 3–4.
[22] Remarks of Carl Hamm, Bureau of Maternal and Child Health, Milwaukee, Wis., Health Dept. Public Health Conference, May 1, 1964, at 4. (Mimeographed.)

case be lost in confusion and by the participation of too many persons with too many different professional points of views. After an incident of abuse has occurred, a plan for handling should be agreed upon. If the plan fails the authority of the court should be invoked immediately. Only if all cases are handled in a court context will such efficiency be achieved.

There is another point. In some states the services of social workers may only be available through the juvenile court. Where that is true, the court's early involvement is obviously desirable.

The case against early juvenile court involvement has been stated in the newly published (by the Children's Bureau) *Standards for Juvenile and Family Courts.*

> The individual or agency who has received the complaint, made the investigation, and requested authorization from the court to initiate a petition is responsible for providing the evidence to support the allegations made in the petition. It seems clear that investigation, as defined here, and the initiating of a petition are not appropriate functions of the court. A court through the use of its own staff should not be placed in the position of investigator and petitioner and also act as the tribunal deciding the validity of the allegations in the petition.

Fundamentally, the properly trained social worker experienced in offering child protection services ought to be the most expert on the question whether, in a given case, the coercive measures of a court are required or whether the family and the child can be adequately cared for by casework or other social services. Juvenile court judges, most of them without special training in social work techniques, are unlikely to be better evaluators of these situations. It is true that offering protective services does invade a family's privacy. Fairness to the parents suggests that they be given an easy way to secure a juvenile court's decision as to whether the offer of service is justified. Yet that fact does not argue for juvenile court supervision of every case which involves protective services.

Providing for reports to the prosecutor is clearly a more unfortunate legislative choice than reporting to the police. Many prosecutors, elected officials, are sure to be conviction-oriented. A large police department might, at least, have a special detail specializing in youth work.

If a state permits the reporter a choice, let us say, of reporting either to the welfare department or the juvenile court, it has arranged for numerous disadvantageous consequences—a certain confusion is created for the reporter, statistics are more difficult to assemble, and, most important of all, similar cases may be handled quite differently, depending upon where the report is sent.

If the practice of exclusive reporting to the department of social welfare were adopted as the best plan, the social investigators ought then to be given a definite set of responsibilities under the law—including the legal power to remove a child temporarily in situations of extreme emergency—just as the police are expressly given in some states, including New York. Child welfare agencies carrying a children's protective service function typically utilize aggressive social casework techniques. The agency "reaches out" into the lives of clients without waiting to be asked. An agency's authority to employ such techniques ought to be clearly defined and limited according to the standards which generally govern the use of authority and power by governmental agencies.

The express directions for action when a case of abuse is reported can be quite complex. The elaborate character of the Nevada law will provide an example. Others can be found in the statutory tables in Appendix B.

In Nevada reports are received by the police department or sheriff's office. These agencies are mandated to investigate and "forthwith refer such report to the local office of the welfare division of the department of health and welfare." Upon receipt of the report the welfare division is instructed to investigate the circumstances surrounding the injury, its cause, the identity of the person responsible, and provide "such social services as are necessary to protect the child and preserve the family." The division is also to advise the law enforcement agency of its investigation. The division is expressly authorized to refer the case to the district attorney for criminal prosecution or to file a petition in dependency in the juvenile court should such action be thought necessary. Obviously the provision for reporting to the law enforcement agency and for an investigation by that agency provides an opportunity for the exercise of law enforcement discretion respecting action to be taken in a case quite independently of whatever law enforcement or prosecutorial action might arise from the welfare department's own investigation. Further, under the Nevada statute a law enforcement official may not remove a child from his home without consulting with welfare unless the police believe immediate removal is required to prevent further injury.

Central Registries

The maintenance of a community-wide or state-wide central registry of reported information in child abuse cases is, in the opinion of many physicians and social workers, an important part of a program designed to deal with child abuse. In six states provision is made for a registry. The purposes which a central index can serve will depend upon what material is placed in it and what persons have access to this information.

Purposes

A registry can provide data for statistical studies. In addition to yielding information about the incidence of child abuse, the reports filed will indicate the age and sex of the abused child, the nature of the injuries, the identity and some characteristics of the child abuser, and other material, which can provide a collection of facts upon which researchers can draw. In the long run, the data might yield conclusions of great practical importance respecting the management of child abuse cases.

A registry can be helpful to the child-protective workers who are investigating the circumstances surrounding a reported case. Information respecting prior reports is obviously useful in deciding how serious the situation may be within a given family. Prior information may help form the basis of a social worker's decision whether he should refer the case to the juvenile court (or the criminal court) for action or whether the offering of protective services is sufficient. A central registry also reduces the possibility that parents who have abused their child on several occasions may hide the situation by moving from doctor to doctor and hospital to hospital. To the extent that "hospital skipping" is a problem, it is important that the registry cover a wide geographical area. It may even become desirable to keep records on a nationwide basis.

Proponents of a central registry have argued that the device may be of assistance in identifying whether a given case brought to a physician's attention is a case of child abuse or whether the injury had probably been incurred in some other way. Thus, a physician who looks at the nature of the injuries, studies the evidence from X rays, and is puzzled by an implausible story given by parents, may still not be persuaded that he has "reasonable cause to suspect" that the injury is not accidental in such a case. To most physicians another doctor's prior report to the authorities will seem relevant at such a moment. A previous incident, similar in kind, may turn doubt to relative certainty in assessing a suspected case.

The uses to which a central registry may be put can be seen by considering the situation in Illinois.

The Illinois Department of Children and Family Services is directed to maintain a central registry of cases "reported under this act." In Illinois practice an oral report either by phone or in person must be made "immediately" to the nearest office of the Department of Children and Family Services, and a written report must be mailed within twenty-four hours after the physician's examination. The Department has provided a form on which welfare workers record briefly the information contained in the oral report. This form, as well as a copy of the later written report, is sent to Springfield and filed in the central registry.

In Illinois the regional office of the Department is responsible for the investigation of the case. Within ten days the regional office is required to report to Springfield headquarters in respect to the results of the investigation and the service which has been initiated as a result of a report respecting suspected child abuse, other information—the report from the field records information about the family, the explanation for the injuries to the child, and any other history of child neglect or abuse that can be discovered—is also recorded on a prepared form and is placed in the central registry. The requirement of the follow-up report is obviously useful in the day-to-day administration of the social service program. It provides a constant check on the promptness of work done by the regional office. If the follow-up report is not forwarded within ten days, the administrator is alerted to inquire about the delay.

The Illinois central registry only includes these reports which are made in compliance with the Illinois reporting law. While the department investigates other reports which are ultimately verified, the facts respecting such investigations are not filed in the Springfield registry but are only recorded in the normal welfare files; they are not classified differently from other protective or general welfare cases, even though physical abuse is clearly involved. Limiting the information recorded in this way can be defended on the ground that the principal purpose of the registry is to provide statistics regarding the effectiveness of reporting legislation in respect to child abuse cases. Yet, statistics based on entries in the registry do not give a full picture of the child abuse problem in Illinois. This practice limits the usefulness of the registry as a general statistical tool, as an aid in diagnosing whether a given case is a case of child abuse, and as a record of the family problems expressed in the infliction of injuries upon the young.

The Illinois registry is strictly confidential. Only case workers and department staff have access to it—not physicians who may be seeking additional evidence to support their suspicions about a given injury. Presumably a physician could receive information about the circumstances surrounding a child's prior injuries by requesting a social worker in the field to obtain information for him. It was reported that in the first four months of the registry's operation, welfare department workers requested information from the central registry in slightly over fifty instances.

There is no procedure for deleting information once it is recorded on the central registry. Illinois department officials are of the opinion that no one is harmed by irrevocable recording because the record is available only to a small group of the professionals responsible. The danger of unjustifiable harm to reputation arising from a mistake in diagnosis is, of course, minimized in Illinois because the results of the department's investigation is recorded along with the reported facts giving rise to the initiation of investigation.

By administrative action additional registries have been established in several places. In New York City a city-wide registry was established by order of the Commissioner of Welfare. In Cincinnati the Community Health and Welfare Council have voluntarily set up a "Red X" file to enable hospitals, physicians, and law enforcement agencies to identify children who have been harmed on more than one occasion. The "Red X" file includes cases where there are suspicious indications of conditions which "could be the result of an inflicted injury or severe neglect" but in which definite evidence cannot be determined immediately. In Denver and in Los Angeles confidential indices are also kept recording cases of "suspicion" not sufficiently definite to justify an immediate social investigation. Some states have set up statewide central registry by administrative decision for statistical purposes.

The existence of a central registry used for anything but statistical purposes raises sensitive issues of privacy. Some means should be found to remove from the registry the cases in which abuse was found not to have occurred. An entry in the registry can bring an unjustified loss of reputation. "Authorized persons" are, after all, human beings who may react adversely to parents listed in the registry; further, no firm assurances can be given that the registry will only be available to authorized persons. In 1966, the Committee on Infant and Pre-School Child of the American Academy of Pediatrics has made a suggestion which may commend itself: "This problem (of removing names from the central registry) might be solved if all reports are held in a temporary file and moved to a permanent one only when the suspicion is found to be based on fact, or when there continues to be doubt as to guilt of the parent." [23]

Another source of possible unfair treatment to parents is presented when a registry is used by a physician who, uncertain whether his present patient has been abused, seeks to discover if another physician has made a report earlier. Although the fact of a prior report is some evidence that the present instance may be a case of abuse, the report may be given undue weight by the physician. The danger is enhanced by the kind of central registry which records instances of reporter's (usually a physician) "suspicion" that there may have been abuse in a given case where the reporter's firmness of opinion is thought insufficient to justify an investigation with its attendant

[23] Committee on Infant and Pre-School Child, American Academy of Pediatrics, 37 PEDIATRICS 377, 380 (1966).

invasion of family privacy. This sort of registry has been described in information from Los Angeles:

> An experimental registry is operated for several Los Angeles hospitals by the State Health Department. This registry is primarily a diagnostic tool—a channel for communication between physicians. Only "mildly suspicious" cases are reported. A participating hospital may check the registry when a new case arrives. The name of the doctor and hospital reporting a previous incident is furnished so that detailed inquiry can be made directly at the reporting source.[24]

In such a scheme, two not very firm opinions might very well add up to "reasonable belief." Considering the fact that belief, formed in this manner, may be the occasion for a serious invasion of family privacy by a public agency, we ought to set up only registries which record opinions strong enough to have triggered some community response.

The Legal Problems of a Reporting Physician

Liability for Violating a Professional Confidence

"There is a Murderer in My Waiting Room," is the title of an emotion-charged article appearing in *Medical Economics* for August 24, 1964. "This is," states a paragraph of puffery preceding the text, "a true and shocking story of child abuse and the legal helplessness of the doctor who was confronted by it." The physician's sense of "legal helplessness" stemmed from the supposed fact that if he were to say "one word to the prosecutor's office about this case," the mother could sue the doctor "right up to the eyeballs for violating a privileged communication." The article goes on to hope that the governor will sign a child abuse reporting law which would make it mandatory for physicians and hospitals to report all cases of suspected child abuse and offer immunity from legal liability to the reporting physician. In this article, as in similar popular literature, the doctor's plight is much overdrawn. He need not have suffered the sense of "legal helplessness" under the existing law, because a doctor who reports in good faith is privileged to do so.

Physicians, although aware of the need to uncover and correct family situations in which children are abused, are concerned whether reporting in the absence of statutory immunity, will involve them in lawsuits with outraged parents. In a sense, this concern cannot be dispelled because no one can predict when anyone will bring an action. Persons may sue, although there is no possibility of success. As we shall see, however, the chances for the parents to recover damages are slim. Parental counterattack in court will not add appreciably to the premium paid for insurance against liability arising out of medical practice.

It is true that a smattering of reported decisions have indicated the existence of a legally enforceable duty binding on physicians not to give out facts or statements respecting their patients learned in the course of a physician–patient relationship. The

[24] Minutes of a meeting called in San Francisco on April 1, 1965, by the Bureau of Maternal and Child Health, Dept. of Public Health of California, at 1. (Mimeographed.)

liability sometimes has been based on a state statute authorizing the licensing of physicians where a license may be revoked because of "unprofessional or dishonorable conduct" which in turn is defined as "a betrayal of a professional secret to the detriment of the patient."[25] Other courts have based similar liability on state statutes establishing a physician-patient testimonial privilege,[26] still others on a judicial consideration of the "ethical concepts" underlying the practice of medicine.[27] Those courts, however, which have recognized civil liability for a physician's breach of confidence have clarified the basis for the imposition of liability by protecting the physician who reports in good faith to serve his patient's interest or the interest of the public.

The tort cases on a physician's duty not to reveal information about a patient comes to this: a basis for legal liability does generally exist but if the disclosure is made to protect certain legitimate interests of the patient or another person affected by the patient's condition the disclosure is privileged.

> Where life, safety, well-being or other important interest is in jeopardy, one having information which could protect against the hazard may have a conditional privilege to reveal information for such purpose. . . .
> One purveying such information about one person to protect another is obliged to consider the likelihood and the extent of benefit to the recipient, if the matter is true, as compared with the likelihood of injury and the extent thereof to the subject, if it proves false, or improper to reveal. Whether the privilege exists, depends upon generally accepted standards of decent conduct. Applying that standard, it exists if the recipient has the type of interest in the matter, and the publisher stands in such a relation to him, that it would reasonably be considered the duty of the publisher to give the information. . . .
> The privilege we are here concerned with is referred to as a "conditional" or "qualified" privilege. The reason for the limiting adjectives is that it must be exercised with certain cautions: (a) it must be done in good faith and reasonable care must be exercised as to its truth, (b) likewise, the information must be reported fairly, (c) only such information should be conveyed, and (d) only to such persons as are necessary to the purpose.[28]

Child abuse reporting laws attempt to provide additional protection for the reporting physician by means of clauses offering express immunity from legal liability for reporting. The various statutes contain three general kinds of immunity clauses.

The reporting laws in the states contain three general kinds of immunity clauses. In some states immunity from civil and criminal liability for reporting and for participating in subsequent judicial proceedings is provided without any express qualification. In another group immunity is given for action taken "in good faith" or "without malice." In still another, meeting the "good faith" standard is aided by a presumption of good faith. The immunity conferred under any statute extends, of course, not only to physicians but to any person who is mandated or permitted to report.

[25] Simonsen v. Swenson, 104 Neb. 224, 177 N.W. 831 (1920).
[26] Berry v. Moench, 8 Utah 2d 191, 331 P. 2d 814 (1958).
[27] Hague v. Williams, 37 N.J. 328, 181 A. 2d 345 (1962).
[28] Berry v. Moench, 8 Utah 2d, 191, 331 P. 2d 814 (1958).

Some statutory variations can be noted. For example, a few jurisdictions do not mention that the immunity extends to liability which might result from participation in judicial proceedings. In Wisconsin the immunity is only given against criminal liability, whereas in Idaho, Maryland, Virginia, and Washington the statutes provide only for immunity in civil cases. The Massachusetts law affirms that reporting "shall not constitute slander or libel"; Nebraska provides that the information in the report "shall be absolutely privileged and shall not constitute slander, libel, breach of confidence, or invasion of any right of privacy." Presumably, these laws too speak only to civil liability. Nevada broadens the immunity to cover any liability which might come from "instituting" an investigation or other action by the welfare department, while Oregon narrows the protection by a requirement that "good faith" reporting gives immunity only when it is based on "reasonable grounds."

These probably unnecessary immunity provisions may encourage reporting simply because they exist and can be publicized to physicians. They may also discourage litigation by plaintiffs otherwise willing to take a gambler's chance on an outcome to be controlled by scattered precedents.

Liability for Failure To Report

A child or parent is unlikely to prevail in his suit against a physician who, in good faith, reports a case of child abuse to the authorities. On the other hand, a physician who fails to report according to a statute which requires him to do so may incur civil liability. In this discussion it is assumed that the reporting statute carries a criminal sanction for failure to report which is contained in the text of the statute itself or is imposed by virtue of a general penal provision found elsewhere but generally applicable to violations of mandatory statutes.

If there were no statute requiring a physician to report cases of suspected child abuse, would a physician be liable in tort for failure to report such a case to the proper authorities on the ground that his inaction had deprived a child of access to protective services and, hence, was a "substantial cause" of subsequent injuries inflicted by the youngster's caretakers? Generally speaking, a doctor, having undertaken treatment of a patient, is under a duty "to act." The action which a physician must undertake is to be judged by the standard of a reasonably prudent physician in the attending physician's general circumstances. Applying such a principle, it is doubtful whether the failure to report (again, absent some special statutory duty) gives rise to an actionable wrong. While many doctors will insist that a physician has a moral duty to report apparently dangerous situations in a young patient's environment, few would agree that it is malpractice not to do so.

The legal consequences of a physician's failure to report when he has a statutory duty to do so are quite different indeed. If the plaintiff is one of the class of persons which a criminal statute was intended to protect and if the harm suffered was of the sort which the statute was intended to prevent, an unexcused violation may be behavior giving rise to a claim for civil damages. In most states a violation of a criminal statute in the circumstances described above is "negligence per se." In other states the violation of the criminal statute raises a presumption of neglect which can be rebutted. In still other jurisdictions criminal behavior is only "evidence" of negligent conduct.

It is true that a violation of the reporting statute does not necessarily put the infant in a worse position than if the doctor had not been consulted. Nevertheless, the doctor has failed to confer a benefit (the reporting of evidence of child abuse) which a statute required. Had the physician carried out his duty, it is possible that further injury to the child might have been avoided through the intervention of the child protective agencies.

Putting aside arguments drawn from the general law of torts, there are cases more specifically applicable to physicians which suggest that a doctor who fails to report indicated child abuse may be liable in tort for subsequent injuries. For example, in *Jones* v. *Stanko*,[29] the administratrix of Stanko brought an action to recover damages resulting from wrongful death caused by the alleged negligence of the defendant physician. The plaintiff's husband performed certain services on behalf of a certain Mr. Thompson who was suffering from smallpox. At the trial, the plaintiff requested an instruction which set forth a portion of the Ohio General Code requiring physicians to report dangerous diseases to the public health officer and which asserted that if the jury found that Thompson was suffering from such a disease and that Dr. Jones had failed to report it, the jury should find for the plaintiff because of the enactment. Refusal to give this charge was held grounds for reversal.

The fact that a defendant's negligence is established by the violation of a statute does not answer the question whether the defendant's misconduct is the proximate cause of the plaintiff's injury. Yet, in some cases, a rather close connection between the failure to report child abuse and subsequent injuries suffered by the child at the hands of his caretakers can be perceived. It is well settled that intervening negligence and intervening criminal acts (of parents or other caretakers), which the defendant might reasonably anticipate, do not supersede or cut off the defendant's liability for his own act or omission.

On balance, it seems likely that reporting statutes which require reporting and which carry criminal penalties create a cause of action in favor of infants who suffer abuse after a physician has failed to make a report respecting earlier abuse brought to his attention. Further, failure to comply with a mandatory reporting law which is not supported by a criminal sanction may result in the imposition of civil liability upon a physician. The analogy to those cases which uphold liability for negligence established by the failure to obey a criminal law is persuasive.

Abrogation of The Patient-Physician Privilege

In a number of states a statute establishes a physician-patient privilege which, some might think, would prohibit a doctor from giving testimony in a juvenile court case or a criminal prosecution arising out of an incident of child abuse. Typically, the statutes prohibit a physician's testimony respecting information, necessary for treatment, which was acquired while the doctor attended the patient in a professional capacity. The privilege, of course, is the privilege of the patient, who may waive it.

This possible difficulty has been met in a large number of the states by legislation abrogating the privilege in child abuse cases. A handful of states retain the privilege although a child abuse reporting law has been enacted. Generally, however, the privi-

[29] 118 Ohio St. 147, 160 N.E. 456 (1928).

lege has limited application in those states. In California and Idaho the doctor-patient privilege is applicable only in civil cases; in West Virginia, only in justice of the peace courts. In New York the privilege is inapplicable if the patient is under sixteen, and information indicates that he is the victim of a crime.

One would expect that states which do not accord the privilege would have no need to "abrogate" it, but Florida has done just that. Even though the Florida laws do not create the privilege, the child abuse reporting act provides that the privilege shall not be grounds for excluding evidence in judicial proceedings resulting from a report. Perhaps the kindest explanation for the legislature's action was given by a Florida student commentator: "This provision was undoubtedly included as a prophylactic against possible future recognition of the privilege."[30]

In any event, the abrogation found in most child abuse reporting legislation is probably unnecessary when in those states recognizing the privilege. The St. Louis Court of Appeals has ruled against a trial court's refusal in a child neglect case to hear the testimony of a physician relating to injuries sustained by the child.

> It is undoubtedly true that under ordinary circumstances a parent, as the natural guardian, would have the right to claim the privilege on behalf of this child when it would be to the best interests of the minor to do so. But the circumstances here were far from ordinary. The child was not a litigant, but the subject of the proceedings, the purpose of which was to protect his interests and safeguard his welfare.
> ... where the privilege is claimed on behalf of the parent rather than that of the child, or where the welfare and interests of the minor will not be protected, a parent should not be permitted to either claim the privilege ... or, for that matter, to waive it.[31]

Conclusion

Generally speaking, the states which have enacted child abuse reporting legislation have not made available added state appropriations specifically intended to extend services to the new cases which reporting might reveal. Letters sent to state welfare departments produced responses not unlike the following from Utah: "My understanding is that the juvenile courts and the Department of Welfare are absorbing any costs that may be involved." Exceptions are Massachusetts, where $100,000 was appropriated, and Illinois, where $50,000 was expended by the state to cover printing, publication, an emergency twenty-four-hour phone service, and an additional staff.

It is, of course, difficult to determine whether appropriations included in the general budget of state and county welfare departments were increased because of child abuse reporting legislation. For example, the Chief of Child Welfare Section of Georgia reported:

> There has been no specific financial appropriation to pay for added service required by the statute. However, an increased amount of money has been made available to the Division for Children and Youth for both administration and direct services for the 1965–66 and 1966–67 fiscal years. This means that increased funds are available for overall child welfare services so that the State has additional funds to help counties pay

[30] 18 Fla. L. Rev. 503, 510 (1965).
[31] In re M.P.S., a minor, 342 S.W. 2d 277, 283 (Mo. Ct. App. 161).

salary and travel for workers. Increased staff in the overall services has meant that there is more staff to give protective services including those situations involving physical abuse. Also, the budget for this same period of time gives us increased funds for boarding care. Again, this means additional funds are available for children who need substitute foster care because of abuse in their own homes.

Without adequate resources to back up a reporting plan the entire effort is an exercise in futility. In urging support for improving the situation in New York, the writer of a *New York Times* editorial said:

> Unless laws are accompanied by provision for preventive and rehabilitative services—that the community will pay for and support—all society is doing is to jail the parents. That is not likely to contribute much to human happiness—or to the protection of defenseless children.[32]

No law can be better than its implementation, and its implementation can be no better than the resources permit.

Acknowledgment

The Study of Child Abuse Reporting Laws received assistance from the United States Department of Health, Education, and Welfare, Child Research and Demonstration Grants Program no. R-194.

Editors' Note

The lawyer, whether he represents the defense or the prosecution, is confronted with a most difficult problem. He must make certain that the legal rights and privileges of his clients are upheld. And yet, who represents the child? Every person involved must constantly keep in mind the child's best interests. By using clever courtroom maneuvers the defense attorney can frequently have a neglect petition denied; this he may define as "winning" the case. But in many situations this, in fact, is not "winning" as far as the child is concerned. The attorney who fails to give as much consideration to the child's welfare as he gives to the legal aspects of the case carries a heavy burden if the child is wrongly returned to battering parents.

All too frequently, we have seen prosecuting attorneys whose disinterest has resulted in an ill-advised, premature reuniting of parents and child. His burden is equally as heavy. Some attorneys who represent child welfare agencies are still insisting on handling a dependency petition as they would a criminal case.

In our experience more satisfactory dispositions are made when attorneys, parents, welfare personnel, and physicians meet together in the judge's chambers and, using proper legal formality, discuss all aspects of the case in question. The judge is then in a much better position to make an intelligent decision resulting in a more satisfactory disposition for all concerned.

[32] N.Y. Times, March 5, 1965, at p. 32 col. 2.

8 | The Role of the Law Enforcement Agency

Jack G. Collins

Department of Police
City of Los Angeles

Law enforcement agencies are required to perform a myriad of diverse duties in accomplishing their prescribed tasks of protecting life and property and maintaining peace and order within communities throughout the country. Frequently these duties are assigned to or assumed by law enforcement agencies on the basis of no more substantial reason than the fact that no one else is doing them. In considering the role of the law enforcement agency with respect to a specific matter within its concern, one must evaluate the relative position of the matter in the wide spectrum of police activities. Those matters that are primarily related to crime or criminal activity and that have a great impact on the total community require the most police concern and involvement.

Law violations of a most serious nature against minors, mainly infants, constitute a grave social problem. The problem of the battered child is not concerned with the discomforts and minor indications of normal or reasonable disciplinary measures imposed by parents but involves such felonious offenses as criminal homicide, assault with deadly weapons, and assault with means or force likely to produce great bodily harm. As pointed out in previous chapters, it is not uncommon to find battered children with broken bones, fractured skulls, brain damage, severe burns on the skin or in body cavities which have been caused by caustic substances, ruptured intestines, or other evidences of vicious attack. Doctors throughout the country who are active in the investigation and treatment of the battered child believe that the infliction of injuries by parents is a significant cause of death in infants and young children.

Mr. Collins is an assistant chief of police in the Los Angeles Police Department. For several years he worked in the juvenile division and was commander of that division.

Experience indicates that many children who survive these vicious assaults are permanently mutilated—partially paralyzed or mentally retarded. For example, the Denver study revealed that 85 of 302 victims of child abuse suffered permanent brain damage.[1] Many believe that seriously abused children cannot escape showing some effect of this violence in their personalities.

The home environment of the abused child must be altered and made safe to avoid repetition of such acts of violence, but experience indicates that the adults responsible for the care of battered children seldom voluntarily change their environment. The failure of the law to intervene constitutes a betrayal of the victims, the children, and fosters a situation potentially hazardous and costly to the community.

The adults involved also need protection from the consequences of their own explosive behavior, as they may eventually commit murder if there is no intervention. There is a movement among some disciplines related to crime and its causation to consider some behavior which was previously classified as strictly criminal in nature as an indication of "sickness." Many authorities concerned with the matter of child abuse by parents imply or express a similar thesis when they advocate the reporting of such cases to child welfare agencies and exclude law enforcement agencies from the initial investigative function. Some contend that the prosecution of parents for violation of these serious criminal offenses should be avoided on the theory that it impedes rehabilitative efforts and hinders the important function of altering the environmental situation of the family (see "Editors' Note" at the end of this chapter). It may be true that the basic and prevalent causes of child abuse by parents are mental or emotional disturbances; in this respect, child abuse might be considered a "sickness." A slight extension of this theory, however, could result in a similar conclusion regarding many, if not all, serious crimes against the person of another.

The law enforcement agencies faced with the battered child problem maintain that these abused children must be protected and that the disposition of such serious criminal offenses and the treatment of parents responsible for such crimes should be prescribed by established courts of law.

Law Enforcement and the Rights of Children

Law enforcement is the function by which the guaranteed rights of individuals and groups are preserved and protected. Legal attitudes toward the rights of children, however, have gone through a process of gradual change over the centuries.

The old Roman law provided that fathers had absolute power over their children, including the right to decide on matters of life or death and slavery or freedom. The state enforced these rights, and no persons or agencies were permitted to intercede on behalf of a child. The common law of England stipulated that fathers had supreme control over their legitimate minor children and were entitled to their custody. Fathers had a duty to support and protect their children, but this obligation was purely moral in nature and was not legally enforceable.

[1] Kempe, C. Henry, Silverman, F., Steele, B., Droegemueller, W., and Silver, H., 1962, The Battered-Child Syndrome, *J. Am. Med. Assoc.*, 181:17–24.

During the Middle Ages the decree that a father could be compelled to fulfill his parental obligations marked the inception of the doctrine of *parens patriae*. The fundamental assumption of this doctrine is that the state has the power to assume parental authority in those cases where parents have failed to fulfill their responsibilities for the care and welfare of their children. In the United States the doctrine of *parens patriae* is found in laws formulated as early as the eighteenth century, but an organized movement for child protection did not develop until the end of the nineteenth century.

During the present century, an increased concern has been demonstrated for the inherent rights of children, and the procedure of using the courts to find solutions for serious conflicts between the rights of children and the rights and responsibilities of their parents has developed. The right of children to live and enjoy normal health despite the actions, wishes, or neglect of their parents is now receiving considerable attention, as communities throughout the nation provide legislation to enable courts to take jurisdiction. Courts have assumed the position that parents are entitled to punish children within the bounds of moderation, but punishment must be for the child's welfare, without maliciously inflicting traumatic injuries. When punishment becomes unreasonable, and unlawful traumatic injuries result, the state must intervene and exert its police power in behalf of the children.

Child Welfare and Law Enforcement Agencies

A problem of such major significance as the battered child requires the organized efforts of all concerned persons and agencies for its ultimate solution. It involves cooperation between the family, social service, medical, law enforcement, judicial, and educational institutions of the community.

The two institutions most important to the solution of the battered child problem are social service and law enforcement. Despite the obviousness of this conclusion, it is the child welfare and the police agencies which generally display the least mutual understanding and tolerance, and it is often unfortunately true that each of these agencies has little knowledge of or indulgence for the actual philosophies, functions, or techniques of the other.

This is not to say that social workers and law enforcement officers are constantly at odds with each other, or that either agency refuses or fails to cooperate or work with the other. It is intended merely to indicate that the underlying philosophies and beliefs of the two are sufficiently different to cause attitudinal problems and suspicions. They generally work in adequate harmony to get the job done, but increased cooperation, confidence, and respect would greatly enhance the performance and success of both groups.

The lack of confidence between the two agencies becomes more understandable when the background and historical development of the child protection agencies are considered. Originally they functioned with "police power" and assumed an authoritarian approach toward both the neglected and abused children and the offending parents. In the beginning this approach was advocated and accepted because of the legalistic foundation for the movement and the climate in which the agencies operated.

Gradually, as the practice of social work developed and new knowledge and under-standing changed the philosophy of child welfare, the protective child welfare agencies moved further and further away from the idea of law enforcement as the only method of protecting children. In the field of child welfare, the law enforcement agency became symbolic of authority and an approach which focused on the prosecution and punish-ment of the offending parents. Those who advocated the case work method of helping parents who neglected or abused their children viewed the authoritarian or punitive approach with disdain.

It seems apparent that the social work profession as a whole has failed to realize that the law enforcement agency's attitude toward the handling of child abuse cases has also undergone a gradual transformation. It is still the belief of the police that pertinent laws must be enforced, but law enforcement has long since recognized the importance and need for referring the various aspects of these most complex cases to those persons and agencies primarily concerned with rehabilitation and the changing of the environment in which the illegal acts occurred. The law enforcement agencies maintain, however, that these referrals and rehabilitation programs must be handled within a legal framework.

The objectives of both the law enforcement and child welfare agencies are the pro-tection of neglected and abused children and rehabilitation of their home situations, but their respective roles and methods of operation are necessarily different. Lack of coordination appears to be the major problem. There is, therefore, a need for greater mutual understanding of philosophies and functions, so that the agencies may comple-ment and supplement each other's efforts. The earlier association of child protection with authoritarian law enforcement should not be allowed to remain as a barrier to cooperation.

Law Enforcement, the Battered Child, the Legal Statutes

As mentioned before, rehabilitative efforts related to the battered child problem must involve a changing of the environment in which the violations occurred. Evidence is accumulating that, unless the environment is changed, the physical assaults with resulting injuries will probably be repeated. But since the adults responsible are seldom willing to change the situation, any successful program of rehabilitation in battered child cases must have a strong legal foundation. Statutory provisions to make legal action possible should include the following:

> Laws forbidding persons from inflicting injuries on children.
> Laws requiring the reporting of injuries to children.
> Laws permitting juvenile courts to declare illegally injured children as wards, regard-less of other legal processes.
> Laws requiring a centralized depository for reports of illegal injuries to children.

The customary statutes involving the offenses of assault with a deadly weapon, assault with means or force likely to produce great bodily harm, and battery are not sufficient to meet the battered child problem adequately because they frequently fail to apply to specific cases. It is not only advisable but also important that there be a section of the law dealing directly with illegal injuries to children. (For example, Section 273a of the Penal Code of the State of California makes it a felony for any person to inflict unjustifiable physical pain or mental suffering on any child in circumstances or conditions likely to produce great bodily harm or death. It is a misdemeanor for any person to commit similar acts in circumstances or conditions other than those likely to produce great bodily harm or death, and Section 273d declares it a felony for any person willfully to inflict upon any child any cruel or inhuman corporal punishment or injury resulting in a traumatic condition.)

It is quite possible that the motivations involved in child abuse cases are of such a nature that they are not responsive to criminal statutes, and that parents subject to such outbursts of violence are not deterred by the prospect of punishment. It is basic to the conduct of an orderly society that persons who violate the personal or property rights of others be prosecuted for their criminal offenses. Obviously, the arrest of child-beating suspects accomplishes an important result—namely, an immediate change in the environment. It is true that this change is often temporary, but by removing the offending adult from the environment, the police protect the child from continued abuse and afford other agencies in the community an opportunity to initiate a more permanent rehabilitative program (see "Editors' Note" at the end of this chapter).

Frequently, it is impossible to criminally prosecute parents responsible for injuries inflicted upon children because of a lack of admissible evidence. Young victims are often unable to communicate because of age or injuries, and sufficient physical evidence is often not available. This fact is illustrated by the dispositions of 201 child-beating cases reported to the Los Angeles Police Department in 1965. Following extensive investigations, 15 of the cases remained unsolved, and in 30 of the cases involving arrests the responsible prosecuting agency refused to issue criminal complaints because of insufficient admissible evidence. Thus, in 22.4 per cent of the cases the police were unable to effect a change in the environment by removing the offending parent.

The Probation Department of Los Angeles County has proclaimed that the decision of a prosecuting agency not to issue a criminal complaint against a parent is not considered evidence that a child was not battered by one or both parents and that, if the evidence supports an allegation that no parent or guardian is exercising proper and effective parental care or control, a petition may be filed on behalf of a minor in juvenile court. In 1959, the presiding judge of the Juvenile Court of Los Angeles County explained that the criminal court case against the adult and the juvenile court case on behalf of the child were parallel cases but not necessarily interdependent. He stated that, under the California Juvenile Court Law, action can be initiated to protect children even though criminal complaints are not filed against adults. The establishment of this philosophy made an important contribution to the protection of babies and children too young to talk or too intimidated to relate the truth when the acts of violence against the child occurred in secret or with no competent witness present.

The benefits of a statewide, centralized depository for reports of child-beating incidents are self-evident. The highly mobile transient population of our urbanized society frequently moves from one location to another, but it is common for families to move between cities within the same state. Parents guilty of child beating, who do not locate in another city, often take their battered children to different doctors in the same area after each incident in an effort to conceal the repetitious nature of their offenses. A statewide, centralized depository for child-beating reports is important to alert concerned protective agencies to repeat cases.

Function of the Law Enforcement Agency

It is the general function of law enforcement agencies to protect life and property and maintain the public peace, and law enforcement officers are restricted to the performance of those tasks or acts which are required or permitted by statutory provisions in the accomplishment of their function. The primary functions of the law enforcement agency in cases involving battered children are to provide immediate protection for the victims and initiate the legal processes through which eventual rehabilitation in the homes may be accomplished.

Policemen are primarily concerned with human behavior and personal conduct in the performance of their duties, and as a result, they encounter an almost endless variety of situations. The intricacies of many of these problems require considerable knowledge and training, which has resulted in much specialization within law enforcement agencies. The assignment of officers to specialize in law enforcement involving juveniles as either perpetrators or victims is so common that professional associations of these officers have been established on a statewide and international basis.

Upon receipt of information concerning suspected infliction of physical injury upon a child by other than accidental means, the juvenile division of the law enforcement agency has two responsibilities after evaluating the validity of the report—first, to initiate appropriate protective action on behalf of the child and second, to determine whether sufficient admissible evidence can be obtained to initiate a criminal action against the person or persons responsible for the inflicted injuries. Arrangements for proper medical examination and treatment of the victim are completed before other phases of the investigation are undertaken. The police generally endeavor to investigate and resolve the case without removing the child from the home. It is frequently necessary, however, to take the victim into protective custody for one or more of the following reasons:

> Both parents have abused the child.
> The non-participating parent sympathized with the violator.
> The non-participating parent encouraged the violator.
> The non-participating parent failed to attempt to intervene or dissuade the violator.
> There is no responsible adult available to assume care and custody of the victim.
> The only parent in the home is the suspected violator.

In such cases it is apparent to the law enforcement officers that the child must be protected against further injury until welfare or social workers can be assigned to the case.

If the investigation discloses sufficient evidence to establish reasonable cause for arrest of those responsible for the traumatic injuries to the child, the police take the suspects into physical custody. The practice of arresting child-beating suspects is criticized by some welfare and social workers, who contend that it hampers their efforts at rehabilitation. In this regard it must be remembered that the strict time limit imposed on law enforcement between the arrest and arraignment of an arrestee provides for an almost immediate judicial review of the police action.

The arrest of child-beating suspects provides a legal framework for the prosecution of felonious offenders. The arrest and prosecution of parents for unlawful acts of violence on their children is not unanimously subscribed to by all persons and agencies concerned with the problem, but it is the only lawful means, from the law enforcement point of view, of ordering and enforcing a program of rehabilitation.

A uniform and effective program for handling child battering cases requires that all such reports be directed to one agency within a single jurisdiction, but there is a lack of unanimity among concerned agencies regarding which agency within a community should receive reports relating to battered children.

Reasons Favoring Reporting to the Law Enforcement Agency

The police are available daily in all areas and communities throughout the nation on a twenty-four-hour basis. When the explosive and violent conduct of an adult results in a traumatic injury to a child, immediate assistance and investigation are required. It is not adequate to refer such matters to an agency that is not available outside normal business hours or on weekends and holidays. Delays can and have resulted in the deaths of children and needless prosecutions of adults for criminal homicide.

The police, charged with the responsibility of protecting all persons within the community, are handicapped in their efforts if traumatic injuries caused by physical assaults are reported to other agencies and not to them. An agency with such a grave responsibility deserves and requires complete cooperation.

It is a traditional pattern of conduct for people to request assistance from the police in criminal matters. People are accustomed to reporting cases of physical violence to the police, and they would doubtlessly consider it incongruous to report serious offenses involving children to an agency other than the police.

Investigations involving battered children and preparation for their formal presentation are laborious and time-consuming. There are numerous indications in the literature that there is an acute shortage of protective and child welfare agencies throughout the nation. In many communities these social agencies are non-existent, and even in most metropolitan areas they are inadequately staffed for the services they are expected to render. It is, therefore, unreasonable to expect the child welfare agencies to assume complete responsibility for child-beating cases.

The legal authority granted peace officers to enter homes on reasonable grounds places the police in a strategic position to protect neglected and abused children from immediate unfit situations.

Child-beating cases involve some of the most serious crimes against the person, crimes which require uncontaminated admissible evidence for a proper and successful court presentation. Such evidence has always been necessary in adult criminal prosecutions, and there is now a definite and accelerated trend in the same direction in juvenile courts. The originally informal, non-adversary atmosphere of the juvenile court is rapidly being replaced by a more legalistic approach. Criminal investigations and court case preparations require experienced investigators knowledgeable in all phases of this exacting work, which has long been the duty of police officers in detective and juvenile assignments. Social agencies are rarely staffed with personnel trained and experienced in this type of investigative work.

The gathering and examination of evidence require rather elaborate and sophisticated photographic and laboratory procedures, such as ballistics tests, examinations of stains, analyses of liquids and substances, and the like. Facilities of this nature are either operated by or available to law enforcement agencies and are not generally accessible to social agencies.

Police action obligates agencies concerned with rehabilitative programs to become involved. When the police take juvenile victims into protective custody and/or arrest adults suspected of inflicting traumatic injuries on children, the attention of other agencies is automatically focused on the problem. Prosecuting attorneys, criminal and juvenile courts, probation departments, and other concerned social agencies must necessarily perform their assigned duties. This results in an official review and consideration of child-beating cases by community agencies charged with the responsibility of developing and implementing rehabilitative programs.

Law enforcement agencies are best equipped to establish and operate a centralized, statewide depository for records. City police departments are either a part of or have access to a statewide communications network, which permits them to exchange information readily. This capability is essential to an effective centralized reporting system.

It is obvious that protection is the common goal of both law enforcement and child welfare agencies with regard to battered children, but the roles of the two types of agencies are quite different. The functions of both agencies are essential to an effective community program of child protection; so it is necessary that the work of each complement and supplement the activities of the other. It is generally recognized that the roles of law enforcement and child welfare agencies are such that neither is equipped to substitute for the other, but, unfortunately, they often simply coexist rather than cooperate. The best possible community program of protection for battered children can be developed only when both law enforcement and welfare services are adequate, and when they consistently demonstrate mutual confidence, respect, and understanding.

Editors' Note

There is a reasonable amount of controversy regarding the manner in which the law enforcement agencies should function. The material presented in this chapter is one point of view. From the information available to the editors it appears that the approach presented is not accepted by all of the law enforcement agencies throughout the country. There are many points in which the editors would agree with the author. There is no question that the only community agency available on a twenty-four-hour basis is the department of police. It is very advantageous to have the police make available highly trained investigators and other police officers to assist the physicians and other members of the community as they are confronted with the problems of child abuse. There is also a great need for increased communication between the police and other community agencies such as child welfare. We would also agree with the belief that "any successful program of rehabilitation and battered child cases must have a strong legal foundation." This legal foundation is supported and carried out by the assistance of the police and juvenile court.

The main difference of opinion that the editors would have with the material presented is the strong emphasis on the criminal aspect of the problem as well as a need for a criminal type of investigation. It is our impression that this type of emphasis impedes the therapy that both pediatricians and psychiatrists are attempting to give to the parents. This point of view is discussed fully in other chapters (2 and 8). We do not believe there is any evidence to indicate that failure to criminally punish parents who injure their children will increase the problem. The author also states that one of the reasons for arresting the parents is to protect the child. It is unusual for the child to require protection by these means. The method that we would prefer is to hospitalize the child. On occasion an immediate referral to child welfare and removal from the home can be carried out. A law enforcement agency should have the authority by law to place a twenty-four to forty-eight-hour "hold" on any hospitalized child who is suspected of having been beaten. The child can usually be protected without the necessity of arresting the parents.

Once the arrest has been made and criminal charges are pending the parents are usually very uncooperative. It is our feeling that the long-term outlook for reuniting the parents with their child and helping them establish a better relationship with him and his siblings is considerably improved if the criminal route is not pursued. After the case has been investigated by the cooperative effort on the part of the police and the child welfare agency we would prefer a dependency action taken by child welfare with a petition to the juvenile court.

An additional deterrent for taking the criminal route is that there is considerable difficulty in proving which particular parent injured a given child or if anything other than an accident truly occurred. Since this is frequently impossible, many of the criminal cases that do reach the courts are settled in favor of the parents. If this occurs, it is most difficult to do anything about the child's severe abuse since there are few juvenile courts who would consider the removal of a child from the home if the parents have already been found not guilty in criminal court.

Finally, we would agree that the registry of child abuse cases should be maintained. For a registry to be completely effective many cases should be included that are never proven to be true child abuse. We do not feel, however, that these cases should be included as part of a police record. Ideally the registry should be kept in the state department of welfare or possibly the state health department.

Concluding Note

"There is probably no aspect of child care that can yield more rewarding results than the proper understanding and approach to the care of the abused and neglected child and his parents" (chapter 2).

The aim of the editors was to present a compilation of views from experts in their respective fields which would illustrate some of the more recent developments in the area of child abuse. From these contributions have evolved both provocative and controversial questions. It is our hope that from these diverse points of view will emerge the information needed by individual readers in their respective fields, enabling them to formulate a broader perspective of the problem.

For many, the most exciting and encouraging aspect of this total problem lies in the area of prevention. We are now beginning to obtain enough insight to provide us with a better understanding of those who batter children. The groundwork has been laid and the data are now available to delve more deeply into the preventive and therapeutic aspects of child abuse. Clearly it is not feasible, or desirable, to separate all abused children from their parents. We must expand our efforts to make available reliable and valid testing instruments which will help in the identification of parents who demonstrate a potential for child abuse. This identification should be followed by meaningful therapeutic intervention. Many treatment programs are developing throughout the country.

It is apparent to the editors, and we hope to the reader, that the complex problems associated with the appropriate care of the battered child and his parents require the attention of the most experienced personnel available—whether they be nurse, social worker, lawyer, law enforcement officer, judge, or physician—who can guide interested nonprofessionals in their involvement with these children and their families. Substantial progress will be achieved as each of these disciplines trains specialists to conduct research programs for the purpose of enhancing our understanding and providing additional answers to many of the prevailing questions.

Even in 1973 it appears that some children are still being ". . . taught to the tune of the hickory stick." It is indeed time that we speak ". . . more of their rights." Progress is slow, but it is evident, and those who will benefit most from this progress are among us.

R.E.H.
C.H.K.

Appendixes

APPENDIX A

A Summary of Neglect and Traumatic Cases

Editors' Note

Dr. Weston has compiled in the tables that follow all of the pertinent facts on the cases discussed in his chapter (4). It is presented here for two reasons: to provide the interested individual with more detailed information on specific cases, but more important to demonstrate the important responsibility and obligation of every medical examiner —this is, that each case requires a most careful and complete investigation into the circumstances surrounding the child's death. A thorough examination must always be performed, and equally as important, painstakingly complete records must be kept. Without such an approach to every case, material and observation such as Dr. Weston's report can never be presented in such detail.

It is careful, complete work such as this that allows the medical examiner to periodically examine his findings, categorize problems, systematize his approaches, and draw meaningful conclusions and recommendations. Only in this manner can we expect change to take place and progress in the most difficult areas to become apparent.

TABLE 1   NEGLECT CASES

AGE (mo)	RACE	SEX	GESTATION	BIRTH WEIGHT (gm)	BIRTH STATUS	DEATH WEIGHT (gm)	RATIO OF WEIGHT TO EXPECTED WEIGHT
1	N	F	Term	2,555	Illegit.	1,725	0.57
2	N	M	Term	2,949	Illegit.	2,210	0.56
2	W	M	Term	2,636	Legit.	2,324	0.63
2	N	M	8 mos.	2,549	Legit.	2,730	0.80
2	N	M	Term	3,061	Illegit.	3,854	0.88
3	N	M	Term	Unknown	Illegit.	2,965	0.78
3	N	M	Term	2,608	Illegit.	2,274	0.55
3	W	F	7 mos.	2,637	Legit.	2,110	0.53
4	W	M	8 mos.	Unknown	Legit.	3,225	0.84
4	N	F	Term	1,927	Illegit.	2,530	0.79
4	N	M	Term	2,609	Illegit.	2,925	0.63
4	W	M	Term	3,572	Illegit.	2,081	0.35
4	N	M	Term	3,260	Legit.	4,705	0.82
6	W	M	Term	Unknown	Illegit.	3,404	0.50
5	W	F	Term	3,089	Legit.	2,575	0.46
6	N	M	Term	3,118	Illegit.	3,140	0.49
6	N	M	7 mos.	2,211	Legit.	2,690	0.57
7	N	M	8 mos.	2,040	Legit.	2,690	0.63
8	W	F	7 mos.	Unknown	Legit.	2,825	0.48
8	N	M	Term	2,834	Illegit.	4,088	0.62
8	N	M	8 mos.	2,439	Legit.	5,022	0.85
10	N	F	Term	3,855	Illegit.	4,097	0.39
11	N	M	Term	2,664	Illegit.	4,310	0.58
13	N	M	7 mos.	2,465	Illegit.	6,544	0.84

DIAPER RASH	SIBLINGS		COMMENTS
	No.	Condition	
...Severe	7	Fair	Extremely dirty; infested with maggots; buried at city expense
...Severe	9	Fair	Buried at city expense; 1 sibling died at 6 weeks
...Moderate	5	Fair, extremely dirty	Filthy; vernix in axilla; buried at city expense
...Moderate	2	Fair	Extremely dirty; parents on vacation; left with 18-year-old aunt who never cared for a baby; home extremely filthy
...Moderate	3	Fair, dirty	Encrusted with dirt; early bronchopneumonia; buried at city expense
...Moderate	11	Poor, one hospitalized	Extremely dirty; organizing bronchopneumonia
...Minimal	3	Good	Acute otitis media at autopsy; buried at city expense
...None	10	Fair	Organizing bronchopneumonia; mother gravid
...None	4	Good	Other children live with grandparents; home extremely dirty; no heat
...Severe	6	Poor, one hospitalized	Macerated skin on thumb from sucking; necrotizing laryngitis; organizing bronchopneumonia; buried at city expense
...Severe	1	Good	Mother told grandmother she had sought medical attention; bronchopneumonia with abscesses in lungs
...Moderate	6	Good, one retarded	History of diarrhea for 1 week
...Severe	3	Fair, dirty	Complete denudation of genitalia; six-hour hospital survival with bradycardia and shock
...Severe	3	Poor, hospitalized	Five-hour survival in hospital; bloody vomitus and feces; string tied around penis; duodenal ulcer at autopsy
...Moderate	5	Good	Baby redressed after death; home clean
...None	6	Fair	Home extremely dirty; human excreta dumped into yard daily
...Severe	2	Poor	Dirt encrustation; maggot infestation; home extremely dirty
...None	5	Poor	Home extremely dirty; other children unclad; excreta on floors
...None	2	Fair	...
...Severe	2	Fair, flea bites, dirty	Extensive dirt encrustation; secondary skin infection; maggot infestation
...Severe	3	Poor, impetigo	Extremely dirty with encrustation; maggot infestation
...Severe	10	Fair	Terminal sepsis from secondary skin infection; bronchopneumonia
...Moderate	2	Fair	Baby scrubbed and redressed after death
...Severe	6	Twin poor, others good	Extremely dirty with encrustation; numerous flea bites secondarily infected; 1 sibling died earlier; this infant 1 of twins

TABLE 2   TRAUMATIC CASES WITH A SINGLE EPISODE OF INJURY

AGE (yrs)	RACE	SEX	ASSAILANT	RECENT EXTERNAL INJURIES	FRACTURES	INTERNAL INJURIES
1/12	N	M	Mother	Small contusions, face and head	Ribs, recent	Contusions—brain, heart, and lungs
1/12	N	M	Mother	Two small bruises on scalp	Skull, recent	Contusion—brain, epidural and subdural hemorrhage
2/12	W	M	Father	Single bruise over lower sternum	None	Laceration of liver
2/12	N	M	Father	Large contusion of face	None	Contusions, brain; laceration of liver; subdural hemorrhage
4/12	N	F	Father	Superficial bruise of scalp	None	Contusions, brain; subdural hemorrhage
4/12	W	F	Father	Contusion, face and lip	None	Subdural hemorrhage
5/12	N	M	Mother	No injury apparent, dirty with severe diaper rash	None	Contusion, brain; subdural hemorrhage
8/12	N	M	Father	Numerous lacerations and contusions, face and mouth	None	Subdural hemorrhage; cerebral contusions
1 5/12	N	F	Unknown	Many bruises over face, neck, and trunk	Ribs, recent	Contusions—brain, lungs, and heart
1 6/12	N	F	Sibling	Thermal burns, lower trunk and lower extremities	None	None
2	N	F	Stepfather	Many bruises and abrasions over face, scalp, and trunk	Ribs, recent	Contusion, brain; subdural hemorrhage
2	N	F	Sibling (age 11)	Many small bruises on scalp and face	None	Contusion, brain; subdural hemorrhage
6	N	F	Sibling (age 12)	Many bruises on head and trunk	None	Laceration of spleen

Cause of Death	Presenting Story	Method of Injury	Reason for Injury
Contusions—brain, lungs, and heart	"Found dead in crib"	Struck with hand	Excessive crying
Craniocerebral injuries	"Fell with baby in arms"	Struck with a plastic toy gun	Excessive crying
Laceration of liver with hemorrhage	"Fell from lap"	Threw feeding bottle at baby	Would not finish feeding
Subdural hematoma	"Fell from crib"	Struck with hand	Excessive crying
Subdural hemorrhage	"Found in crib, choking"	Banged baby's head against crib while shaking	Baby was fussy
Subdural hemorrhage	"I hit the baby"	Struck with hand	Excessive crying
Subdural hemorrhage	"Found dead in bed"	Threw into bassinet, which overturned—baby's head struck baseboard	Excessive crying
Subdural hemorrhage	None—baby found in sewer pit	Struck with hands	Excessive crying
Contusions—brain, lungs, and heart	"Fell downstairs"	Unknown	Unknown
Shock with thermal burns, unattended	"Placed baby's bottom in hot water, then fell and dropped baby in overturned water"	Same as indicated	Baby soiled floor
Subdural hemorrhage	"Fell from bed and downstairs"	Beat with hair brush	Child had diarrhea for 1 week and messed bed
Subdural hemorrhage	"Beat up by brother"	Spanked, swung around striking door	Urinated on floor
Laceration of spleen with hemorrhage	"Fell from toilet seat"	Struck with vacuum cleaner pipe and fists	Was leaning out window

TABLE 3   Traumatic Cases with Multiple Episodes of Injury

Age (yrs)	Race	Sex	Assailant	Recent External Injuries	Remote External Injuries	Fractures
2/12	W	M	Mother	One small bruise on head	Three small healing bruises on head	Skull
2/12	N	F	Mother	Malnourished; numerous bruises on head, trunk, and extremities	Numerous healing and healed linear bruises and scars, trunk	Skull—recent
4/12	W	M	Father	Thermal burns, lower trunk and lower extremities	None—confessed to previous beating	Skull—healed
8/12	N	F	Mother	Numerous bruises and abrasions, head and trunk	Numerous healing bruises over trunk and extremities	Skull—recent Ribs—recent
9/12	N	M	Mother	Two small abrasions, posterior trunk	None—confessed to previous beating	None
10/12	N	F	Foster mother	Numerous bruises of face, laceration of lip	Healing linear abrasions, buttocks and lower extremities	Humerus—healing Skull—recent
11/12	N	F	Unknown	Superficial contusion, face	None	Humerus—recent
1 6/12	W	M	Male paramour	Extremely dirty; numerous bruises, head, trunk, and extremities	Healing and healed linear scars, extremities	Skull—recent
1 6/12	N	M	Sibling (age 15)	Numerous bruises on abdomen	Numerous linear scars on extremities	None
1 6/12	N	M	Mother	Numerous bruises and abrasions, head and trunk; laceration of lip	Healed pattern burn on buttocks; healed linear scars, trunk and extremities	None
1 9/12	N	F	Unknown	Numerous bruises on face and trunk; laceration of lip and loose teeth	Healing contusion, face and bridge of nose	Femur—healed
2	N	F	Mother	Linear abrasions and loop abrasions, lower extremities	Healing burns of hands	None
2	W	M	Mother	Numerous bruises on face, head, and neck	Old burns, buttocks, healing and healed abrasions, contusions and lacerations of head and trunk	None
2	N	M	Mother	Extremely dirty; numerous bruises, head, face, and extremities	None—admission of repetitive episodes	None
2	N	F	Father	Numerous bruises, face and abdomen; postmortem burns, lower trunk and legs	Healed circumscribed scars, head and lower lip	None
3	N	F	Father	Numerous bruises and abrasions on head, trunk, and extremities	Few linear scars on trunk and extremities	Ulna—healed Humerus—recent
3	N	F	Sibling (age 16)	Several small bruises on anterior trunk	Scattered linear scars on buttocks and thighs	Ribs—recent
3	N	M	Father	Malnourished; numerous loop and linear fresh abrasions; numerous bruises, face and head; laceration of lip	Numerous healed and healing loop and linear abrasions and scars	None
3	N	M	Stepfather	Numerous bruises, face and trunk; large laceration, lip; numerous linear and loop abrasions, trunk	Healing and healed linear and loop abrasions; healing burn, buttocks	Rib—recent

Internal Injuries	Cause of Death	Presenting Story	Method of Injury	Reason for Injury
Congenital hydrocephalus; cerebral contusion	Resolving and recent subdural hemorrhage	"Car bed collapsed on her, banging head"	Struck with fist, banging head against wall	"Crying at feeding time"
Contusion, brain; subdural hemorrhage	Subdural hemorrhage	"Found dead in crib"	Struck with hand	"Cried too much"
Bronchopneumonia; Curlings' ulcer; Waterhouse-Friderichsen syndrome	Waterhouse-Friderichsen syndrome	"Overturned bottle of hot water on table where baby was"	Immersed in sink of hot water	"Cried too much"
Contusion, brain; subdural, epidural hemorrhage	Intracranial hemorrhage	"Fell out of crib"	Struck by hand, fist and shoe	"Cried too much"
Subdural hemorrhage; cerebral contusion	Subdural hemorrhage	"Fell from sofa"	Slapped and knocked from table to floor	"Soiled pants and spit out food"
Contusions, brain; subdural hemorrhage	Subdural hemorrhage	"Baby fell from table"	Beat with hand, cord, and wooden ruler	"Excessive crying after fracture of humerus when first handled"
Recent and remote cerebral contusions	Cerebral contusion	"Fell off sofa"	Unknown	Unknown
Contusion, brain; subdural hemorrhage	Subdural hemorrhage	"Fell downstairs"	Beat by hands and belt	Unknown
Lacerations, liver and mesentery	Laceration of liver with hemorrhage	"Found dead in crib"	Beat by fists	"Would not eat his food"
Contusion, brain; subdural hemorrhage	Subdural hemorrhage	"Fell from potty chair"	Placed on gas burner; beat with stick and hands	"Wet pants"
Laceration and contusion, mesentery	Laceration of mesentery with hemorrhage	"Fell downstairs"	Struck by fists in face and abdomen	Unknown
Subdural hemorrhage	Subdural hemorrhage	"Head banged floor while shaking"	Shook violently; beat with cord	"Feces smearing"
Contusion, brain; subdural hemorrhage	Subdural hemorrhage	"Fell from chair and beat child"	Yanked chair from beneath him	"Would not eat"
Contusion, brain; subdural hemorrhage	Subdural hemorrhage	"Fell downstairs"	Beat by hands and fists	"Baby had temper tantrums"
Contusions, brain and lung; laceration, liver	Laceration of liver with hemorrhage	"Found in bath tub"	Struck by fists; banged head on tub	"Splashed water"
Contusions, brain and liver	Cerebral contusion	"Fell downstairs after beating"	Beat with hand and belt	"Messing in pants"
Contusions, brain, heart, and lung; subdural hemorrhage; healed scar, liver	Subdural hemorrhage	"Fell from bed"	Beat with fists and banged head	"Wet pants"
Contusion, brain; subdural hemorrhage	Subdural hemorrhage	"Dog jumped on him and he fell down"	Beat with strap; struck with fists and fell	"Drinking sibling's bottle"
Laceration, liver; contusions—lung, mesentery, and jejunum	Laceration of liver with hemorrhage	"Fell downstairs"	Placed on hot radiator to dry pants; beat with belt and switch; struck with hands	"Wet and messed pants"

TABLE 3 (*continued*)

AGE (yrs)	RACE	SEX	ASSAILANT	RECENT EXTERNAL INJURIES	REMOTE EXTERNAL INJURIES	FRACTURES
3	W	M	Mother	Numerous bruises and abrasions, head, trunk, and extremities	Numerous healing bruises, trunk and extremities	None
3	N	F	Babysitter (age 14)	Numerous bruises of head and trunk	Scattered healing abrasions, posterior trunk and thighs	None
3	W	M	Father	Bruises, linear and loop, on face, trunk, and extremities	Healed linear scars, lower extremities	None
5	N	M	Foster parents	Numerous bruises on scalp, face, and trunk	Healed and healing linear and loop scars, trunk	None

Internal Injuries	Cause of Death	Presenting Story	Method of Injury	Reason for Injury
Laceration, mesentery	Laceration of mesentery with hemorrhage	"Beat child"	Struck by hands	"He needed love and attention"
Lacerations and contusions, liver and mesentery	Laceration of liver with hemorrhage	"Found on floor near bed"	Beat by fists	"Wet her pants"
Severe cerebral edema; cerebral contusion	Cerebral contusion	"Fell downstairs"	Beat with wire coathanger	"Strewing contents of cabinet"
Subdural hemorrhage	Subdural hemorrhage	"Fell from bed"	Beat with hand, fists, and belt	"Wetting and messing pants"

APPENDIX B

A Summary of Child-Abuse Legislation, 1973

Revised by
Brian G. Fraser
National Center for Abuse and Neglect
1001 Jasmine
Denver, Colorado 80220

Editors' Note

The reporting laws in the United States are continually being revised. Contained herein is the latest version from each of the states, as of the day we went to press. Mr. Fraser has completely revised this section in an effort to provide the reader with undated reference material. The New York Statute should be given close attention. Their 1973 law is completely new and contains some of the most up-to-date thinking of a legislative body and their advisors.

*   *   *

Explanatory Notes

Statute: the appropriate citation to the state's statutory law where the child-abuse reporting law can be found.

Age: the age of children concerning whom reports are to be made.

Who Reports: who the reporters are in each state and, in parentheses, the circumstances under which reports are to be made. The symbol (H) refers to the existence of a provision that hospital administrators are to report when "notified" by a physician. It should be noted that under some statutes hospitals are directed to report independently. "Physician" has been used in general to include also medical interns and residents.

Nature of Injury: the nature of reportable injuries. The symbol (RH) refers to a provision which states that parents do not abuse their children by resorting to some form of religious healing, such as Christian Science.

To Whom Reported: the person, official, or institution to whom reports are made.

Legislative Directions: the directions, found in the legislation, respecting what is to occur when a case of child abuse is reported. Three types of declarations of purpose are found in the statutes of the state: The first (Type I) is exemplified by the formulation found in the Delaware statute merely sets forth the aim of child protection, "The purpose of this Chapter is *to provide for the protection of children* who have had physical injury inflicted upon them." The second (Type II) contains additional language identical with, or substantially similar, to the italicized portion of a clause found in the Children's Bureau model:

> The purpose of this Act is to provide for the protection of children who have had physical injury inflicted upon them . . . . Physicians . . . should report . . . thereby *causing the protective services of the State to be brought to bear* in an effort *to protect the health and welfare of these children and to prevent further abuses.*

The third (Type III) contains language identical with, or substantially similar to, the italicized portion of the Colorado Statute:

> In order to protect children whose health and welfare may be adversely affected through the infliction, by other than accidental means, of physical injury . . . the general assembly hereby provides for the mandatory reporting . . . by doctors and institutions . . . . It is the intent . . . that, as a result of such reports, *protective social services shall be made available in an effort to prevent further abuses, safeguard and enhance the welfare of such children, and preserve family life wherever possible.*

Immunity: the immunity from legal liability given to the reporter.

Abrogation of Evidentiary Privileges: the evidentiary privileges abrogated by the reporting statute.

Central Registry: indicates the states which maintain a central registry by statute and describes where the registry is kept. In some states registries are kept on a state-wide basis by administrative order. Some local registries also exist.

Maximum Penalty for Failure to Report: the states which impose criminal sanctions and the penalty imposed. The symbol (V) indicates that the offense is simply "violating" the statue; (K) indicates that the violation must be "knowingly" done; (W) refers to a "willful" violation; (KW) refers to a "knowing and willful" violation.

ALABAMA

Statute: Ala. Code tit. 27 §§ 21–25 (Supp. 1971 cumul.)

Age: under 16.

Who Reports: hospitals, clinics, sanitariums, doctors, physicians, surgeons, nurses, school teachers, pharmacists, social workers, or any other person called upon to render aid or medical assistance (if there is suspicion that injury was caused by abuse or neglect or if the child appears to be suffering from starvation or sexual abuse or attempted sexual abuse).

Nature of Injury: wound or injury which appears to be unusual or of such a nature so as to indicate or raise a suspicion that it was caused by physical abuse, child brutality, child abuse, or neglect. (RH)

To Whom Reported: chief of police or to the sheriff who files report with the department of pensions and security which will offer child protective services.

Legislative Directions: no provision.

Immunity: unqualified.

Abrogation of Evidentiary Privileges: physician-patient.[1]

Central Registry: . . .

Maximum Penalty for Failure to Report: 6 months or $500. (K)

ALASKA

Statute: Alaska Stat. §§ 47.17.010–47.17.070 (Supp. 1972)

Age: under 16.

Who Reports: mandatory reporting by a practitioner of the healing arts, peace officers, school teachers, social workers, administrative officers in institutions (has cause to believe that a child has suffered harm as a result of abuse or neglect, or starvation).

Nature of Injury: physical harm or starvation other than by accidental means or neglect.

To Whom Reported: nearest office of the Department of Health and Social Service.

Legislative Directions: Type III. The department shall investigate and cause such action as prescribed by law as may be necessary to prevent further injury to the child or to insure the proper care and protection of the child.

Immunity: if in good faith.

Abrogation of Evidentiary Privileges: physician-patient and husband-wife.

Central Registry: maintained by Department of Health and Social Services.

Maximum Penalty for Failure to Report: . . .

ARIZONA

Statute: Ariz. Rev. Stat. Ann. § 13-842.01 (Supp. 1972 and 1973)

Age: under 16.

Who Reports: any physician (whose examination of any minor discloses evidence of). (H)

Nature of Injury: injury or physical neglect not explained by the available medical history as being accidental in nature.

To Whom Reported: to a municipal or county peace officer.

Legislative Directions: no provision.

Immunity: unqualified.

Abrogation of Evidentiary Privileges: physician-patient.

Central Registry: State Department of Public Welfare. Arizona rev. stat. § 8-546.03 (1973)

Maximum Penalty for Failure to Report: $100 and/or 10 days. (V)

---

[1] "The doctrine of privileged communication shall not be a ground for excluding evidence." This language would seem to affect the confidential communication between husband and wife as well.

ARKANSAS

Statute: Ark. Stat. Ann. §§ 42-801–42-806 (Supp. 1971)

Age: under 16.

Who Reports: any physician, dentist, coroner, osteopath, intern, resident, pharmacist, nurse, chiropractor, laboratory technician, or superintendent or manager of a hospital (having reasonable cause to suspect that any child has had . . .). Any person *may* report (having knowledge or reason to believe abuse). (H)

Nature of Injury: serious physical injury resulting from abuse or neglect and caused by other than accidental means by a parent or other person responsible for his care. (RH)

To Whom Reported: appropriate police authority, with copy to County or State Welfare Department.

Legislative Directions: declaration of purpose Type II. Welfare to offer protective services.

Immunity: if in good faith; statutory presumption of good faith.

Abrogation of Evidentiary Privileges: physician-patient and husband-wife.

Central Registry: Family Services Division, State Welfare Department.

Maximum Penalty for Failure to Report: $500 and/or 6 months. (KW)

CALIFORNIA

Statute: Cal. Pen. Code § 11161.5 (Supp. 1972)

Age: minor.

Who Reports: physician, surgeon, dentist, resident, intern, podiatrist, chiropracter, religious practitioner, registered nurse in employment of public health agency or school, superintendent, supervisor of child welfare and attendance, certified pupil personnel employee, principal, or teacher of any public or private school, licensed daycare worker, administrator of public or private summer day camp or child care center, and any social worker.

Nature of Injury: physical injury or injuries which appear to have been inflicted upon him by other than accidental means by any person.

To Whom Reported: local police authority and to juvenile probation department.

Legislative Directions: none.

Immunity: unqualified.[2]

Abrogation of Evidentiary Privileges: . . .

Central Registry: State Bureau of Criminal Identification and Investigation.

Maximum Penalty for Failure to Report: misdemeanor. (V)

COLORADO

Statute: Colo. Rev. Stat. Ann. §§ 22-10-1–22-10-8 (1972) See also 22-3-1 and 22-3-5

Age: under 18.

Who Reports: physician, medical institution, nurse, school employee, social worker or any other person who has reasonable cause.

[2] "No mention of immunity from liability resulting from participation in judicial procedures."

Nature of Injury: abuse. (See 22-10-1(4), abuse.)

To Whom Reported: proper law enforcement agency.

Legislative Directions: declaration of purpose Type III. Law enforcement shall refer report to county welfare department which shall investigate and advise law enforcement agency. The department shall provide the necessary social services and may take further legal action.

Immunity: unqualified.

Abrogation of Evidentiary Privileges: physician-patient, husband-wife.

Central Registry: . . . in division of public welfare of the department of social services.

Maximum Penalty for Failure to Report: . . .

CONNECTICUT

Statute: Conn. Gen. Stat. Ann. §17-38 (a)–§17-38 (h) Public Act No. 73-205 (effective 1 October 1973)

Age: under 18.

Who Reports: physician, surgeon, any resident physician or intern, registered nurse, licensed practical nurse, medical examiner, dentist, psychologist, school teacher, school principal, school guidance counselor, social worker, police officer, and clergyman. (H)

Nature of Injury: physical injury or injuries inflicted upon him other than by accidental means or has injuries which are at variance with the history given of them or is a condition which is a result of maltreatment such as, but not limited to, malnutrition, sexual molestation, deprivation of the necessities or cruel punishment.

To Whom Reported: the State Welfare Commissioner or his representative, or the local police department or the state police.

Legislative Directions: to protect children whose health and welfare may be adversely affected, to strengthen the family and make the home safe for children, and provide a temporary or permanent nurturing and safe environment for children when necessary.

Immunity: civil or criminal, if in good faith.

Abrogation of Evidentiary Privileges: the privilege against the disclosure of communications between husband and wife shall be inapplicable and either may testify as to any relevant matter.

Central Registry: the Welfare Commissioner shall maintain a registry of the reports received pursuant to this section and shall adapt regulations to permit the use of the registry on a 24-hour daily basis to prevent or discover abuse of children.

Maximum Penalty for Failure to Report: any person required to report under the provisions of this section who fails to make such report shall be fined not more than $500. (V)

DELAWARE

Statute: Del. Code Ann. Vol. 9 tit. 16 §§ 1000–1007 (effective 1 May 1973)

Age: under 18 (chronologically under the age of 18 or mentally retarded).

Who Reports: any physician and osteopathic physician, dentist, intern, resident, nurse, school employee, social worker, psychologist, medical examiner, or other person. (H)

Nature of Injury: serious physical injury or injuries inflicted upon him by other than accidental means by a parent or other person responsible for his care. (R.H.)

To Whom Reported: Division of Social Services.

Legislative Directions: declaration of purpose Type I. Upon receipt of such a report the family court may refer the matter to a probation officer, any institution receiving state aid, or any other welfare agency.

Immunity: if in good faith.

Abrogation of Evidentiary Privileges: physician-patient and husband-wife or any other except attorney-client.

Central Registry: Division of Social Services

Maximum Penalty for Failute to Report: $50. (KW)

DISTRICT OF COLUMBIA

Statute: D.C. Code Ann. §§ 2-161-2-166 (1971 Supp.)

Age: under 18.

Who Reports: any physician having reasonable cause to believe. (H)

Nature of Injury: serious physical injury or injuries inflicted by other than accidental means or has suffered serious physical harm due to neglect. (RH)

To Whom Reported: Metropolitan Police Dept. of the District of Columbia.

Legislative Directions: declaration of purpose Type III.

Immunity: if in good faith.

Abrogation of Evidentiary Privileges: physician-patient and husband-wife.[3]

Central Registry: . . .

Maximum Penalty for Failure to Report: . . .

FLORIDA

Statute: Fla. Stat. Ann § 828.041 (1)–828.041 (11) effective 1 July 1971 (1972 and 1973).

Age: under 17.

Who Reports: physician, nurse, teacher, social worker, or employee of public/private facility serving children. (H)

Nature of Injury: (*abuse*—see definition)

To Whom Reported: department of health and rehabilitation services.

Legislative Directions: declaration of purpose Type III.

Immunity: if in good faith; presumption of good faith.

Abrogation of Evidentiary Privileges: physician-patient, any privilege except attorney-client.

Central Registry: department of health and rehabilitation services. (K.W)

Maximum Penalty for Failure To Report: "misdemeanor of 2nd." (828.042—negligent treatment of children, effective 1 January 1972)

---

[3] Provided the juvenile court "determine such privilege should be waived in the interest of public justice." The privileges are abrogated only in juvenile court proceedings.

GEORGIA

Statute: Ga. Code Ann. § 74-111 (Supp. 1971).

Age: under 12.

Who Reports: any physician or osteopath, dentist, podiatrist, public health nurse, or welfare worker (having reason to believe). (H)

Nature of Injury: physical injury or injuries inflicted other than by accidental means by a parent or caretaker.

To Whom Reported: child welfare agency providing protective services or in absence of such agency, to an appropriate police authority. Public health nurse or welfare worker shall report to county health officer or, if none, to licensed physician.

Legislative Directions: declaration of purpose Type III.

Immunity: if in good faith.

Abrogation of Evidentiary Privileges: . . .

Central Registry: . . .

Maximum Penalty for Failure to Report: . . .

HAWAII

Statute: Title 20 §§ 350-1–350-5 (1972).

Age: any minor.

Who Reports: any person licensed by the state to render services in medicine, osteopathy, dentistry, or any of the healing arts; or registered nurse, school teacher, social worker or coroner (having reason to believe). (H)

Nature of Injury: any injury inflicted upon him (the minor) as a result of abuse or neglect. (RH)

To Whom Reported: The Department of Social Services.

Legislative Directions: declaration of purpose Type II. The Department of Social Services shall investigate and if the facts so warrant, shall report to the prosecuting attorney.

Immunity: if in good faith.

Abrogation of Evidentiary Privileges: physician-patient and husband-wife.

Central Registry: Department of Social Services.

Maximum Penalty for Failure To Report: . . .

IDAHO

Statute: §§ 16-1624, 16-1625, 16-1641, and 9-203 (which relates to confidential communications).
(16-6624, 16-1625 and 16-1641 amended and effective April 1973)

Age: under 18.

Who Reports: any physician, resident on a hospital staff, intern, nurse, coroner, school teacher, day care personnel, social worker or other person having reasonable cause.

Nature of Injury: has been abused or observes the child being subjected to conditions or circumstances which would reasonably result in abuse.

Abuse (16-1625[m]): Any case in which a child exhibits evidence of skin bruising, bleeding, malnutrition, sexual molestation, burns, fracture of any bone, subdural hematoma, soft tissue swelling, failure to thrive, or death, and such condition or death is not justifiably explained, or where the history given concerning such condition is at variance with the degree or type of such condition or death, or the circumstances indicate that such condition or death, may not be the product of accidental occurrence.

To Whom Reported: proper law enforcement agency.

Legislative Provisions: protective services of the state be brought to bear, to prevent further abuses and strengthen the family unit wherever possible.

Immunity: from criminal and civil proceedings and any other such judicial proceedings or as a result of such report.

Abrogation of Evidentiary Privileges: any privileged communication except lawyer-client.

Central registry: none

Penalty: none

ILLINOIS

Statute: Ill. Ann. Stat. ch. 23 §§ 2041-47 (Supp. 1972).

Age: under 16.

Who Reports: any physician, surgeon, dentist, osteopath, chiropractor, podiatrist, or Christian Science practitioner (having reasonable cause to believe); any hospital. (H)

Nature of Injury: injury or disability from physical abuse or neglect inflicted upon him other than by accidental means, or shows evidence of malnutrition.

To Whom Reported: to the nearest office of the Department of Children and Family Services. Reports may in addition be made to the local law enforcement agency. If report is made to law enforcement agency, the reporter shall so inform the department.

Legislative Directions: the department shall investigate and offer protective social services. The department may utilize protective services of voluntary agencies. Whenever it believes removal of the child to be necessary, the department shall file a petition with one appropriate court.

Immunity: if in good faith with presumption of good faith.

Abrogation of Evidentiary Privileges: physician-patient.

Central Registry: Department of Children and Family Services.

Maximum Penalty for Failure to Report: . . .

INDIANA

Statute: Ind. Ann. Stat. §§ 52-1426–1431 (1972).

Age: under 16.

Who Reports: any person who has reason to believe.

Nature of Injury: physical injury or injuries inflicted other than by accidental means by a parent or other person responsible for his care.

To Whom Reported: to the county department of public welfare or the law enforcement agency having jurisdiction.

Legislative Directions: declaration of purpose Type II. County Department of Public Welfare shall investigate and if the facts so warrant shall report to the prosecutor.

Immunity: not maliciously as in bad faith.[4]

Abrogation of Evidentiary Privileges: physician-patient and husband-wife.

Central Registry: . . .

Maximum Penalty for Failure to Report: $100, 3 days. (K)

IOWA

Statute: Iowa Code Ann. §§ 235A.1–A.8 (Supp. 1971).

Age: under 18.

Who Reports: every health practitioner, defined to include any physician, surgeon, osteopath, dentist, optometrist, podiatrist, or chiropractor, and any registered nurse attending a child in the absence of such a practitioner (who has reason to believe or believes). Permissive reporting by "any person." (H)

Nature of Injury: physical injury inflicted as a result of abuse or willful neglect.

To Whom Reported: required reports—oral to county department of social welfare. If reporter believes immediate protection of child is advisable, he also shall report to an appropriate law enforcement agency. Written report to county department of social welfare and county attorney. Nonmandatory reports—to county welfare or county attorney or county law enforcement agency. The latter two are to refer such reports promptly to county welfare.

Legislative Directions: declaration of purpose Type I. County department of social welfare shall promptly investigate, primary purpose of which shall be the protection of the child. Department shall make a written report of the investigation to the juvenile court and county attorney and the appropriate law enforcement agency. Detailed provision on nature of investigation and further action.

Immunity: if in good faith.

Abrogation of Evidentiary Privileges: physician-patient and husband-wife.

Central Registry: . . .

Maximum Penalty for Failure to Report: . . .

KANSAS

Statute: Kan. Stat. Ann. §§ 38-716–721 (Supp. 1972).

Age: under 18.

Who Reports: every physician, dentist, osteopath, psychologist, chiropractor, social workers, every teacher, school administrator and every registered nurse or school nurse, examining, attending, or treating such a child in the absence of a physician or surgeon, teacher, school administrator, or employee of school which such child is attending, or law enforcement officer. (H)

---

[4] The qualification applies to "anyone participating" in reporting, in addition, doctors and hospital staff members are given unqualified immunity from any liability for the disclosure of matters which might be considered confidential because of the doctor-patient relationship.

Nature of Injury: serious injury or injuries inflicted as a result of physical or mental abuse or neglect.

To Whom Reported: juvenile court, juvenile judge, state department of health.

Legislative Directions: declaration of purpose Type I.

Immunity: participate without malice.

Abrogation of Evidentiary Privileges: physician-patient or similar privilege.

Central Registry: state department of social welfare.

Maximum Penalty for Failure to Report: misdemeanor. (KW)

Note: § 38-720 of 1972 senate bill no. 636 indicates the amendment of K.S.A. 1971 supp. 38-720, but this section was not involved in the bill. Some question of whether or not there is a penalty clause.

KENTUCKY

Statute: New Ken. Rev. stat § 199.335 (1973).

Age: under 18.

Who Reports: any physician, nurse, osteopath, teacher, school administrator, social worker, coroner, medical examiner or other person (having reasonable cause to suspect.) (H)

Nature of Injury: That a child . . . serious physical injury or injuries inflicted other than by accidental means by a parent or whose health appears to be endangered from malnutrition, sexual abuse, or gross neglect which would affect either the physical, mental or emotional well being of the child.

To Whom Reported: oral report to representative of Department of Child Welfare, followed by written report.

Legislative Directions: declaration of purpose Type II. Department of Child Welfare shall investigate.

Immunity: acting upon reasonable cause.

Abrogation of Evidentiary Privileges: physician-patient and husband-wife.

Central Registry: . . .

Maximum Penalty for Failure to Report: $100.[5] (KW)

LOUISIANA

Statute: La. Rev. Stat. § 14-403 (1973)

Age: under the age of 17 years.

Who Reports: licensed physicians, interns or residents, nurses, hospital staff members, teachers, social workers, and other persons or agencies having the responsibility for the care of children, *shall* report.

Nature of the Injury: the infliction of physical or mental injury or the causing of the deterioration of a child shall include exploiting or overworking a child to such an extent that its health, moral or emotional well-being is endangered.

To Whom Reported: to the Parish Child Welfare Unit, or the Parish agency responsible for the protection of juveniles, or to any local or state law enforcement agency.

[5] "Not less than" $10, "nor more than" $100.

Legislative Directions: type III.

Immunity: from liability, civil and criminal, in any participation in any judicial proceeding resulting from such report.

Abrogation of Evidentiary Privileges: the privileged status of all confidential communications abrogated except in the case of attorney-client confidential communications.

Central Registry: Baton Rouge by the Department of Public Welfare.

Maximum Penalty for Failure to Report: 6 months and/or $500.00 (KW).

MAINE

Statute: Me. Rev. Stat. Ann. tit. 22 §§ 3851–55 (Supp. 1972 and 1973).

Age: under 16.

Who Reports: any physician, osteopath, or chiropractor (having reasonable cause to believe). (H)

Nature of Injury: physical injury or injuries inflicted other than by accidental means by a parent or caretaker.

To Whom Reported: State Department of Health and Welfare, Division of Child Welfare, and to the county attorney.

Legislative Directions: declaration of purpose Type III.

Immunity: if in good faith.

Abrogation of Evidentiary Privileges: . . .

Central Registry: . . .

Maximum Penalty for Failure to Report: $100 and/or 6 months. (KW)

MARYLAND

Statute: Md. Code Ann. Art. 27 § 35A (effective 1 July 1973).

Age: under 18.

Who Reports: physician, surgeon, psychologist, dentist and any other persons authorized to engage in the practice of healing, registered nurse, licensed practical nurse attending or treating a child in the absence of a practitioner, teacher, counselor or other professional employee of any school, public, parochial or private, or any caseworker or social worker or other professional employee of any public or private social, educational, health or social service agency or any probation or parole officer or any professional employee of a correctional institution, police officer, state trooper. (H)

Nature of Injury: abuse defined to be any physical injury or injuries sustained by a child as a result of cruel or inhumane treatment or as a result of a malicious act or acts.

To Whom Reported: the local department of social services or to the appropriate law enforcement agency. The agency to which the report is made shall immediately notify the other agency.

Legislative Directions: declaration of Purpose, Type I. The purpose being the protection of children who have been the subject of abuse by mandating the reporting of suspected abuse.

Immunity: from any civil liability or criminal penalty that might otherwise be incurred or imposed, if made in good faith.

Abrogation of Evidentiary Privileges: the husband and wife when such proceedings involve the abuse of a child under 18 years, pursuant to 35A of Article 27 of this Code.

Central Registry: the State Department of Social Services.

Maximum Penalty for Failure to Report: none

MASSACHUSETTS

Statute: Mass. Ann. Laws § 119-39 (1972).

Age: under 16.

Who Reports: every physician (who has reasonable cause to believe). 119-39 (C) any social services worker or school official having reasonable cause.

Nature of Injury: serious physical injury or abuse inflicted by a parent or other person responsible for the care of such child.

To Whom Reported: Department of Public Welfare.

Legislative Directions: none.

Immunity: if in good faith.[6]

Abrogation of Evidentiary Privileges: . . .

Central Registry: division of child guardianship, department of public welfare.

Maximum Penalty for Failure to Report: . . .

MICHIGAN

Statute: Mich. Compiled Laws Ann. §§ 14.564 (I) 1 and 2 (new), 3, 4 (1972).

Age: under 17.

Who Reports: any physician (who examines or provides medical treatment for a child who has . . .). (H) 14.564 (I) 1, registered nurse, social worker, school principal, assistant school principal, counselor, law officer. (H)

Nature of Injury: physical injuries which were or may have been intentionally inflicted by any person responsible for his care.

To Whom Reported: triplicate report; copy to prosecuting attorney, to local department of social welfare, and State Department of Social Welfare.

Legislative Directions: no provision except authorization that hospital may detain child until next day for hearing in Probate Court.

Immunity: if in good faith;[7] presumption of good faith.

Abrogation of Evidentiary Privileges: physician-patient and husband-wife.

Central Registry: Lansing, Michigan State Dept of Social Services.

Maximum Penalty for Failure to Report: misdemeanor (V).

---

[6] Reporting "shall not constitute slander or libel."

[7] No mention of immunity from liability resulting from participation in judicial proceedings.

MINNESOTA

Statute: Minn. Stat. Ann. § 626.554 (1)–(7) (Supp. 1971).

Age: minor.

Who Reports: any physician, person authorized to engage in the practice of healing, superintendent or manager of a hospital, nurse and pharmacist (injury appears to have been caused by abuse).

Nature of Injury: physical injury where the injury appears to have been caused as a result of physical abuse or neglect. (RH)

To Whom Reported: appropriate police authority and county welfare agency. Police authority, upon receiving such a report, shall notify county welfare agency.

Legislative Directions: declaration of purpose Type I. County welfare agency shall investigate and offer protective social services.

Immunity: if in good faith.

Abrogation of Evidentiary Privileges: physician-patient and husband-wife.

Central Registry: . . .

Maximum Penalty for Failure to Report: misdemeanor. (KW)

MISSISSIPPI

Statute: Miss. Code of 1942 recompiled (1972 Supp.) §§ 7185-02, 7185–05, 7185–06, 7185–13.

Age: under 18.

Who Reports: physician, dentist, registered nurse (reasonable cause to suspect). (H)

Nature of Injury: a "battered child" defined as a child upon whom a parent, custodian, or person legally responsible for his care has inflicted serious physical injury other than by accidental means as a result of abuse or neglect.

To Whom Reported: "any person designated" by the juvenile court judge, and the county welfare department.

Legislative Directions: whenever any person informs the juvenile court that a child is a "battered child" the court shall make a preliminary inquiry to determine whether the court shall take further action.

Immunity: if in good faith; statutory presumption of good faith.

Abrogation of Evidentiary Privileges: physician-patient and other similar privileges.

Central Registry: . . .

Maximum Penalty for Failure to Report: . . .

MISSOURI

Statute: Mo. Ann. Stat. §§ 210.105, 210-108 (Supp. 1970), 210.107.

Age: under 17.

Who Reports: reporting by any physician, surgeon, dentist, chiropractor, podiatrist, Christian Science or other health practitioner, registered nurse, school nurse, teacher, social worker or other with responsibility for care of children for financial remuneration (having reasonable cause to believe) (H) shall report 210.105(1).

Nature of Injury: injury or disability from physical abuse or neglect.

To Whom Reported: county welfare office or county juvenile officer.

Legislative Directions: none.

Immunity: if in good faith.

Abrogation of Evidentiary Privileges: physician-patient and husband-wife.

Central Registry: . . . State Welfare Office, Jefferson City.

Maximum Penalty for Failure to Report: misdemeanor. (V)

MONTANA

Statutes: 10-901–10-905 (10-901, 10-902, and 10-903 amended and effective 1 April 1973).

Age: under the age of majority.

Who Reports: physician, nurse, teacher, social worker, attorney, law enforcement officer, or any other person who has reason to believe.

Nature of Injury: serious injury or injuries inflicted upon him as a result of abuse or neglect, or has been willfully neglected.

To Whom Reported: department of social and rehabilitative services (its local affiliate) and county attorney of the state where the child resides.

Legislative Provision: cause protective services of the state to seek to prevent further abuses, protect and enhance welfare of these children, and preserve family life wherever possible.

Immunity: presumed to be acting in good faith and immune from civil and criminal liability.

Abrogation of Evidentiary Privileges: all-inclusive (physician-patient privileges or any other similar privilege against disclosure).

Central Registry: Department of Social and Rehabilitative Services.

Maximum Penalty for Failure to Report: none.

NEBRASKA

Statute: Leg. Bill No. 207, 83ᵈ Legislature (effective 2 September 1973).

Age: any child.

Who Reports: physician, medical institution, nurse, school, employee, social worker, or other person.

Nature of Injury: knowingly, intentionally, or negligently permitting a minor child to be (a) placed in a situation which may endanger his life or health; (b) tortured, cruelly confined, or cruelly punished; (c) deprived of the necessities; or (d) (if under the age of 6) left in a motor vehicle unattended.

To Whom Reported: law enforcement agency.

Legislative Directions: none.

Immunity: unqualified, if in good faith.

Abrogation of Evidentiary Privileges: physician-patient and husband-wife.

Central Registry: Department of Public Welfare.

Maximum Penalty for Failure to Report: $100. (W)

NEVADA

Statute: Nevada Revised Statutes, § 200.501 to § 200.507 (1973) [8]

Age: any child under 18 years of age.

Who Reports: any physician, surgeon, dentist, doctor of osteopathy, chiropractor, optometrist, every nurse licensed to practice professional nursing, attorney, clergyman, social worker, school authority and teacher, and every person who maintained or is employed by a licensed child care facility or children's camp. (H)

Nature of the Injury: serious injury or injuries inflicted on him as a result of abuse or neglect.

To Whom Reported: to the local office of the Welfare Division of the Department of Health, Welfare, Rehabilitation, to any county agency authorized by the juvenile court, or to any police department or Sheriff's office.

Legislative Directions: declaration purpose Type I, the law enforcement agency shall investigate forthwith and refer such reports to the local welfare division of the Department of Health and Welfare. The division shall investigate, provide social services, advise law enforcement of its investigations, and begin court actions if necessary.

Immunity: immunity from civil or criminal liability if made in good faith. [9]

Abrogation of Evidentiary Privileges: physician-patient.

Central Registry: none.

Maximum Penalty for Failure to Report: misdemeanor. (KW)

NEW HAMPSHIRE

Statute: N.H. Rev. Stat. Ann. §§ 571:25–30 (1971).

Age: under 18.

Who Reports: any person who becomes aware (having reasonable cause to suspect). (H)

Nature of Injury: serious physical injury or injuries inflicted other than by accidental means by a parent or other person responsible for his care, or a child who has been neglected. (RH)

To Whom Reported: bureau of child welfare of the division of welfare of the department of health and welfare, which shall notify an appropriate police authority.

Legislative Directions: declaration of purpose Type I.

Immunity: if in good faith.

Abrogation of Evidentiary Privileges: physician-patient and husband-wife.

Central Registry: State Division of Welfare.

Maximum Penalty for Failure to Report: not less than $200, not more than $500. (K)

NEW JERSEY

Statute: N.J. Stat. Ann. §§ 9:6-8.1–8.7 (Supp. 1972 and 1973), 9:6-8.8 to 9:6-12 (Supp. 1973). Seem to be almost parallel acts.

[8] Assembly Bill No. 184, enacted into law as chapter 101 of the Statutes of Nevada 1973, effective July 1, 1973.

[9] Immunity also from any liability for "instituting" an investigation and action by the Welfare Department.

218   *Appendix B*

Age: under 18.

Who Reports: any physician or osteopath (having reasonable cause to suspect) (H) (and/or any person, 9.6-8.10).

Nature of Injury: new abuse def. N.J.S.A. § 9:6-1 (effective 1 June 1973).

To Whom Reported: county prosecutor of the county in which the child resides (and/or Bureau Children's Services, 9.6-8.10)

Legislative Directions: declaration of purpose Type I. County prosecutor shall investigate and proceed in the manner prescribed by law relevant to criminal prosecution or file a complaint with the Bureau of Children's Services.

Immunity: unqualified.

Abrogation of Evidentiary Privileges: . . .

Central Registry: Bureau of Children's Services, Trenton.

Maximum Penalty for Failure to Report: misdemeanor (KW) (and disorderly person, 9.6-8.14).

NEW MEXICO

Statute: N.M. Stat. Ann. §§ 13-14-14.1–13-14-14.2 (1973)

Age: any individual who is less than 18 years of age.

Who Reports: any licensed physician, resident or intern examining, attending or treating a child, any law enforcement officer, registered nurse, visiting nurse, school teacher or social worker acting in his or her official capacity or any other person.

Nature of the Injury: serious injury or injuries have been inflicted upon a child as a result of abuse, neglect or starvation.

To Whom Reported: county social services offices of the health and social services department in the county where the child resides or the probation services office of the judicial district in which the child resides.

Legislative Directions: None.

Immunity: Presumption of good faith and shall be immune from liability, civil or criminal.

Abrogation of Evidentiary Privileges: total abrogation of evidentiary privileges (shall not be excluded on the grounds that the matter is or may be the subject of a physician-patient privilege or similar privilege or rule against disclosure).

Central Registry: . . .

Maximum Penalty for failure to Report: any person failing, neglecting, or refusing to report shall be guilty of a misdemeanor and shall be punished by a fine of not less than $25.00 nor more than $100.00.

NEW YORK

Statute: McKinney's Consolidated Laws of New York Ann., Social Services, Title 6, §§ 411 to 428.[10]

[10] *McKinney's Consolidated Laws of New York Annotated,* Social Services Act, Title 6, §§411–428, effective 15 June 1973. This act repeals §383A of the Social Services Law and §383C of the Social Services Law; 1032, 1033, and 1034 of the Family Court Act are similarly repealed by this act.

The new N.Y. act is so extensive and far-reaching and so innovative that it is very difficult to summarize it in any form that we've chosen here (e.g., central registry, color photos and x-rays, local community plans).

Age: an "abused child" means a child under 16 years of age defined as an abused child by the Family Court Act and a "maltreated child" includes a child under 18 years of age.

Who Reports: any physician, surgeon, medical examiner, coroner, dentist, osteopath, optometrist, chiropracter, podiatrist, resident, intern, registered nurse, hospital personnel engaged in the admission, examination, care, or treatment of persons; Christian Science practitioner, school official, social services worker, day-care center worker, or any other childcare or foster care worker, mental health professional, peace officer, or law enforcement official. Note: § 414 refers to any other person who may make a report.

Nature of Injury: abused child means any child under 16 years of age, defined as an abused child by the Family Court Act. The second subsection refers to a maltreated child, and this is defined as a neglected child by the Family Court Act or any child who has had serious physical injury inflicted upon him by other than accidental means.

To Whom Reported: oral reports are made immediately to the statewide central registry of child abuse and maltreatment unless the appropriate local plan calls for an oral report to be made to the local child protective service. If the oral report is made in a particular locality to the local child protective services or service, local child protective service immediately makes an oral or an electronic report to the statewide central registry. Written reports are made to the appropriate local child protective service.

Legislative Directions: the purpose is to encourage a more complete reporting of suspected child abuse and maltreatment and to establish in each country a child protective service capable of investigating reports swiftly and in providing protection of the individual child.

Immunity: total immunity from any liability, civil or criminal, for the purpose of any proceeding, the good faith of any person required to report cases of child abuse or maltreatment is presumed in New York.

Abrogation of Evidentiary Privileges: found in another section apart from Mandatory Reporting of Child Abuse, but the abrogation of evidentiary privileges is extensive.

Central Registry: new electronic statewide central registry.

Maximum Penalty for Failure to Report: any person who is so required to report and willfully fails to do so is guilty of a Class A misdemeanor.

NOTE: § 420(2) establishes civil liability for any person required to report under the provisions of this act who knowingly and willfully fails to do so.

NORTH CAROLINA

Statute: N.C. Gen. Stat. § 110-115–122 (Supp. 1972).

Age: under 16.

Who Reports: any professional personnel, physician, surgeon, dentist, osteopath, optometrist, chiropractor, podiatrist, RN, PN, hospital administrator, Christian Science Practitioner, medical examiner, coroner, social worker, law enforcement officer, school teacher, school principal, school attendance counselor (or other professional personnel in public or private schools).

Nature of Injury: physical injury inflicted by parents or allowed to be inflicted by other than accidental means. Statute also requires reporting of substantial risk of physical injury created or allowed to be created by parents and the committing or permitting to be committed (again by parents) of any sex act on the child, and neglect.

To Whom Reported: director of social services of county (1) where child resides or (2) where found.

Legislative Directions: Type III. Director shall investigate, seek removal of child from home if necessary, arrange for protective services, petition juvenile court if necessary.

Immunity: unless person acts in bad faith or with a malicious purpose.

Abrogation of Evidentiary Privileges: physician-patient and husband-wife.

Central Registry: State Department of Social Services.

Maximum Penalty for Failure to Report: . . .

NORTH DAKOTA

Statute: N.D. Cent. Code §§ 50-25-01–05 (Supp. 1971).

Age: under 18.

Who Reports: any physician, osteopath, chiropractor, or public health nurse (having reasonable cause to believe).

Nature of Injury: serious injury or physical neglect not explained by the available medical history as being accidental in nature.

To Whom Reported: director of the Division of Child Welfare of the Public Welfare Board. If circumstances are such as may warrant immediate action, the report may be made to the appropriate juvenile commissioner or state's attorney.

Legislative Directions: the director of the Division of Child Welfare shall investigate any initial report made directly to him, shall report to the juvenile court, and shall offer protective services. Juvenile Commissioner or state's attorney shall take suitable action and shall report to the director of the Division of Child Welfare.

Immunity: if in good faith (except for perjury).

Abrogation of Evidentiary Privileges: physician-patient and husband-wife.

Central Registry: . . .

Maximum Penalty for Failure to Report: . . .

OHIO

Statute: Ohio Rev. Code Ann. § 2151.42.1 (Baldwin Supp. 1972).

Age: under 18 or any physically or mentally handicapped child under 21 years.

Who Reports: any physician, podiatrist, dentist, person rendering spiritual treatment, any registered nurse, visiting nurse, school teacher, school authority, or social worker acting in his official capacity (having reason to believe). (H)

Nature of Injury: any wound, injury, disability, or condition of such a nature as to reasonably indicate abuse or neglect of such child. (RH)

To Whom Reported: municipal or county peace officer.

Legislative Directions: peace officer shall refer report to the appropriate county department of welfare or children services board. Department or board shall investigate. Investigation in cooperation with law enforcement agency which shall have primary responsibility. Department or board shall report to law enforcement and offer social services—also may recommend regarding prosecution.

Immunity: unqualified.

Abrogation of Evidentiary Privileges: physician-patient.

Central Registry: State Welfare Department shall maintain.

Maximum Penalty for Failure to Report: (2151-99) Not more than $500 or imprisonment not more than one year, or both. (V)

OKLAHOMA

Statute: Okla. Stat. Ann. tit. 21, §§ 845–48 (Supp. 1972 and 1973).

Age: under 18. (21-846)

Who Reports: every physician, dentist, osteopath, and every registered nurse examining in the absence of a physician or surgeon (having reason to believe) (H) and every other person having reason to believe—*shall.*

Nature of Injury: physical injury or injuries inflicted as a result of abuse or neglect.

To Whom Reported: county office of Department of Institutions, Social and Rehabilitative Services.

Immunity: if in good faith.

Abrogation of Evidentiary Privileges: physician-patient or similar privilege (21-848).

Central Registry: Child Welfare Division of Department of Institutions, Social and Rehabilitative Services.

Maximum Penalty for Failure to Report: misdemeanor. (KW)

OREGON

Statute: Ore. Rev. Stat. §§ 418.740–775 (1972)

Age: under 15

Who Reports: any physician and dentist (having reasonable cause to suspect). (H) (146.750 [3]: school teacher, school nurse, school principal, public health nurse, employee of Public Welfare Service, police officer—*shall.*)

Nature of Injury: physical injury or injuries defined as caused by blows, beatings, physical violence, or abuse where there is some cause to believe that such physical injury was intentionally or wantonly inflicted and includes wanton neglect as revealed by physical examination which leads to physical harm to the child (or physical injury caused by a knife, gun, pistol, inflicted by other than accidental means.)

To Whom Reported: law enforcement official.

Legislative Directions: none.

Immunity: if in good faith.[11]

Abrogation of Evidentiary Privileges: physician-patient and husband-wife.

Central Registry: Children's Services Division.

Maximum Penalty for Failure to Report: none.

---

[11] Immunity further limited to those having "reasonable grounds" for making report.

PENNSYLVANIA

Statute: Pa. Stat. Ann. tit. 11 §§ 2101–9, 4330 (Supp. 1972–73)

Age: under 18.

Who Reports: any physician, osteopath, or school nurse, teacher whose examination discloses evidence of gross physical neglect or injury.

Nature of Injury: 11-2103 begins with "discloses evidence of gross physical neglect or injury not explained by available medical history as being accidental in nature" or suffering any wound or other injury inflicted by his own act or by the act of another by means of a knife, gun, pistol, or other deadly weapon (or in any other case where injuries have been inflicted upon any person in violation of any penal law of the Commonwealth)

To Whom Reported: public child welfare agency.

Legislative Directions: Type III. Investigate, offer child protective services, petition juvenile court if necessary.

Immunity: unqualified.[12]

Abrogation of Evidentiary Privileges: physician-patient.

Central Registry: Department of Public Welfare.

Maximum Penalty for Failure to Report: $300 in default, 90 days. (V)

RHODE ISLAND

Statute: R.I. Gen. Laws Ann. §§ 40-11-1–10 (Supp. 1971).

Age: under 18.

Who Reports: any physician or osteopath (who has cause to believe). (H)

Nature of Injury: physical injury or injuries which may adversely affect his health and welfare, inflicted upon him other than by accidental means by a parent, legal guardian, or any other person having custody or care of such child.

To Whom Reported: department of social welfare, division of community services and law enforcement agency.

Legislative Directions: declaration of purpose Type III. Department shall investigate to determine the circumstances. The department shall advise the law enforcement agency and shall provide such social services as are necessary to protect the child and preserve the family. Law enforcement agency to investigate further and take action.

Immunity: if in good faith.

Abrogation of Evidentiary Privileges: husband-wife, physician-patient, and any other except attorney. (40-11-9)

Central Registry: Department shall (40-11-4)

Maximum Penalty for Failure to Report: . . .

SOUTH CAROLINA

Statute: S.C. Code Ann. §§ 20-302.1–302.4 (Supp. 1971).

Age: under 16.

---

[12] No mention of immunity from liability resulting from participation in judicial proceedings.

Who Reports: all physicians, staff members of hospitals and similar institutions and medical officers of the United States on duty in this state (having cause to believe).

Nature of Injury: physical injury inflicted other than by accidental means by a parent or person having the care, control, or custody.

To Whom Reported: to the proper authority of the county having jurisdiction over minors or to the sheriff of said county.

Legislative Directions: no provision.

Immunity: if in good faith; presumption of good faith.

Abrogation of Evidentiary Privileges: . . .

Central Registry: . . .

Maximum Penalty for Failure to Report: $100 or 30 days. (V)

SOUTH DAKOTA

Statute: South Dakota Compiled Laws, § 26-10-10 to 26-10-15 [13]

Age: any child under 18 years of age.

Who Reports: any physician, surgeon, dentist, doctor of osteopathy, chiropractor, optometrist, podiatrist, psychologist, social worker, hospital intern, resident, or law enforcement officer having reasonable cause (H). (there is provision made for any other person who has reasonable cause to suspect abuse).

Nature of the Injury: has been starved or has had serious physical injury or injuries inflicted upon him by abuse or wilful neglect other than by accidental means. (It should be noted that reference is made to the emotional injury or injuries as a result of abuse or wilful neglect. *South Dakota Compiled Laws*, § 26-10-10 [1973])

To Whom Reported: to the judge of the district county court of the child's residence.

Legislative Directions: none.

Immunity: immunity from any liability, civil or criminal if in good faith.

Abrogation of Evidentiary Privileges: physician-patient and husband-wife.

Central Registry: Department of Public Welfare.

Maximum Penalty for Failure to Report: misdemeanor (KW).

TENNESSEE

Statute: Tenn. Code Ann. §§ 37-1201–1211 (Ch. 81, Public Acts of 1973, eff. August 1973)

Age: under 18 years of age or who is reasonably presumed to be under 18 years of age.

Who Reports: any person having knowledge of or called upon to render aid to any child. (H)

Nature of Injury: sustained any wound, injury, disability or physical or mental condition which is of such a nature as to reasonably indicate it has been caused by brutality, abuse or neglect.

To Whom Reported: to the judge having juvenile jurisdiction over the county office of the department or to the office of the sheriff or the chief law enforcement official of the municipality where the child resides.

[13] South Dakota Compiled Laws, §26–10–10 and §26–10–12 are amended and become effective March 27, 1973. Substitute Bill 193, Legislature of South Dakota.

Legislative Directions: to protect children whose physical and mental health and welfare are adversely effected by brutality, abuse or neglect. It is intended that as a result of such reports, the protective services of the state shall be brought to bear on the situation to prevent further abuses.

Immunity: presumption of acting in good faith and shall thereby be immune from any liability, civil or criminal.

Abrogation of Evidentiary Privileges: The husband-wife privilege, the psychiatrist-patient privilege, the psychologist-patient privilege.

Central Registry: the department (i.e., the Tennessee Department of Public Welfare) shall maintain a state central registry.

Maximum Penalty for Failure to Report: who knowingly fails to make a report is guilty of a misdemeanor and upon conviction may be fined not more than $50 or imprisoned for not more than 3 months or both.

TEXAS

Statute: Texas Family Code, Title Two, §§ 34.01–.06 (1973)

Age: under 18.

Who Reports: any person having cause to believe . . . shall report.

Nature of Injury: child's physical or mental health or welfare has been or may be further adversely affected by abuse or neglect.

To Whom Reported: county child welfare unit or county agency responsible for protection of juveniles or any local or state law enforcement agency.

Legislative Directions: none.

Immunity: immunity unless made in bad faith or with malice.

Privileges: all waived except for the attorney-client provision.

Central Registry: Texas State Welfare Department, Austin, Texas.

Penalty: none.

UTAH

Statute: Utah Code Ann. §§ 55-16-1–6 (Supp. 1971).

Age: minor.

Who Reports: any person (having cause to believe). (H)

Nature of Injury: physical injury as a result of unusual or unreasonable physical abuse or neglect—now includes negligence (55-16-1, purpose).

To Whom Reported: local city police or county sheriff or office of the Utah State Welfare Department (Division of Family Services).

Legislative Directions: declaration of purpose Type III.

Immunity: if in good faith.

Abrogation of Evidentiary Privileges: physician-patient.

Central Registry: . . .

Maximum Penalty for Failure to Report: misdemeanor. (KW)

VERMONT

Statute: Vt. Stat. Ann. tit. 13 §§ 1351–55 (Supp. 1972).

Age: under 16.

Who Reports: any physician, osteopath, or chiropractor (having reasonable cause to suspect). (H)

Nature of Injury: serious physical injury or injuries inflicted upon him other than by accidental means by a parent or other person responsible for his care.

To Whom Reported: the department of social welfare.

Legislative Directions: declaration of purpose Type II.

Immunity: if in good faith.

Abrogation of Evidentiary Privileges: . . .

Central Registry: . . .

Maximum Penalty for Failure to Report: $25. (V)

VIRGINIA

Statute: Va. Code Ann. §§ 16.1-217.1–217.4 (1972).

Age: under 16.

Who Reports: any person licensed to practice medicine or any of the healing arts, or any registered nurse, visiting nurse, public school nurse, registered social worker, associate social worker, probation officer, receiving information in his or her professional or official capacity (having reason to believe). (H)

Nature of Injury: serious bodily injury or injuries or who has suffered harm by reason of neglect or sexual abuse which may be the result of abuse or neglect. (RH)

To Whom Reported: juvenile and domestic relations court or to the sheriff or chief of police.

Legislative Directions: after the report is received by the police, he shall investigate and take such action as he determines necessary for the protection of the child. He shall file a report to the appropriate juvenile and domestic relations court.

Immunity: if in good faith.[14]

Abrogation of Evidentiary Privileges: physician-patient and husband-wife.

Central Registry: Bureau of Vital Statistics.

Maximum Penalty for Failure to Report: . . .

WASHINGTON

Statute: Wash. Rev. Code Ann. §§ 26.44.010–080 (Supp. 1972).

Age: under 18, and any mentally retarded person.

Who Reports: any chiropodist, chiropractor, dentist, doctor of osteopathy, Christian Science practitioner, teacher, counselor, school nurse, school administrator, registered nurse, psychologist, pharmacist, clergyman, employee of health and social services, shall report, mandatory (reasonable cause to believe).

[14] Immunity from civil liability only. This immunity extended unless reporter "acted in bad faith."

Nature of Injury: physical injury or injuries inflicted other than by accidental means or suffering from physical neglect or sexual abuse.

To Whom Reported: proper law enforcement agency, or social health services.

Legislative Directions: declaration of purpose Type II.

Immunity: unqualified.[15]

Abrogation of Evidentiary Privileges: physician-patient [16] and husband-wife.[17]

Central Registry: State Department of Public Assistance.

Maximum Penalty for Failure to Report: misdemeanor. (K)

WEST VIRGINIA

Statute: W. Va. Code Ann. § 49-6A-1–4 (1972).

Age: under 18.

Who Reports: any physician or doctor of healing arts or any registered nurse, any visiting nurse, any school teacher, or any social worker acting in his or her official capacity (having reason to believe). (H)

Nature of Injury: serious injury or injuries inflicted upon him or her as a result of abuse and neglect.

To Whom Reported: prosecuting attorney.

Legislative Directions: declaration of purpose Type I. Prosecuting attorney shall investigate and take such action as may be necessary to prevent any further injury and to punish person or persons responsible.

Immunity: if in good faith; statutory presumption of good faith.

Abrogation of Evidentiary Privileges: . . .

Central Registry: . . .

Maximum Penalty for Failure to Report: . . .

WISCONSIN

Statute: Wis. Stat. Ann. § 48.981 (1971).

Age: child

Who Reports: a physician, surgeon (in situations where the examination creates a reasonable ground for an opinion), or a dentist, hospital administrator, nurse, social worker, or school administrator (having reasonable cause to believe).

Nature of Injury: physical injury or other abuse inflicted by another other than by accidental means.

To Whom Reported: to a county child welfare agency or the sheriff of the county.

Legislative Directions: the recipient shall notify the other receiver of reports within 48 hours. Provision for investigation and further action by sheriff and investigation by county child welfare agency.

[15] Immunity from civil liability only.

[16] In addition, reporting "shall not be deemed a violation of the patient-physician relationship or confidence."

[17] In criminal case growing out of child abuse.

Immunity: if in good faith—civil and criminal (49.981 [2])

Abrogation of Evidentiary Privileges: . . .

Central Registry: . . .

Maximum Penalty for Failure to Report: $100 and/or 6 months. (KW)

WYOMING

Statute: Wyo. Stat. § 14-28.7–13 (1972).

Age: under 18.

Who Reports: physician, surgeon, dentist, osteopath, chiropractor, podiatrist, intern, resident nurse, druggist, pharmacist, social worker or any other person (having reasonable cause). (H)

Nature of Injury: physical injury or injuries inflicted other than by accidental means by a parent or caretaker. (14-28.7)

To Whom Reported: Department of Health and Social Services of County.

Legislative Directions: county welfare department shall investigate and shall render a written report to the county attorney.

Immunity: if in good faith.

Abrogation of Evidentiary Privileges: physician-patient, husband-wife.

Central Registry: State Department of Health and Social Services.

Maximum Penalty for Failure to Report: $100 and/or 6 months. (KW)

VIRGIN ISLANDS

Statute: Vir. Isl. Code Ann. tit. 19, §§ 171–76 (Supp. 1971).

Age: under 15.

Who Reports: any physician or osteopath (having reasonable cause to suspect). (H)

Nature of Injury: serious physical injury or injuries inflicted other than by accidental means by a parent or other person responsible for his care.

To Whom Reported: an appropriate police authority.

Legislative Directions: declaration of purpose Type II.

Immunity: if in good faith.

Abrogation of Evidentiary Privileges: physician-patient and husband-wife.

Central Registry: . . .

Maximum Penalty for Failure to Report: $500 and/or 1 year. (KW)

APPENDIX C

Report of the New York State Assembly Select Committee on Child Abuse April 1972

Douglas J. Besharov

Executive Director
Select Committee on Child Abuse
270 Broadway
New York, N.Y. 10007

Perry B. Duryea

Speaker
New York State Assembly

Editors' Note

In 1969 the tragic death of Roxanne was reported in great detail in a New York City newspaper. Every facet of the mother's problems, the boyfriend's sickness, and finally the discovery of the child's body in the East River was covered in depth. A judge was "tried" by the press and "convicted" by the public. Blame was passed from one agency or individual to another, and yet no one person was to blame, not even the parents. It was the "system" which permitted little or no involvement by any single, helpful person—a situation very reminiscent of the case of Mary Ellen in the same city nearly one hundred years earlier (see introduction to first edition). Like Roxanne, some 1,000 other children in the U.S. died in 1969, and 1,000 more in 1970 and again in 1971. So that Roxanne might not have died in vain, Perry B. Duryea, Jr., Speaker of the New York State Assembly, appointed a Select Committee to suggest resolutions to this vast and growing problem. In New York there were some 400 reported cases of suspected child abuse and neglect in 1966, and almost 3,200 in 1971.

The Select Committee did its work in a thorough and painstaking manner. The final report, prepared by Douglas J. Besharov with the assistance of Susan H. Besharov, is one of the most complete summaries of the problems of child abuse to date. Now begins the long and difficult task of implementation: keeping what's good of the old while fighting to weed out the tradition and hierarchical structure of "the system."

During the one hundred years between Mary Ellen's death and that of Roxanne, we have learned much. Many dedicated individuals in this vast state are now trying to mold these experiences into therapeutic programs that have the potential of stemming the tide in the next decade.

The editors feel that the specific findings and recommendations made by the Select Committee are appropriate not only for New York but for every state concerned about the problem of child abuse.

*   *   *

Introduction

To deny that child abuse is in part both a consequence and a symptom of broad societal and cultural problems sweeping the nation—of the brutality and violence of our age, and, to an extent, of poverty—is to deny reality.

This committee has heard testimony by professionals that the condition of poverty is by no means the sole cause of parental abuse or neglect and that most children of even the very poor are neither abused nor neglected, as we use the term. They did, however, advise the committee that poverty can make it more difficult for a borderline parent to cope with the pressures of raising a child.

In early 1972 a detailed study of the fifty-four child fatalities in New York City suspected to be the result of parental abuse or maltreatment was performed for the New York City Task Force on Child Abuse and Neglect by the office of Mrs. Barbara Blum, Deputy Administrator of the Human Resources Administration. The study revealed that

> more than half of these families were known to social service agencies prior to the death of the child and that eight cases were known to various sections of the Bureau of Child Welfare. One case was being serviced by child protective service at the time of death, and six cases had been closed in the Child Protective Service prior to time of death. The study has extremely important implications for determining the future of Child Protective Services. (1)

We now know that thirty-nine of these families were known to other agencies prior to the child's death and another nine were known to the Bureau of Child Welfare at the time of death. Bureau of Child Welfare records indicate that in at least seven of the thirty-nine cases the other agency had prior knowledge that a situation of abuse or neglect existed or that something was wrong in the family, but did not report it. Though actively involved with the family, they did not report the child's situation to the Bureau of Child Welfare.

Though New York State seems to have the most comprehensive legislative treatment for the adjudication of child abuse and neglect in the Nation, this committee concludes, as do most responsible people in the field, that children who are in danger still receive inadequate protection and limited benefit from the myriad of expensive programs now in existence in New York State.

During the Select Committee's investigation, we repeatedly came upon situations that reflected the inadequacy of care to children in the broadest sense. For example, the study of suspected child abuse fatalities raised questions about the efficiency of the Aid to Dependent Children welfare grant in providing protection and care for children. The purpose of the ADC grant is to maintain not adults but children. In the fatality cases that involved families on welfare, the ADC grant obviously did not ensure the survival of the child. The grant was used for other things, especially in cases where the children died of starvation, and it did not prevent situations of neglect or abuse from claiming the life of the child.

Although generalizations about sixty-two separate counties can be tenuous, it is fair to say that we have found a pervasive inability on the part of childcare agencies to respond both programmatically and administratively to the needs of the children they are meant to serve. We have found that New York State has an expensive, mismanaged or unmanageable child welfare system that only imperfectly fulfills the important child protective responsibilities given it.

According to the conventional wisdom, the failure of our institutions is caused by a dreadful lack of facilities, of social workers, of judges, of shelters, of probation workers, and of all sorts of rehabilitative social and psychiatric services. Undoubtedly, if we poured millions of dollars more into existing programs the picture would be less bleak. But this committee has become convinced that existing facilities and services, if properly utilized, could go a long way toward filling the need for service. In fact, we believe that unless existing services are first put in order, additional sums of money could not be properly utilized. Nowhere is this more sadly in evidence than in the complete failure of the state Department of Social Services to fulfill its legislatively mandated responsibilities to plan, supervise, and administer child protective programs.

Forceful direction is needed to coordinate and channel existing child welfare services in a manner more beneficial to the children they are meant to serve. The legislature can provide that leadership, in cooperation with the executive branch, by developing the guidelines and framework for better child welfare services. It is no longer adequate for the legislature merely to respond passively to the recommendations of others who may have a vested interest in the status quo. Neither is it adequate for the legislature to be forced to respond in an ad hoc manner to crisis situations, as it did two years ago in relation to child abuse proceedings in the Family Court.

Much of what is said in this report others have said before; many of the recommendations made have also been made by others. We acknowledge the work of all those who have gone before. That the inadequacies we have found have been known for years and that solutions were proposed for them years ago suggests not only that the changes which the committee proposes are long overdue but also that there is something terribly wrong with a system that fails to correct its own obvious shortcomings.

In its first two years the committee proceeded under the assumption that if child protective agencies were given the legal tools with which to protect children, children would be protected. But we have seen that New York's laws, the most comprehensive in the nation, have not been enough. We have striven not to interject the committee and the legislature into administrative affairs. Instead our proposals seek to reorient and focus the accountability and planning responsibilities of child welfare officials in an attempt to compel the system to respond on its own to administrative and programmatic needs.

Findings and Recommendations

The Select Committee on Child Abuse views with alarm the seeming inability of child protective agencies to deal with the rise in child maltreatment in New York State. The recognition, reporting, investigation and treatment of child abuse must be accorded a priority in our child welfare system which it does now not receive.

The committee therefore makes the following findings and recommendations.

Recognition and Reporting

1. *Child abuse is much more prevalent than is revealed by current statistics; substantial numbers of children are being abused and neglected without being brought to the attention of the appropriate authorities.*

The New York legislature passed its first child abuse law in 1964. It mandated the reporting of suspected cases of abuse observed by physicians and others, and the investigation and treatment of these cases by local Departments of Social Services. Since then there has been a steady increase in the number of cases reported, as can be seen in table 1.

TABLE 1

CASES OF CHILD ABUSE REPORTED IN NEW YORK, 1964–71

Year	New York State	New York City	Upstate and Long Island	N.Y.S. Deaths
1 Aug. 1964–31 Jan. 1965	211	152	60	unknown
1 Feb. 1965–31 Dec. 1965	573	446	127	unknown
1966	416	301	115	unknown
1967	706	505	201	unknown
1968	987	733	254	36
1969	2,169	1,737	432	65
1970	3,027	2,543	484	93
1971	3,224	2,532	692	125

SOURCE: New York State Department of Social Services

Most disquieting of all, this committee has found that substantial numbers of children have injuries suggestive of child abuse not reported to the authorities despite being observed by physicians, nurses, social workers, or teachers. This committee's study of child abuse fatalities disclosed a number of cases in which children have been killed after such persons failed to report observations of abuse. The case of Larry R. illustrates this pattern:

> In the early part of 1971, two-year-old Larry was brought to a hospital emergency room by his parents. He had multiple bruises, multiple scars on his buttocks, and healing lesions on his upper and lower lips. Less than an hour after his arrival in the hospital, Larry died of laceration of the liver—hemo-peritinem—which the coroner called homicidal.
>
> A week before Larry's death, his mother had taken him to the same hospital for treatment of a broken arm. The hospital record indicated that numerous marks and scars were observed on Larry's body. There is no indication that any physician or other hospital personnel raised any question concerning these injuries. And no report of suspected abuse was made.

At one of the committee's hearings (Syracuse, 16 November 1971), the commissioner of social services of Auburn reported on a survey his department performed by examining, after the fact, Medicaid payment forms of children treated in hospital emergency rooms. Out of 195 cases surveyed, 26, or approximately 13 percent of the emergency room treatments recorded were found to be of "suspicious injuries" that should have been reported—none were. They therefore concluded that the number of potential abuse cases *might* be double or triple the number presently reported.

In a study by a hospital in nearby Rochester, approximately 10 percent of all children under the age of five who came into the emergency room fell into the battered child category, and another 10 percent into the category of neglect (2). Until the intensive evaluation which these cases had derived from the study, many had gone unreported.

Patterns of nonreporting seem to vary from community to community. Our investigation indicates that except from "inner-city hospitals," reporting is sporadic and not uniformly conducted. The statistics, for example, indicate that abuse or neglect among the affluent is seldom reported, while such reporting is common with regard to poor people living in cities. Suburban hospitals as well as doctors either are not aware of the symptoms of child abuse and neglect or are not willing to report such abuse and neglect.

2. *Restrictive policies of the state Department of Social Services discourage and limit reports of suspected child abuse.*

Testifying before the committee, the commissioner of the state Department of Social Services cited a number of factors which, the department contends, limit the reporting of suspected child abuse.

> While it is not possible to account for the problem of underreporting, and particularly the disparity in reports between New York City and the rest of the state with absolute certainty, several factors seem to be influential. Although many persons will casually accept the possibility that some children may be subjected to abuse, it appears that only the tragedy of the death or severe maiming of a child in one's own community, with its ensuing publicity and notoriety, provides the stimulus for reporting the suspected abuse of other children. Other factors would seem to be: more restrictive definitions being applied upstate—that is, the tendency to report abuse only when injury is severe; diagnostic capabilities not sufficiently well developed, particularly in areas where medical centers are not involved; reluctance to become involved due to fear of criminal prosecution of parents or automatic removal of children (more personal relationship with one's neighbors in rural communities mitigates against being willing to speak out even though this will protect a child); frustration that reports have not in fact resulted in the desired goals—that is, rehabilitative treatment for the child and family, or successful adjudication in Family Court; lack of organized, vigorous programs of casefinding and interpretation. (3)

3. *Failure to conduct a continuing program to educate all those required to report suspected abuse is the most significant reason for underreporting.*

Perhaps the most recurrent theme that was expressed at the committee's hearings was that of the lack of sensitivity on the part of childcare professionals and the community to the problem of child abuse. This insensitivity is the result of both lack of education in this area and disbelief that such maltreatment actually occurs. In addition, difficulty in diagnosis was frequently cited.

The committee concludes that the single most effective method of encouraging fuller reporting is to educate professional personnel who are mandated to report under the law. Childcare professionals, including physicians, nurses, social workers, and teachers, must be sensitized to the occurrence of child abuse; must be trained in its identification; and must be instructed in reporting procedures. An educational program would also seek to explain that child protective procedures are not punitive in nature—that their purpose is the protection of the child and rehabilitation of the family.

4. *The refusal to accept "nonmandated" reports of suspected child abuse has presented a distorted view of the problem in this state.*

The committee was surprised to learn of a rule of the Department of Social Services which prohibits reports from what it calls "nonmandated" sources. A nonmandated source is any source not listed in the child abuse reporting law. Among nonmandated sources are the police. Thus, if the police find a child severely beaten and they have a confession or other clear evidence that a parent or parents are responsible, a report will not be accepted by the state's central register. Unless the case comes in contact with a mandated source and unless the mandated source happens to make a report, it will never be listed in the register. It is extremely unlikely for such a report to be made in that case. The mandated source would assume that after police action, an appropriate report would already have been made to the central registry.

The committee has been informed of cases where nurses and other hospital personnel were actually instructed not to report children whom they suspected to be victims of maltreatment. Since they are not mandated sources under the law, they cannot report their suspicions without permission of the hospital administrator, who is the mandated source for the hospital. While the direct responsibility in such situations now lies with the hospital administrator, we decry the fact that the department's rules can be used in this way to prevent reporting.

We recommend legislation that ends these senseless and dangerous practices by adding all law enforcement agencies as mandated sources and by requiring the state central register to accept and record all reports of suspected child abuse it receives, whatever the source. New York City, at the urging of the Task Force on Child Abuse and Neglect, violates this state mandated rule, and accepts reports from police and other nonmandated sources. This sensible practice should be statewide policy. In accordance with present law, immunity from civil and criminal liability should be granted to these nonmandated sources for good faith reports. Immunity is indispensable to the working of the reporting law because it removes the fear of an unjust lawsuit for attempting to help protect a child.

The committee recognizes that many of these reports that the register will receive will be unfounded—indeed a large number of reports from mandated sources appear to be unfounded. Hence, in the section of this report dealing with the operations of the central register we propose that provision be made for amending or expunging unfounded or untrue reports.

5. *The rigid interpretation of "serious abuse or maltreatment" adopted by the Department makes diagnosis of suspected abuse difficult and therefore limits reports.*

The Social Services Law (Section 383-a) mandate that reports must be made to the state Department of Social Services on children who have "had serious physical injury inflicted upon [them] by other than accidental means, or whose condition gives indication of other serious abuse or maltreatment" has been seriously undercut by an interpretation which excludes cases of "neglect," no matter how severe, from this mandate. There is no requirement in law for this exclusion, and its wisdom is questionable.

There is a great deal of misunderstanding about the difference between abuse and neglect. Similar cases are differently categorized as either abuse or neglect on the basis of individual judgment, understanding, and experience with little regard to the legislative purpose.

Distinctions between abuse and neglect have no place in the decision of whether or not to report a case of child maltreatment to the authorities. This committee introduced the distinction between child abuse and neglect into the laws of this state. That distinction, however, was made in the Family Court Act as a procedural device to insure priority treatment and speed of action for cases involving severe and immediate danger to children. As such, it has no role to play in the decision of whether or not society should intervene to protect a child—it was intended only to assign a *priority* to child abuse cases within the context of the family court's overburdened resources.

Another prime cause of this failure to report seems to be a reluctance of physicians and other childcare professionals to label parental conduct "abusive," especially when they are not certain whether the suspected maltreatment is caused by abuse or neglect.

Unless the central register is mandated to accept reports of neglect as well as abuse, there is little hope of determining the true incidence of child maltreatment. Such information is vital if we are to discern adequately and at an early stage patterns of behavior detrimental to the welfare of children.

Many respected authorities have suggested that *all* childhood injuries be reported; currently, reports concern only those cases where abuse is suspected. This, it is said, avoids a number of the factors which seem to limit reporting—for example, reluctance to accuse, difficulty in diagnosis, and lack of sensitivity. An "all trauma" register of this type is being tested experimentally in Monroe County. In light of the difficulties in administering the present central register, discussed in the next section, this suggestion to record millions of reports would be impossible to implement on a statewide basis without a massive reorientation of resources. The vast expenditure of funds necessary to put such a system into operation would be unjustified until its implications were fully explored.

6. *The local department's evaluation of the report of abuse should be given to the person who made the original report.*

In later sections of this report the fragmentation of services as it weakens the delivery of protective services will be discussed. Fragmentation also tends to discourage reporting. At the present time a person who makes a report of suspected abuse is rarely informed of the local Department of Social Services' disposition of his report or even whether the investigation verified his suspicion. Sometimes his request for information is refused on the grounds of confidentiality. As a result, he feels isolated from the department's efforts to protect the child; he does not know the validity of his diagnosis; and he does not know the effect of his report. Why should there be any surprise when the next time he observes a child possibly suffering from maltreatment, he decides not to make a report?

We propose legislation that would require the results of the department's investigation be made available to the person who made the original report. Of course, the amount of information provided would be limited by the child's and his family's right of privacy and would also depend upon the source of the report. Thus we envision that only a minimal report would be furnished to nonprofessional sources.

7. *The reporting law needs to be simplified and clarified.*

By reason of numerous amendments, the existing child abuse reporting law (Social Services Law §383-a) has become confusing to both lawyer and layman. As a consequence, medical and child care professionals, looking to it for guidance, become confused or are misled as to their responsibilities and powers. Hence, a first priority is the simple redrafting of section 383-a to clarify its meaning and facilitate its readability.

8. *There must be explicit civil and criminal liability for failure to report suspected child abuse.*

This committee is appalled at the lack of sensitivity and callous disregard of the law exhibited by those who continue to violate the legal mandate to report cases of suspected abuse. Society cannot countenance such blatant disregard of its law. Although this committee would prefer to rely upon education and voluntary compliance, we are convinced that those who refuse to fulfill their duty must be penalized. We therefore propose that the reporting law (Social Services Law §383-a) be amended to provide for civil liability for failure to report an appropriate case; we further propose that the child's guardian be given standing to bring such a suit. The failure to report already raises the possibility of civil liability. Through an explicit statement of liability, we hope to bring added pressure on those required to report.

For the same reason we also propose to make explicit the existence of criminal liability. In its review of child abuse fatalities the committee found numerous cases of criminally negligent failure to follow legally mandated procedures.

The Central Register

9. *The New York State Central Register contains inaccurate and insufficient information.*

The purposes to which the central registry can be put largely depend upon the material it contains and the method of its dissemination. By receiving and processing reports immediately, it could provide a foolproof method of insuring that investigations are performed and services provided. It could also monitor the provisions of such services by other agencies.

At the very least, however, the central registry should provide the kind of statistical data necessary to reach management and policy decisions concerning the delivery of child protective services. Unfortunately, we have found glaring inaccuracies in the actual information recorded in the register.

10. *The statewide central register must be made consistent with legislative intent. If it is to help protect the lives and well-being of children, it must be capable of receiving and responding to telephoned reports of child abuse twenty-four hours a day, seven days a week.*

It is often difficult to diagnose a case of suspected child abuse without information concerning a child's prior injuries or lack thereof. Abuse and neglect are often continuing and repetitive. Because children are often taken from hospital to hospital, doctor to doctor, or social agency to social agency, it is virtually impossible for an individual to know whether a child has previously suffered a suspicious injury—impossible, that is, unless the individual has access to some sort of data bank which could provide such information. That individual should be a telephone call away from information regarding whether the injured child or another child in the same family has been the subject of prior reports. A previous incident, similar in kind, can turn supple doubt into relative certainty. Prior reports can provide information necessary in determining the seriousness of a given family's situation and can be an important factor in determining whether the child should immediately be removed from his home. We recommend that the information contained in the register be available to all persons with "need to know."

The central register should be responsible for notifying the appropriate local authorities to perform an investigation and for monitoring the delivery of protective service to the child and family involved.

Finally, this committee recognizes that many of the reports received by the central registry are unfounded. There should be a method of amending reports and removing them from the register under appropriate circumstances. Even in those cases where the suspicion of abuse has been verified, the confidentiality of the information in the register must be carefully protected. To insure that only authorized persons are given information on the telephone, a system of authorization numbers might be instituted.

Investigation, Verification, and Intervention

There are three more or less clearly defined steps or phases in any program of services to abused and neglected children and their families which must be performed after the initial recognition and report of abuse or neglect is made. In chronological order, they are:

1. Investigation and verification of reports;
2. Protection of the child from further abuse, including, when necessary, immediate removal of the child from the home environment;
3. Provision for the long term needs of the child by (a) rehabilitating the parents (or other guardian) wherever possible so that the "home is made safe" for the child, or (b) when necessary, to place the child for adoption.

Experts in child abuse agree that the most critical time for help to both the child and his parent is within the first seventy-two hours after a report of possible abuse is filed. The immediate danger to the child should be gauged within twenty-four hours and the offer of service made within the next forty-eight hours.

11. *Fragmentation of child protective responsibility causes critical delays in service and sometimes leads to a dangerous lack of information necessary to protect children from further abuse.*

The most immediate consequences of the fragmentation of child protective responsibility are delays in services caused by continuous "referrals" to the next individual in the assembly line and the possibility that communication and cooperation will break down at a critical juncture. Anywhere from three to eight agencies can be involved in a particular case.

The constant shifting of agencies and personnel in the middle of cases—coupled with the repetition of interviews which it requires—can be confusing, threatening, and annoying to the families and children involved, making worker-client relationships almost impossible. While diversity may theoretically encourage creativity, the present atomization of responsibility and patchwork of services limits the vision of individual components and stifles meaningful assistance. Unable to see and sometimes unwilling to deal with the broader objective—that is, the welfare of the child—each discharges his individual responsibility with little consideration of the consequences of his actions.

The result of what a recent New York City Department of Social Services report called "a patchwork system of delegated responsibility, often poorly defined, often based on vague and superficial considerations" (4, p. 10) is the continued jeopardy of children even after their danger has been observed by some governmental or social service agency. The committee's study of suspected child abuse fatalities disclosed too many situations in which one agency was in possession of critical information concerning a child's care and well-being that would have prevented a child's death had it been communicated to and accepted by the "appropriate" agency. The death of Vincent H. exemplifies the consequence of such failures:

> In early January the police responded to the call of a mother of five who reported that her 8-month-old son, Vincent, had stopped breathing while she was feeding him. About five minutes later the police arrived; attempted resuscitation failed. Cause of death was reported as malnutrition, immaturity, and terminal aspiration.
> One week before, a neighbor had found Vincent and his four brothers and sisters home alone. She phoned her own public assistance caseworker who immediately went to the apartment to verify the complaint. The worker found the H.'s apartment dirty and the children seemingly underweight and in need of medical attention; she also observed that two of the children had feces on their legs. At that time, the neighbor commented that she had called the police in the past to report similar incidences, but they had never responded.
> The public assistance worker reported what she had observed to the child protective staff of her own agency, which rejected her report and forwarded it to the H.'s own public assistance worker for investigation since the public assistance staff was the "appropriate" agency to investigate. There is no record of any investigation being performed.
> The original public assistance worker had also attempted to get information from a neighborhood health center where, according to the neighbor, the family had received medical care. The center informed the worker that they had never heard of the family and, furthermore, did not service the area where they lived.
> At that point, the social worker gave up; a week later, Vincent was dead.

Two days afterward, the Department of Social Services began an investigation, during which time it was discovered that the family and its problems were well known not only to the neighborhood clinic but also to a Health Demonstration Project in the neighborhood.

12. *Investigations as presently performed by child protective agencies inadequately determine the existence and severity of abuse.*

The advantage of using social workers instead of police to perform these "investigations" resides in their presumed ability (1) to make psychological evaluations of the parents in order to determine if abuse or maltreatment is occurring; (2) to convince parents of their problems; and (3) to offer assistance on a voluntary basis. Unfortunately, our study of suspected child abuse fatalities reveals a systematic inability to successfully perform basic investigations.

Investigative caseworkers appear to have difficulty in getting genuine information about families. Some records in such cases have no official information from other agencies involved in the case. The only information they contain comes from the hearsay reports of relatives or from the parents themselves. The record in these cases often shows no effort to verify these unofficial reports, which are accepted as fact.

Table 2, prepared from information supplied from the state Department of Social Services, reveals the large number of cases in which no action is taken because of a "lack of evidence."

TABLE 2

RESULTS OF CHILD PROTECTIVE INVESTIGATIONS*

RESULT OF INVESTIGATION	PERCENT OF TOTAL	
	1969	1970
Abuse confirmed	44.3	42.0
Social investigation	33.4	33.4
Court decision	10.8	8.6
Abuse ruled out	21.1	28.1
Social investigation	20.1	25.6
Court decision	1.0	2.5
Abuse uncertain	34.6	29.9
Lack of evidence	25.0	23.1
Case pending in court	9.7	6.8

* SOURCE: New York Department of Social Services.

13. *Child protective investigations suffer because social workers do not clearly understand their role and responsibility to protect children.*

We have found that the attitude of "child protective" workers is often a barrier to effective investigation. Because of their sympathy for the parents of the dead child, they often did not ask the hard, pertinent questions which might embarrass or upset the parents.

Part of the problem lies in the fact that child protective workers do not clearly understand that their primary role and responsibility is to protect children from further injury and maltreatment. The research of the New York City Task Force on Child Abuse and Neglect documents this failing:

> When asked what do you see as the role of the investigator in abuse and neglect cases, the vast majority (85%) made reference to developing a casework relationship with the client. One of every three respondents mentioned diagnostic study, while less than twenty percent felt that a child protective worker's role was to protect the child. Most respondents (67%) felt that their colleagues had the same role definitions as they did. (5, p. 98)

Clear and realistic goals must be laid down for those responsible for child protective services. To make the home "safe for the child's return" is an admirable statement of intention, but it contains no guidelines upon which child protective judgments may be made. Although primarily an administrative concern, the need to correct attitudes and establish criteria requires legislative attention. The committee recommends that the present social services law be amended to set forth clear guidelines for corrective action.

14. *Many family court child abuse cases continue to go uninvestigated.*

Another consequence of fragmentation of responsibility for child protective cases is that many cases are heard by the family court without benefit of a pretrial investigation. Because no one agency is responsible for the investigation of all child protective cases, no agency is institutionally concerned when some child protective cases go uninvestigated.

At the trial stage of the proceeding, the absence of evidence that could have been obtained through investigation can force the family court judge to dismiss the case. Indeed, dismissal rates in child protection cases are extremely high—over 26 percent are dismissed, over 21 percent withdrawn (6, p. 353).

Precourt investigations also act as a device to screen and divert cases before they reach the family court by either establishing them to be unfounded or resolving them through voluntary acceptance of social service. The absence of investigation needlessly adds to the workload of an already overburdened family court. Many of the cases the court is thus shouldered with are based on frivolous, unfounded complaints brought by a distraught spouse having marital difficulties. For cases in which the Department of Social Services is not originally involved, a number of family court judges have adopted the practice of ordering the department to investigate the allegations of abuse and neglect. Although without clear legal basis, these orders are generally respected, and their use should be encouraged until unambiguous legal authority is established by an act of the legislature.

15. *There must be a highly trained and specialized staff to investigate* all *child protection cases.*

Since most abused children are too young or too frightened to relate what happened to them, and since most acts of abuse and maltreatment take place in the privacy of the home, without an identifying motive, the gathering of evidence in such cases is probably more difficult than in adult murder cases. Therefore, those who are given the grave responsibility for such investigation must be highly qualified.

This committee has received a number of suggestions that the investigatory function be transferred to local police departments. They have a large body of highly trained, experienced, and properly equipped professional investigators. Available twenty-four hours a day, seven days a week, they have access to all phases of forensic science and have available from local precincts a wealth of information about the communities and people involved.

In light of the grave deficiencies found in the investigations performed by local departments of social services and the advantages of police investigation, the suggested use of police was studied carefully. The committee, however, was reluctant to surrender the many real benefits of social work investigation without first attempting to improve the performance of the social worker investigators. For example, depending on the community, from 30 to 60 percent of the cases reported to the central register are resolved by an out-of-court offer of social services. This is not to say, however, that the presently offered social services are sufficiently helpful in preventing future abuse or maltreatment.

Therefore, before considering such a fundamental reorientation, the committee recommends that we should first attempt to improve investigations presently performed by child protective agencies. The first priority must be to end the existing fragmentation of child protective agencies. There must be a specialized, unitary staff responsible for the investigation of all reports of maltreatment in a community. The advantages will be immediate and clear-cut. Agencies and individuals in the community will look to one place for advice and assistance in child protective cases. The caseworkers will be more sensitive to the needs and problems of the family because continued contact will encourage rapport while also easing problems of information communication and inter- and intra-agency coordination. Agency and individual accountability for the protection of children will finally be clearly established.

16. *There will be a greatly increased need for qualified protective workers. The consolidation and coordination of existing protective agencies would produce efficiencies to fill this need and result in substantial revenue savings.*

Local departments of social services, societies for the prevention of cruelty to children, family courts, family court probation, hospitals, and a variety of other public and private agencies share, divide, and duplicate scarce resources. This waste of manpower, effort, expertise, record keeping, administration, and policy planning caused by the existing fragmentation of services has never been justified. It cannot be tolerated in this period of severe budgetary constraint. If existing workers from the many public agencies now playing a role in child protection are consolidated or at least coordinated, the resulting efficiencies of operation will allow for a greatly expanded total case load.

Much can be done to encourage private or voluntary agencies to provide more services to children with little or no increase in state and local expenditures. For instance, hospitals make from 60 to 80 percent of all child abuse referrals to the Department of Social Services. In this process a social worker on the hospital staff—usually someone with a master's degree in social work—makes the referral with a full report to a Department of Social Services caseworker, who has less professional training. The department caseworker then duplicates much of the hospital social worker's efforts. With appropriate legislation, the hospital social worker could be designated a special representative of the department, assuming adequate safeguards, and could thus receive the appropriate federal reimbursement for a job which for almost all purposes he has already done.

Rehabilitation and Foster Care

17. *Abused and neglected children are in urgent need of therapeutic services.*

We usually think of abused and neglected children only as the recipients of physical injury. However, the damage of abuse and neglect to a child's emotional development is often equally severe. Hence, therapeutic services are crucial for these children if they are to grow up to be happy, normal, and law-abiding individuals.

Dr. Shervert Frazier, deputy director of the New York State Psychiatric Institute and professor of clinical psychiatry at Columbia University, gave dramatic testimony on the very high incidence of childhood abuse found in the histories of adult and adolescent murderers. Dr. Frazier was involved in one study of all the murderers in the state of Minnesota. They were interviewed along with each living relative, generally three to five persons. Their study began with no hypothesis. He explained in his testimony that they were interested in acting-out behavior and that "the ultimate in acting-out in anything would be murder. So we began studying acting-out behavior in murderers. And then it came up: the findings, just by collecting data, that they had all been subjected to physical brutality."

The plight of abused and neglected children, whose life experience has been one of deprivation and attack, deserves society's attention. However, if humanitarian considerations in themselves do not succeed in mobilizing sufficient resources to help these children, these consequences to society of the failure to provide for maltreated children must be considered.

A full range of services is required. Some children will have to be removed temporarily and will require foster homes that are carefully supervised to help the foster parents handle their difficult behavior. For other young children therapeutic nurseries or therapeutic day care centers are needed—again with personnel oriented toward the unusual demands and needs of these children.

18. *If we wish to combat child abuse, we must attempt to rehabilitate parents.*

Removal of an abused child from his home is often the only way to protect his health and well-being. Thus, short- and long-term foster care are important social services which must be available for abused and neglected children.

However, removal of a child from his home and the use of foster care is not a solution to child abuse. There may be other children in the household who may subsequently become the object of an attack. In addition, even if all existing children are removed permanently from the home, our review of child abuse fatalities and information from concerned hospital social workers reveal that many abusive mothers continue to have children after having their earlier children removed. Thus, the pattern of child abuse is repeated in the same household, with the same perpetrators, but with new victims.

Hence, the existence of a rehabilitative program capable of breaking these genera-tional patterns of abuse and maltreatment is of extreme importance to the community. From a cold dollars-and-cents point of view, it is less expensive to make a child's home safe for his return than to keep him in prolonged foster care.

To be successful, a rehabilitative program must have easy access to a range of counseling and concrete services designed to alter or modify many of the specific psy-chological and environmental conditions which lead parents to abuse their children. The services frequently necessary to modify patterns of abuse include:

casework and supervision of families;
psychiatric counseling;
group therapy;
lay therapists and surrogate mothers;
visiting nurse service;
abusive parents anonymous;
short-term placement;
long-term placement;
homemaker services;
day care;
babysitting;
family planning;
job counseling, training, and referral;
adequate housing.

19. *The present fragmented and uncoordinated child welfare complex is unable to deliver sufficient protective and rehabilitative services to abused children and their families.*

The patchwork of child welfare agencies is responsible for lack of communication, inefficiency, and inadequate service. A list of agencies in itself reveals the splintering of services. A family in trouble too often gets lost in the maze of agencies. Repeating their problems over and over again to social worker after social worker becomes frustrating, annoying, and destructive to any helping relationship. Our fatality study clearly demonstrates how the involvement of too many social workers dilutes the re-sponsibility any one person takes for a family.

The effectiveness of the multitude of social workers in child welfare agencies, family service agencies, welfare centers, hospitals, psychiatric clinics, schools, courts, neigh-borhood houses, and poverty programs is restricted because cooperative community structures are lacking. Too often agencies are able to help with one aspect of a family's difficulties only to find the family remains in crisis because other services are either nonexistent or inaccessible.

Even when a social worker engaged in counseling a family is painfully aware of a concrete problem, he may find himself as impotent as the family in getting the needed service. A social worker in a clinic or hospital may spend many frustrating hours try-ing, without success, to obtain adequate housing for a family desperately in need of such help. Homemaker services, day care, or jobs may also be inaccessible to social workers.

20. *Efforts to supervise the safety of children who remain in or are returned to their homes are often inadequate to detect and prevent further abuse.*

It is claimed that the reason for inadequate supervision is lack of sufficient staff. While it is undoubtedly true that smaller caseloads would improve supervision, the real problem seems to be the quality of the supervision being provided. One well-conducted home visit is worth two or three superficial ones. The committee's study of child abuse fatalities disclosed numerous home visits conducted in such a fashion as to reveal no real information concerning the current condition and status of the children and families involved. These are the same weaknesses that plague protective investigations—namely, inadequately trained and inexperienced caseworkers who lack the skills requisite to perform their responsibilities competently and efficiently.

21. *The efforts of childcare agencies suffer from inadequate casework and administrative practices. Too many children remain in foster care for too long.*

There are many highly dedicated and skilled people in the field of child welfare. However, caring for over 50,000 children outside of their homes is a Herculean task. Despite the sincere and energetic efforts of childcare professionals, the quality of care is uneven.

We found alarming evidence of the negligence of some childcare agencies to carry out their fundamental responsibilities toward the children in their care. One agency had no recording on some cases for over three years. Caseworkers leave this agency without recording any information at all about some of their contacts with the children, parents, and foster families in their care. Such negligence obviously renders thoughtful planning impossible. In another agency, within one year, seven children were placed one after another in one foster home and then removed with no record to explain why so many children were unable to get along there. It was thus impossible to know what kinds of children, if any, to place there in the future.

Childcare professionals have informed us in discussions that many agencies maintain only minimal contact with the natural parents of the children in their care. Many agencies have retained their child-focused approach to such an extent that they make no effort to work with parents of children who are in their care for years. We want to emphasize that there are some agencies in which creative and highly constructive rehabilitative efforts are made with natural families, but these seem to be the exceptions to typical practice.

22. *Foster care places a child in a painfully ambiguous situation, with an uncertain future, and therefore it should be used as little as possible.*

The use of foster care should be kept to a minimum, because even when the quality of care is adequate, it is very troubling to children. Children frequently blame themselves for the separation from their parents and hence harbor feelings of guilt. At the same time if they relate the separation to some fault of the parents, their identification with the parents causes them to see themselves as similarly "bad." In addition, the very nature of foster care adds to a child's concerns about his worth.

The child's position in foster care is further complicated by the policy prohibiting foster parents and the children from becoming too emotionally involved. This policy is based on the theory that foster care is temporary with the return of the child to his natural parents the ultimate objective. Undue affection on the part of the foster parent, it is asserted, could cause emotional ambivalence if and when the child is returned to his natural home. It is not unusual for agencies to remove children from a foster home because foster parents have shown too much love. One agency precipitously removed a nine-year-old and an eleven-year-old from a foster family in which they were thriving, because after three years of placement the agency believed that the foster parents were becoming unsuitably attached to these children. The children were placed in an institution.

Unfortunately, we have drifted into a system where foster care is the main mode of "treating" the problems of abuse and neglect as well as parental inadequacy in general. Society cannot afford to tolerate a system that for so many children has such destructive consequences.

23. *Children who could and should be freed for adoption instead languish in foster care.*

Some parents of children in foster care will never have the interest or capacity to care for their children. In formulating plans for children in foster care, adoption should be actively explored as early as possible in all cases in which it is unlikely that the children will return to their natural families. The behavior of many parents who leave their children in care suggests that they might agree to release their children for adoption if this alternative were actively explored.

Throughout the state we find agencies negligent in providing the stability of an adoptive home for large numbers of these children. Even after an affirmative decision to terminate parental rights, the adoption process is very often torturously slow. It requires the cooperation and successful interaction of many agencies and individuals not always able or willing to do so.

Speed in terminating parental rights and placing children with adoptive parents is crucial to maximize the adoptability of children. Prospective adoptive parents generally prefer infants. Although they tend to be somewhat more flexible today, their preference for young children continues to limit the adoptability of children older than three or four, particularly from minority groups or with physical handicaps or behavioral problems.

24. *Children, especially abused and neglected children, who for their own safety should be removed from their homes, are sometimes not removed because of the quality of foster care.*

The often indiscriminate continuation of placement and the quality of foster care makes more difficult the already difficult decision to place a child. The decision to remove a child from his home is colored by the limited availability of good placement facilities. Judges in making dispositional decisions and social workers in working with families cannot help but weigh the alternatives of the quality of care outside the home with the possibility of danger within it. This leads some judges and social workers, quite understandably, to try to avoid or delay placement. Concerned with the possibility that children will be in mediocre placement situations longer than necessary, they may hesitate to remove a child from a dangerous situation.

25. *Foster care has become an overused response to the problems of child abuse and other parental inadequacy. For the majority of New York children in need, child welfare has meant child placement.*

Although no firm figures seem to be available, sources in the state Department of Social Services and among child welfare professionals estimate that there are over 50,000 children in placement outside of their homes as a result of parental inadequacy. When compared to the rest of the nation, New York's use of foster care in relation to other child welfare services is extremely high—twice as high, in fact.

The reasons for child welfare's reliance on foster care as opposed to helping children within their families are complex and stem from attitudes ingrained over many years. The nation's child welfare system was developed to care largely for orphans or children whose parents were ill. It was originally designed to come to the rescue of "innocent," well-adjusted children beset by sudden tragedy. The focus on caring for helpless children has not adjusted sufficiently to the conditions of modern society. Today placement is more often due to the inability of parents to give their children adequate supervision, care, or emotional support.

The traditional skills of child welfare fail to meet many of the needs of today's urban society. The child welfare system has been particularly resistant to change. Perhaps this is partly because it is more pleasant and more manageable to help individual children than it is to grapple with patterns of pathological interaction in families and the distasteful problems of addicted parents, or impulsive, immature parents, or slightly retarded parents.

Although foster care is sometimes the best plan for children, the New York State child protective network is overdependent on its use. Foster care should be used only when the gravity of a family's problems make other services insufficient to render a home safe for a child. This committee is alarmed by the disproportionately large role foster care plays because of the consequences it has on the safety and well-being of children in need of protection.

26. *The enormous amounts of money allocated to child welfare are consumed by expensive custodial foster care programs instead of being available for treatment and rehabilitation.*

Not only is foster care troubling to children but it is also extremely expensive. While enormous amounts of money are used in foster care, funds are lacking for other child welfare programs geared toward rehabilitation. A recent detailed analysis of the costs of foster care in New York reveals that a child entering the foster care system in 1971 and remaining in substitute care until age 18 will cost the public $122,500. (This figure is based on an anticipated annual 5 percent increment.) Thus, foster care costs about five times as much as raising a child in its own family—an expense which, on a low-cost, urban budget, is estimated to be $25,560 (6).

The enormous cost of maintaining children in foster care underscores the savings realized when children are discharged to their own families or adoptive parents. From their calculations, Fanshell and Shinn (7) projected that 100 families with children in care would cost 14 million dollars, while 100 discharged would cost 2 million, and the same number adopted, one-half million dollars. We join with them in the hope that a realization of the enormous extra expense of foster care will promote a more rational system.

27. *There must be a statewide computerized information system that monitors the care and treatment provided children and their families.*

The problem of children remaining in foster care due to inadequate efforts to work with parents toward their return home or to free them for adoption has been recognized by the legislature in the past. In an attempt to ameliorate the situation, legislation was enacted requiring a review of all foster care cases by the family court every twenty-four months. The need for some review is certainly great but it has yet to be seen whether such a large task can be handled by an already overburdened court. This is an important step, but intense efforts should be made to arrive at permanent plans for a child before he has been in care for two years.

28. *For most abusive parents, the present child protective system in New York will never be able to* prevent *child abuse.*

This committee is deeply concerned by the picture of family disintegration presented during its investigations. Our efforts are doomed to failure unless we deal with this fundamental reality. If we hope to begin combatting child abuse at its roots, we must provide means, now absent, whereby families can receive the help they need.

Where a family-oriented service proves an effective method of treatment, current expenditures for high cost foster care can be reduced. Treating the real problems of the child and of his family will serve the best interests of our society as well as of the child.

This committee is still considering this most significant problem and intends to issue its recommendations as soon as possible. At that time we will propose what we believe is necessary to ensure that appropriate facilities are established.

The Family Court of the State of New York

Although, as was indicated in the previous section, most reported child abuse cases do not reach the family court, the family court is nevertheless the linchpin upon which the entire out-of-court system depends. Only if social agencies can ultimately turn to the court can we realistically expect their offer of assistance to be accepted. Moreover, the cases that do reach the family court are often the most severe and require speedy and firm action.

Although child abuse and neglect are crimes (Penal Law 260.10 [2]), the family court has no criminal (that is, punitive) jurisdiction. Instead, it has civil (child protective) jurisdiction "to help protect children from injury or mistreatment and to help safeguard their physical, mental and emotional well-being" (§ 1011). The criminal court can only protect the child by jailing the offending parent. While this is sometimes necessary and appropriate (§ 1014), in most cases the abuse or neglect is a problem arising from and exacerbated by the constellation of familial relations and tensions. In such cases, the remedial actions of the family court are much more effective than those of the criminal court in preventing future abuse or neglect. Hence, the family court protects children by providing social and psychological assistance, albeit often involuntarily imposed, to families and households in order to "assure that the home satisfies at least the minimal requirements of a suitable place for a child to grow" (committee comments to 1962 act, § 34, repealed). We reaffirm our faith in this state's dedication to the notion that the problems of child abuse and neglect are primarily social and psychological and that they are therefore subject to amelioration through social and psychological assistance.

The family court, however, is only a court. Its role is the central, though limited, one of "determining when the state . . . may intervene against the wishes of a parent on behalf of a child so that his needs are properly met" (§ 1011). It is thus the role of the family court to impose, in proper cases, a treatment or protective measure on a family or household when voluntary adjustments are insufficient or unsatisfactory. Viewed in this light, the court cannot and should not be held responsible for the detection, reporting, and investigation of child abuse and neglect.

29. In many ways the state's most important trial court, the family court, has been consigned to second-class status, and its efforts have been undermined by inadequate supporting services.

In any one day a family court judge can decide that a neglected or abused child should be placed in foster care for years; that a child should be placed in a state training school; that a father or mother should be prohibited from returning to a home; that a child's custody should be transferred from one parent or relative to another; that a child's paternity has not been established; that a parent's rights over a child should be permanently terminated; or that a child should be adopted. These decisions, of immense importance to the individuals before the court and to society as a whole, are at least as important as the determinations made by any other trial court in the state. Yet, the family court traditionally has been considered a court of secondary importance to which priority resources need not be assigned—the importance of its work underestimated and its personnel demeaned.

Compounding the difficulties confronting the family court judge is the absence of adequate supporting services. From adjudication to disposition, the family court judge is "dependent upon the cooperation and assistance of other municipal agencies and private social agencies, so often understaffed and ill equipped to meet even the minimum needs and demands of this court, [contributing] heavily to its inability to become the social forum it was designed to be" (8, p. 2).

30. The family court's ability to adjudicate cases of abuse and neglect is compromised by inadequate child protective services.

The family court can only act upon cases which are brought to it. It depends on local departments of social services, police, and other agencies and interested parties to bring cases of abuse and neglect to its attention. Likewise, the adjudicatory process is dependent upon the evidence discovered by the investigations of these agencies and their effective presentation in court.

31. *The provision for a separate child abuse part in the family court must be maintained and strengthened.*

No problem facing the urban family courts of New York state, or all our urban courts for that matter, is more deplorable than that of overburdened and overcrowded court facilities. The backlogs, delays, and rushed proceedings this causes can have tragic consequences if, as a result, an adequate inquiry into a child's safety is postponed or precluded.

In recognition of these conditions which afflict the court, the 1969 child abuse legislation, which this committee drafted, established a special "child abuse part" in the family court to "be held separate from all other proceedings of the court" and "charged with the immediate protection of [abused children]" (repealed § 1013 [1]).

Earmarking a case as child abuse, putting it in a special part, and noting on the summons, warrant, and petition that it is a "child abuse case," acts as a red flag to indicate a case requiring immediate and careful consideration. Moreover, such special parts develop and enhance the expertise and sensitivity of the judges, attorneys, social workers, and other personnel who man them.

32. *The family court does not have access to the specialized services necessary to fulfill its rehabilitative purpose.*

Dean Paulsen's summary of the condition facing the nation's juvenile courts applies with equal vigor to the family court of the state of New York.

> The dreams were inflated dreams—cut off from the hard realities of the world. The cities, counties, and states were never willing or able to provide the juvenile court with the resources its theory required. Few judges have reached the level of performance that the reformers expected. Probation staffs have been inadequately staffed and given such large numbers to supervise that nothing but the most perfunctory attention can be given most cases. Most courts do not have access to either adequate auxiliary services or to a wide range of institutions for the help of the adjudicated delinquent. (9, pp. 30, 46)

If a parent abuses or neglects a child, the family court judge has basically two choices: (1) he or she can remove the child from the parents' custody, perhaps permanently; or (2) he or she can warn, order, and implore the parent to discontinue the abuse. The court has little or no psychiatric or treatment facilities available to it.

The only counseling or supervision of a household that most courts can offer is the monthly visit of an untrained probation officer. A 1970 grand jury in New York County investigating the child abuse murder of a little girl made this finding:

> The testimony before the Grand Jury showed that when a family is placed on probation, which is the alternative to placement of the child or children, very often there is no supervision of that family. This is due to the understaffing of the Probation Department of the City of New York attached to the Family Court. The result is that there is no such procedure as "supervision of the court." (10, p. 3)

33. *There should be a revised system of judicial administration for the family court of the state of New York.*

If the family court is to assume its rightful place among the courts of this state, the court must first possess the authority and capability of dealing with its own internal problems. But too many of our family courts, perhaps handling as much as three-quarters of the court's total caseload, suffer from antiquated and cumbersome administrative procedures, almost nonexistent calendaring practices, poor record keeping, no on-the-job training of personnel, inappropriate or inefficient use of personnel, little program development, and haphazard administrative accountability.

34. *There should be greater contact between family courts in order to devise, exchange, and implement solutions to their common problems.*

Both the Association of Family Court Judges and the Judicial Conference conduct seminars and conferences in which new concepts in judicial administration and family court law and procedure are discussed and developed. Attendance of as many judges as possible is essential. The modest amount of expense involved is more than justified by the interchange of ideas and intellectual stimulation and improved judicial morale which will result.

35. *In many areas of the state, the institution of law guardian has proven to be an inadequate protection for children in the court process.*

The nature of the role of law guardian seems to vary from attorney to attorney, but most distinctly from urban to rural or suburban areas. In a number of areas, the attorneys who fulfill the role of law guardian conduct an active pretrial investigation and take a forceful role in the court proceedings. When they are convinced that a child is abused or neglected, these attorneys take on a prosecutor-like role as they press for a court adjudication and appropriate disposition. Unfortunately, such attorneys are only a minority of the attorneys who act as law guardians.

In urban counties, where the law guardian function is performed by the local Legal Aid Society, many law guardians perform no pretrial investigations, collect little evidence, and play a passive, watching role during the court proceedings—save to make occasional recommendations to the judge. In effect, the law guardians have assumed the role of second judge, of weighing and testing the evidence. This was not the role intended for law guardians, who as the title suggests, were expected to work actively to protect their clients' physical well-being.

36. *A new legal officer, the "children's attorney," should be created and made responsible for the effective investigation and presentation of child protective cases.*

Given the continuing failure of the majority of law guardians to fulfill the role envisioned for them, the committee now concludes that a new legal officer, the "children's attorney," be established in every county and be given responsibility for the effective investigation and presentation of *all* child protective cases.

The presence of an effective advocate—someone to gather, marshal, and present evidence—is crucial to the successful adjudication of child protective cases.

In addition, the presence of a full-time staff of attorneys can be expected to improve the operating efficiency of the family court and all agencies that appear in it. By handling calendars, arranging witness and case coordination, and furnishing other legal aids to the court, these attorneys can be expected to have a significant impact on family court processes. An experimental project in New York City funded by the federal government, the Family Court Law Officer Project, has already succeeded in reducing the average number of adjournments before trial from six to three while at the same time more than doubling the rate of successful adjudication of cases.

Future Planning

37. *With only a few notable exceptions, there is a pervasive, statewide inability of child welfare agencies at all levels of government to respond programmatically or administratively to the needs of the children they are meant to serve.*

Although generalizations about sixty-two separate counties can be tenuous, it is fair to say that we have found a pervasive inability on the part of childcare agencies to respond both programmatically and administratively to the needs of the children they are meant to serve. We have found that New York State has an expensive, mismanaged, or unmanageable child welfare system that only imperfectly fulfills the important child protective responsibilities given it. Furthermore, although increased facilities and new programs are necessary, if we in New York State are to provide the best possible protection for abused children, this committee has become convinced that existing facilities and services, if properly utilized, could go a long way toward filling the need for service. In fact, we believe that unless existing services are first put in order, additional sums of money cannot be properly utilized. Nowhere is this more sadly in evidence than in the complete failure of the state Department of Social Services to fulfill its legislatively mandated responsibilities to plan, supervise, and administer child protective programs. However real the need for additional funds may be, it is evident that we are simply not getting what we should out of the money presently being spent. Part of the explanation is the suffocating bureaucracy, the callousness and insensitivity that the system encourages, and our inadequate understanding of how to influence human behavior.

More fundamentally, though, the reason for the growing irrelevancy of society's institutions is an insistence on a policy of developing programs instead of developing a policy focus. Too often we have attempted to solve problems by establishing a detailed and comprehensive program. We have for too long attempted to plan and provide for all facets of a program from a centralized, management perspective. We have assumed that implementation would be effected as predicted and that the nature of the problem, as diagnosed from a distance, would not change. Given the enormity and complexity of our problems, this approach has resulted in the institutionalization of roles and processes often irrelevant to the individual child. It was bound to fail.

38. *There is an urgent need for a group or agency that can speak for or advocate the needs of children and work toward the coordination and strengthening of child welfare programs.*

There is no one and no one agency in government who speaks solely for the needs of children. From the highest to the lowest levels of government, no one speaks on behalf of the overall needs of the child. The thousands of children who rely upon our child welfare complex for care, treatment, and protection are unrepresented in government planning circles. The planning and policy-making phases of child welfare are as fragmented and uncoordinated as its other phases. The state and local departments of social services—the primary sources of child protective services—are preoccupied with the problems of welfare administration and family assistance planning. The few interested staff are overwhelmed by the other responsibilities of these departments. They cannot give the comprehensive direction that is necessary; they cannot assign priorities for the investment of scarce child protective resources.

39. *There should be a statewide office of child guardian responsible for the protection of children from further abuse and neglect and for the evaluation and coordination of child protective efforts.*

The child guardian, on an ongoing basis, would advise the legislature and the governor on the problems of children in the state by (1) constantly updating, examining, and evaluating information concerning the needs of children and (2) monitoring the implementation of existing laws and determining the need for additional legislation. The child guardian would review the programs and budgets of all agencies responsible for providing children's services.

We are convinced that the advocate for children's needs should also be an advocate of individual children. He should be able to act as an advocate on behalf of children deprived of services essential for their safety and development. His power would thus include hearing grievances and requests for action. In responding, the child guardian would clarify the nature of the problem, initiate action to secure appropriate services, gather data to see if such grievances reflect a pattern, report lapses in the delivery of services to the responsible agencies, make recommendations for more effective alternatives, and take any other appropriate action. He could also hold public hearings, take testimony, have the power to subpoena witnesses, and require production of all relevant documents. On the basis of his findings, he could refer matters to the appropriate law enforcement agency and, in addition, he would have standing to sue for the enforcement of legislative mandates.

We expect that, as a result of the child guardian's activities, the manner in which child abuse and neglect cases are handled would be made known to the public. Under no circumstances should information be released that would tend to identify the child or family. The public, however, should become better informed about the manner in which cases of child abuse are handled within the system, the types and severity of injury being sustained by our children, and the ultimate disposition of these cases.

An urgent priority is the improvement of communication and planning of all agencies concerned with child welfare. A first priority of the child guardian would be the convening of a consultative group made up of the heads of the appropriate state departments to ascertain the ways in which services to children can be better integrated and coordinated throughout the state.

The child guardian's duties would include the development of local advocate committees throughout the state; providing these committees with technical assistance and information; and generally acting as a central clearinghouse, coordinating the development of these local groups. He would also develop a compendium of New York State laws relating to children, accessible to all concerned parties, which would stimulate the development of programs to secure services for children and their families. He would develop monetary guidelines; engage in review and evaluation of programs and training of personnel; and, finally, submit an annual report to the governor and legislature on "The State of Child Welfare in New York."

This broad power and responsibility requires that the child guardian have the broadest possible mandate to act. He must be absolutely independent of any existing agency. For these reasons, and also because of the child guardian's ombudsman-like role, the committee recommends that the child guardian be appointed by the legislature.

To recapitulate the responsibilities we would place on the child guardian:

Research and Development
  1. Gather and analyze facts.
  2. Propose and evaluate new programs, approaches and concepts on both a pilot and an institutional basis.
Institutional Administration
  1. Encourage consistency, systemization, and rationality in the delivery of child welfare services.
  2. Encourage the improvement of information services.
  3. Encourage research utilization and innovation.
Child Protective
  1. Act as the individual's and the public's court of last resort to assure speedy, just, and efficient treatment by child caring agencies.
  2. Act as an arbiter between bureaucracies and agencies.
  3. Utilize public complaints in order to discover dysfunctions within the system before they reach crisis proportions and to work toward their amelioration.
Legislative
  1. Propose legislation when necessary and appropriate to meet welfare goals.
  2. Evaluate all other proposals for legislative change in the field of child welfare in this and other states.

Establishment of the Office of Child Guardian would furnish a means for providing the children of the state with the services they require—the services to which they are entitled. At its maximum efficiency, the Office of Child Guardian could examine the broad needs of our children, find out where those needs are not being met, and channel the necessary resources into the areas where they can best be utilized, making full use of available community resources. Coordination in the delivery of services to children will be vastly improved and a comprehensive, unified system created to fulfill the various needs of children and their families.

Because of the innovative nature of this proposal, legislation is not proposed at this time to establish the office of child guardian. Instead, an application for anticrime and social rehabilitation funds will be made to the appropriate federal agencies. In this way, there will be a period in which to test the feasibility of specific functions we suggest for the child guardian.

40. *In every county in the state there should be a citizens' committee to monitor local operations, make suggestions for improvement, and gain public support for reform.*

The committee has been impressed by the accomplishments of local citizens committees in Onondaga and Broome counties. We have concluded that the creation of similar local citizens committees in every county would help coordinate local child welfare efforts as well as create grass roots support for fulfilling the needs of abused and neglected children. These committees would do fact-finding to provide information to the community about the local child welfare system. They would identify community needs and mobilize community concern around gaps and needs and initiate action to effect requisite change. As a side benefit, this community education can be expected to stimulate local agency action.

The local committees would also mount a continued effort to inform, advise, and educate the public of the serious nature of child abuse and of the necessity of reporting such cases.

It can be expected that these local committees would receive complaints from children and their families about inadequate services and engage in fact-finding about such complaints. If the problem cannot be resolved at the local level, the committee could then refer it to the child guardian.

The committees would be appointed by the county legislature or executive officer and would consist of a highly responsible group of medical, social, and legal personnel as well as concerned citizens. We expect the local family court judges, and particularly the administrative judge, and the children's attorney to play leading roles in the development of these committees.

*   *   *

Statistics on Child Abuse and Neglect, New York City, 1971–72 (revised and completed 1973)

TABLE 3

CHILD ABUSE AND NEGLECT REPORTS, BY MONTH, FOR NEW YORK CITY, 1971–72

MONTH	1971		1972							
	ABUSE AND NEGLECT		ABUSE		NEGLECT		ABUSE AND NEGLECT	
	Children	Families	Children	Families	Children	Families	Children	Families
January	189 [a]	173 [a]	249	209	406	210	655	419
February	188	169	243	233	533	248	776	481
March	540	377	265	232	842	412	1,107	644
April	496	327	198	178	644	272	842	450
May	458	278	246	219	900	410	1,146	629
June	510	370	274	241	802	361	1,076	602
July	421	291	200	175	601	269	801	444
August	484	317	214	195	752	317	966	512
September	461	325	194	166	594	248	788	414
October	602	403	196	179	554	248	750	427
November	626	436	206	185	560	286	766	471
December	722	502	225	198	467	230	692	428
TOTAL	5,697	3,968	2,710	2,410	7,655	3,511	10,365	5,921

[a] Abuse only.

TABLE 4

<small>CHILD ABUSE AND NEGLECT, PREVALENCE BY COUNTY, NEW YORK CITY, 1971–72</small>

	1971		1972							
	ABUSE AND NEGLECT		ABUSE		NEGLECT		ABUSE AND NEGLECT	
COUNTY	Children	Families	Children	Families	Children	Families	Children	Families
Bronx	1,728	1,226	832	728	2,094	970	2,926	1,698
New York (Manhattan)	1,534	1,105	689	632	1,482	758	2,171	1,390
Kings (Brooklyn)	1,735	1,158	825	738	2,440	1,052	3,265	1,790
Queens	615	416	303	261	1,059	640	1,362	901
Richmond	85	60	61	54	222	97	283	151
TOTAL	5,697	3,965	2,710	2,413	7,747	3,517	10,457	5,930

TABLE 5

<small>CHILD ABUSE AND NEGLECT, PREVALENCE BY AGE AND SEX, NEW YORK CITY, 1971–72</small>

	1971			1972		
AGE	Female	Male	Total	Female	Male	Total
Under 1	642	657	1,299	677	747	1,424
1–4 years	699	770	1,469	1,334	1,351	2,685
5–9 years	674	756	1,430	1,371	1,530	2,901
Over 10	835	654	1,489	1,475	1,357	2,832
No age information			7	30	39	69
No sex information			3			546
TOTAL	2,850	2,837	5,697	4,887 [a]	5,024 [b]	10,457 [c]

[a] Abuse: 1,370. Neglect: 3,517.
[b] Abuse: 1,329. Neglect: 3,695.
[c] Abuse: 2,710; no sex information, 11. Neglect: 7,747; no sex information, 535.

TABLE 6

SOURCES OF ABUSE AND NEGLECT REPORTS IN NEW YORK CITY, 1971–72

REPORTING SOURCE	1971 Abuse and Neglect	1972 Abuse	Neglect	Abuse and Neglect
Municipal hospitals	1,297	867	481	1,348
Voluntary hospitals	1,140	846	479	1,325
Private physicians	2	4	5	9
Schools:				
Principals		368	0	368
Teachers	826	0	884	884
Nurses	23	4	5	9
Physicians	17	1	1	2
Department of Social Services:				
Public Assistance	790	85	728	813
Bureau of Special Services	53	0	0	0
Bureau of Child Welfare	193	45	144	189
Family Court	274	72	269	341
Police	161	92	222	314
S.P.C.C.:				
Manhattan	248	10	129	139
Brooklyn	133	59	90	149
Bronx	12	1	15	16
Queens	53	34	189	223
Public and private agencies	418	172	384	556
Nurses	5	3	12	15
Physicians	6	5	14	19
Medical examiner	6	19	3	22
Other:				
Non-mandated		0	2,956	2,956
Welfare Inspector General		23	258	281
Anonymous complaint		0	479	479
Miscellaneous	36			
C.H.A.N.C.E.	4			
TOTAL	5,697	2,710	7,747	10,457

Postscript

On September 1 the Child Protective Services Act of 1973, sponsored by Speaker Duryea and the Select Committee, took effect. Its many provisions are already having a profound effect on the quality of protection we in New York provide for abused and neglected children. The Child Protective Services Act of 1973 establishes an improved state Central Register of Child Abuse and Maltreatment and requires reporting of all suspected child abuse cases by doctors, school officials, police, and other professional persons.

It requires that the central register be manned on a round-the-clock basis. It permits any citizen to report abuse cases to the register and then requires state and local social services departments to investigate and make findings on each report to the register. Photographs are required to be taken of battered and abused children at the time of injury for later use in resultant court action.

It makes persons required to report civilly liable in damages for willfully failing to report.

It permits persons such as a parent or guardian who is the subject of a finding on a report to have a fair hearing before the state Department of Social Services in order to have the report amended or expunged.

It directs every local department of social services to establish a child protective service.

It requires each local department to adopt yearly a local plan for child protective services after consultation with juvenile court and child welfare officials and after a local public hearing.

The new statewide system for reporting child abuse and maltreatment has already received reports on 3,886 children who were suspected victims in September—that is more than the total of suspected abuse cases reported in all of 1972. Before the central register was expanded to oversee investigations into child neglect, it received reports concerning 3,319 children who were suspected victims of abuse.

As legislators, we know too well the limitations of legislative action to remedy deepseated social problems. We in New York have the nation's most extensive child abuse laws. We like to think they are also some of the best. Indeed, most commentators have said so. But we acknowledge that laws are only the beginning. They provide a legal and institutional framework for professional and community people to act. No set of laws—no matter how well intentioned and no matter how well drafted —can succeed without the understanding, cooperation, and active assistance of professionals and the public. A law lives in the manner in which it is used.

As in every area of public action, more money and more staff are undoubtedly needed by our child protective system. However, in too many communities the existing system is like a sponge. It absorbs more and more of our limited resources without improving its shape. It merely becomes more bloated. We therefore believe that forceful legislative direction is needed to rationalize existing child protective services before channeling into them large amounts of additional funds. We believe that we in New York have begun to do so.

References

1. *New York Times*, 14 February 1972, p. 58, col. 3, and *New York Daily News*, 14 February 1972, p. 10, col. 1.
2. Holter, Joan L., and Friedman, Standford B. 1968. Child abuse: Early casefinding in the emergency department. *Pediatrics* 42, no. 1.
3. Testimony before Select Committee on Child Abuse. 5 October 1971. Albany, New York.
4. *Initial quarterly progress report to Criminal Justice Coordinating Council.* 1972. Child abuse grant C55934.
5. New York City Task Force on Child Abuse and Neglect. 1970. *Task force report.*
6. *Annual report of the judicial conference.* 1972.
7. Fanshel, David, and Shinn, Eugene. 1972. *Dollars and sense in foster care.* Pamphlet. Child Welfare League.
8. *Report to the Senate Judiciary Sub-Committee on the family court.* 3 March 1960.
9. Paulson, Monrad. 1968. Children's court: Gateway or last resort. In *Gault: What now for the juvenile court,* edited by Virginia D. Nordin. Ann Arbor: Institute of Continuing Legal Education.
10. *State of New York* v. *John Doe.*

Index